ESSENTIAL

psychology

david cohen

BLOOMSBURY

This paperback edition published in Great Britain 1994

Copyright © by David Cohen, 1990

Cover illustration: case containing 60 phrenological heads,
by courtesy of The Science Museum/Science & Society Picture Library

Bloomsbury Publishing Plc,
2 Soho Square, London W1V 5DE

British Library Cataloguing in Publication Data

A CIP catalogue record for this book
is available from the British Library

ISBN 0 7475 1947 1

10 9 8 7 6 5 4 3 2 1

Designed by Penny Edwards

Printed in Britain by Cox & Wyman Ltd, Reading, Berks

Contents

Introduction

Psychology is firmly established in industry, schools, hospitals and universities and in the media. It may sometimes appear that the main achievement of psychology has been to change the way in which we talk about ourselves. In the 1800s, those uncluttered pre-psychological times, nobody had 'insight' or an 'Oedipus complex' because no one had conceived these concepts that, it now seems, we cannot live without.

In the United States, there are currently about 115,000 psychologists. In Britain, the British Psychological Society has over 15,000 members. Israel alone has 4000, which is not bad for a country with a population of only 4 million. Psychologists give advice, construct experiments, assist in designing campaigns, offer help in schools, in business, in the health services and in prisons. In personnel departments, psychologists have been very persuasive: companies often rely on them when hiring people and also to ease the process when employees are made redundant. The work of many other professions also involves psychology, and a great deal is included in the training of policemen, probation officers, nurses and social workers.

Within the discipline itself, there are many different kinds of psychologists, including:

- clinical psychologists
- cognitive psychologists
- community psychologists
- educational psychologists
- experimental psychologists
- environmental psychologists
- industrial psychologists
- neuropsychologists

- personnel psychologists
- physiological psychologists
- radical psychologists
- social psychologists

And, of course, many psychiatrists and psychotherapists also employ psychological theories and techniques.

Psychology, it would appear, has become established. However, If I were writing a survey of another established discipline – say, biology, physics or even history – I wouldn't feel compelled to devote most of an introduction to an outline of the ways in which rival biologists, physicists or historians snipe at their colleagues and heap ideological abuse on each others' views. Within all academic disciplines, there are controversies, but in most, there is relative agreement on what ought to be studied, how it ought to be studied and what constitutes an important finding.

Not so in psychology.

Psychologists can't even agree when their discipline started. Some agree that the Greeks – and especially Aristotle and Plato – had important psychological insights, and philosophers such as Descartes and Hume made useful contributions, especially to the study of thinking. Others, who tend to describe themselves as 'real' scientists, date the start of 'proper' psychology only to 1879 when >Wilhelm Wundt, a German physiologist, started an experimental psychological laboratory in Leipzig. However, this 'real science' division of history as either pre- or post-psychology is not straightforward. Carreras Patsos, in a 1979 study of the French psychologist >Jean Piaget wrote:

I cannot prevent myself asking one question of Piaget. His experiments were extremely simple and the means for carrying them out were available to all the great thinkers from the Greeks on. How does Piaget explain that it was not until the twentieth century that someone understood what he undertook?

For some, therefore, the start of experimentation was the start of psychology. A few famous psychologists are worshipped by one group and abused by others. >Sigmund Freud is the classic example of that ambivalence. To some, the founder of >psychoanalysis was the most important psychologist ever. To others, such as >Hans Eysenck, Freud was a charlatan who had a splendid prose style. Eysenck has quipped that what Freud said was true wasn't new, and what he said that was new wasn't true. In other sciences, there are more facts, less vitriol. Physics has moved on since Einstein, biology since Pasteur, but in neither discipline are these great pioneers dismissed in a comparable way. Eysenck feels comfortable badmouthing Freud because he doesn't see Freud's approach as really scientific. Freud relied simply on talking to patients and focused on such inner entities as dreams, the unconscious mind and our hidden motives. Eysenck for one sees no real experimental evidence that points to the importance of these. There are other victims. >B. F. Skinner, the behaviourist, who claims that only observable behaviour should be studied and that we are products of what we have done and what has been done to us, has been criticized as both superficial and sinister. Noam Chomsky has even damned him as inconsequential.

Conflict is evident both in the areas on which some psychologists focus and in the methods they use. To get some idea of the differences, it is worth comparing >behaviourism, >psychoanalysis, developmental psychology (>child development), social psychology and >cognitive psychology.

- **Behaviourism** is a school of psychology founded by >J. B. Watson in which it is claimed that the only viable way of studying psychology is through the observation of behaviour. It rejects the concept of >consciousness. Watson went so far as to argue that thinking is just silent speech – in other words, thinking isn't really a private process that takes place inside the mind but something which, in principle, can be observed. All you need is sophisticated enough methods to pick up the very soft speech that the thinker mumbles only to him or herself. Behaviourism set the agenda for much contemporary psychology because of its insistence on rigorous scientific methods.

- **Psychoanalysis** is the very opposite of behaviourism in a variety of ways but not in some of its underlying assumptions. Psychoanalysis was conceived by Sigmund Freud, who discovered not just that we all have unconscious minds but that unconscious processes are extremely important in explaining much of our conscious behaviour. Although chiefly famous for his theory that dreams are actually a form of wish fulfilment, Freud devised a rich, complex and enormously influential theory which highlighted many of the areas that the behaviourists said couldn't be studied – thoughts, feelings, intentions as well as dreams. Yet Freud saw himself as a scientist (he was trained as a neurophysiologist) and, like the behaviourists, he believed that human beings didn't really have free will.

  Occasional attempts have been made (such as those by Miller and Dollard in 1950) to use experimental methods to tease out how psychoanalytic concepts show themselves in actual behaviour. Such studies are very interesting, but many disagree on how to interpret them.

- **Developmental psychology** – that is, the study of the psychological development of children – has always involved more of a reliance on observation in real settings, initially in schools and latterly in the home. Even thinkers such as Piaget who suggested a rigorous theory of how children develop never became quite as dogmatic as behaviourists or psychoanalysts.

- **Social psychology** is essentially the study of how people (usually adults) behave in groups. Social psychologists rely heavily on artificial situations in laboratories as well as on the use of questionnaires. The problem is that it is hard to know how meaningful their results are when applied to real life.

- **Cognitive psychology** studies mental processes. Its exponents are the heirs of the old experimental tradition in psychology and they use experimental approaches. However, they are also interested in studying concepts such as mental functioning which behaviourism ruled out of order.

It's tempting, of course, to lump these theories together and conclude that psychology is the study both of human behaviour and of human intentions and feelings. Unfortunately, this isn't possible, largely because the methods used to study behaviour are very different from those used to study intentions and feelings.

In theory at least, it's easy to observe behaviour. I can watch Andrew walk to the supermarket, browse and then buy a tube of toothpaste. Any other sensible observer would see the same – Andrew's behaviour is self-evident. However, his feelings and intentions are not – there is no way that I, or anyone other than Andrew, can observe them directly. At best, we can observe their consequences. As I watch Andrew go into the supermarket, I can imagine what he is thinking about. I can draw on my own experiences of what I feel like when I go to the supermarket thinking of buying toothpaste. But these thoughts may be very different from Andrew's and from those of another observer. I have no way of knowing how Andrew feels unless he chooses to tell me. Andrew might tell me that he intends to buy toothpaste because he has a date tonight and wants to avoid bad breath. But Andrew may be lying; or he may change his mind and buy a bar of chocolate; or, even if he thinks he knows why he is buying toothpaste, he may be wrong. He may not realise the causes of his actions.

Behaviourists would argue that Andrew's intentions don't cause his tooth-paste-buying at all. Rather, it's his history of >reinforcement: as a child, his mother told him off if he didn't clean his teeth; he therefore learned to clean his teeth to earn her approval. Psychoanalysts, on the other hand, might suggest that he was being obsessive about buying toothpaste to ward off deep anxieties; perhaps his date reminds him unconsciously of his mother. Such theories might differ in many ways and yet agree that Andrew isn't buying the toothpaste of his own free will. His past determines his actions; his intentions don't count for that much. He is probably not aware of the real reasons for his purchase.

Fundamentally, these different views reflect differences about whether human beings have free will or whether their thoughts and actions are predetermined. The ideas that most of us have of our motives for doing things are dismissed by some academics as mere folk psychology or illusions of common sense. Not all psychologists are so contemptuous. Many rely on history: for thousands of years, people have spoken and written as though they thought their intentions did actually cause their actions. Is all this to be discounted as self-important illusion? We may think that there is a 'ghost in the machine', an inner being who decides what we do, but some psychologists say that that's only because we are deluded. Since the seventeenth century, many thinkers have argued that the human body is a machine and that machines don't have minds or free will.

Others, including >humanistic psychologists, claim that we do have free will and that we act rather than react. They maintain that human beings can decide to change and 'grow'. The notion of using scientific insight to achieve the 'perfectability of man' dates back to the Enlightenment and has continued to influence the less scientific schools of psychology. But it isn't just 'personal growth' faddists who claim that free will matters. Many sober psychologists maintain that >determinism has failed because of their colleagues' own lack of success in specifying precisely what determines any action. Recently, with the development of ever more complex computers and the vogue for >cognitive theory, a third approach has surfaced. This accepts that we are machines but these machines are so wonderful and so complex that they (and we) may well actually have something like free will.

Such differences also affect what experts think the task of psychology is. Mechanists (those who argue we are nothing but biological machines whose workings can be revealed by experiment) tend to want psychology to reveal the general laws of human behaviour. They want answers to questions such as:

- What are the general principles that govern learning?

- Is there a link between people's personalities and their style of thinking?

- What social and psychological factors account for prejudice?

Those who believe in free will tend to be more interested in using psychology to understand individual cases. After all, if free will really exists, general laws can at best apply only to certain areas of human behaviour. Effort should be devoted instead to explaining why Araminta is so cranky, difficult and uninterested in a sexual relationship.

It isn't actually possible to prove that any of these approaches is correct. Chomsky has noted with a modesty rare among psychologists that it may well be that understanding how the human brain works is beyond the capacity of the human brain. This is no reason to give up trying but a reason for a modicum of humility.

Given the different approaches to psychology, it isn't surprising that many textbooks reflect a chronic lack of consensus. As early as 1945, a book called *Seven Psychologies* commented on the odd fact that there should be so many different ones. Things haven't improved: a recent book on personality theory, *Perspectives on Personality* (Carver and Scheier, 1989) examined 15 different approaches to the study of personality, and weighed each in terms of its own strengths and weaknesses. The authors, however, were unable to decide which theory is true. Rather, they speak of different 'metaphors' in different theories having different 'focuses of convenience'.

A number of textbooks reveal the depth of these disagreements. I mention a few here to give an idea of the extent of the rivalries in psychology, but this list is far from exhaustive.

- Nehemiah Jordan in *Themes in Speculative Psychology* (1968) argued that psychology has been a complete failure: it discovers plenty of facts but can't knit these facts together into any coherent theory of human action.

- Liam Hudson in *The Cult of the Fact* (1972) echoed some of Jordan's conclusions but added the twist that psychologists desperately want to produce elegant solutions to elegant problems. Yet there is little that we have produced in the last 50 years that is in any sense of that complex word, relevant.

- Donald Broadbent's *In Defence of Empirical Psychology* (1974) argued persuasively that the empirical methods that Jordan detests and Hudson snipes at are perfectly adequate for furthering psychology.

- More recently, psychologists have taken to offering an analysis that accepts these differences and seeks to explore some reasons for them. Books such as *A Science in Conflict* (Kendler, 1982), *Models of Man* (Chapman, Jones, 1980) and my own *Psychologists on Psychology* (1977) try to outline these differences systematically. Richardson in *Understanding Psychology* (1989) has noted that students often complain of this lack of consensus – they'd like their psychology simple. Unfortunately, as the entries in this dictionary will reveal, that isn't possible.

It's important to analyse the reasons for the lack of consensus. First, psychology studies the behaviour of human beings at very many different levels. In this book, there are entries that cover things that wouldn't seem strange in a book on anatomy – what the brain consists of, how the retina of the eye works, and how the nerve endings in the skin affect the perception of touch and pain. But there are also entries on complex social movements such as the behaviour of crowds, and others covering important but very individualistic activities such as going to encounter groups and religious services. Many researchers also work with animals as well as (or instead of) people. Quite different levels of analysis are needed for understanding these various topics. Yet they all fall under the heading of psychology.

The second reason for the controversies that are endemic in psychology is that human beings are not just conscious but self-conscious. From 1913, when J. B. Watson published his behaviourist manifesto, psychologists tried to pretend that we are just like any other species and that we can be studied just like a rat can be studied, but eventually, 60 years later, common sense won out. It wasn't just idiocy that led psychologists to this former view. They were desperately eager to have their discipline recognized as a real science, and so they moved most of their investigations into the laboratory, arguing that it was possible to adapt the methods of physics and chemistry. Irritatingly, however, human beings can't be studied like chemical solutions or even quirky sub-atomic particles. We are more complex and, above all, we are conscious and self-conscious. I not only eat a hamburger but I know that I'm eating a hamburger and can, if required, explain why. This makes me somewhat different from a mouse nibbling a piece of cheese or a pigeon pecking at a pellet of Bird-o-Food.

As a result, the methods of the physical sciences can't be applied to all sections of psychology. A comprehensive psychology has to cover vastly different sorts of investigations. Again, the following list is not exhaustive, but the psychologist may examine:

- ways in which we are like animals.

- ways in which all human beings are alike – eg we all need to eat, drink, sleep.

- ways in which groups of human beings are alike but different from other groups – eg what makes Jews different from those of other faiths?

- ways in which each of us is unique – eg why does Joan feel compelled to ring radio chat shows to talk about her sexual problems while Leonard won't even admit to himself that he has any.

- ways in which some of us seek spiritual consolations that others deride.

The task of psychology is complicated by our capacity for deception and self-deception. As complex social beings, we can pretend and deceive – and, indeed, there's considerable evidence that subjects often do that in psychology labs. They often give responses that they think the experimenter wants (>response bias) or >socially desirable responses that make them look good; subjects also don't necessarily reveal the truth about themselves. As a result, the rather simple methods used by psychologists often fail.

Often, experiments are badly designed and assume that people who take part in them enter a totally artificial world without realizing it. For example, some social psychology studies depend on subjects playing games such as the 'prisoners game'. In this, whether you get two years or ten years in jail depends on how accurately you predict the behaviour of a fellow prisoner. In real life, such a game would be desperately serious. In the psychology lab, it is, of course, played as a lark; nothing is really at stake. Can it then really tell us much about how people handle stressful and important decisions?

In 1969, Stanley Milgram assembled a number of subjects at Yale University. They were told to give painful electric shocks to experimental 'stooges' in another room when the latter failed to solve maths problems. They apparently went along with this cruel procedure: stooges duly failed and screamed, but the subjects went on giving shocks. Milgram argued that this revealed our craven capacity for obedience. However, ten years later, Rom Harré countered that it was nothing of the sort. Subjects knew quite well that Yale was a sober university where people weren't tortured. They just went on playing what was obviously some kind of game, humouring the researchers.

A dictionary of psychology can either ignore these arguments and just define what terms mean or put definitions in context. I have tried to indicate critical thinking on key issues so that readers get a sense of the varying positions and, indeed, rows. Some concepts, such as >regression, only occur in particular theories. With some central concepts such as >consciousness, the controversies are vital, especially as now some psychologists are reintroducing it.

Material that was once taboo is making its way back into psychology. This has been helped by the new methods of investigation that have arisen in the last 15 years or so – for instance, the video camera, which has made it possible to record behaviour very accurately and very cheaply. Self-reports, in which people explain what they feel or why they do something, have become more accepted. Developmental psychologists are even beginning to ask how children come to have a 'theory of mind'. Traditionally, this theory has sought to explain what it means to be conscious, how we know other people have minds and are not automatons. It also enquired how we carry out subtle actions such as promising. The inadmissible mind is back. However, the developmental psychologists who are now studying these areas don't rely only on the >introspection that was a driving force in the early days of psychology. They certainly ask children what they think, but they also try to use experimental designs and a great deal of naturalistic observation to arrive at conclusions. In reality, they are beginning to study how children become self-conscious, adapting the methods of empirical psychology which once saw consciousness as irrelevant.

The impact of computers in psychology has been great. Practically, it's made it easier to analyse large batches of data in more complex ways. Theoretically, psychologists have learned to make comparisons between the way computer programs work and how the brain does. Cognitive psychology, which examines problem-solving, how we think and how we think about how we feel, has been one of the most interesting developments since the mid-1970s.

However, it is important not to wax lyrical about a few signs of greater tolerance! Exponents of different brands of psychology still behave rather like the manufacturers of different brands of detergent. Competitors boost their own claims and abuse those of their rivals: Insight X really doesn't illuminate at all compared to our own wonderful, thought-shattering Insight Y.

The very breadth of psychology helps explain why it is so hard to achieve a consensus. As one leading psychologist, David McClelland, told me, one reason that psychologists are so argumentative is, he suspects, because they love vying for power. Another reason could be that the theories psychologists have about human nature have to have some implications for their own views of themselves – or vice versa. It is impossible to claim that all human beings are machines apart from oneself who, being the ultimate psychologist, is somehow different and above it all. Personal involvement may make such intellectual disputes more heated. Psychologists' theories are about themselves, too.

I have been very critical of the progress that psychology has made, but it would be silly to pretend there has been none. Let me itemize just three positive developments.

- The design of instruments in aircraft cockpits was improved radically after it was discovered that the needles on antimeters confused aircrew easily and that this led to accidents. The recent spate of airline crashes has focused attention again on how best to design instruments so that pilots can read them quickly under pressure.

- Psychological research has helped to make it clear that there is considerable value in talking to the families of psychiatric patients and in treating such patients with respect. Otherwise, they all too easily become helpless and dependent on the institutions such as hospitals in which they are cared for, and they become frightened of leaving them.

- Studies of conversation have also shed unexpected light both on how parents and children interact and how men and women do. We now know, for example, that mothers and fathers endlessly repeat phrases for their children so that they learn the patterns of social interaction. Less cosily, we know that the way men carry out conversations makes it hard for women to have an equal chance to speak. Males tend to interrupt continually, while females tend to listen and to interject encouraging little sounds, looks and smiles which reinforce the male ego. When women talk together, however, they do so on a much more cooperative basis, with a great deal of give and take.

It would be wrong to see psychology as a total failure. Despite much theoretical confusion and acrimony, it has offered practical help in many areas.

Yet, there is a certain sense of disappointment in what it has achieved. The early pioneers of psychology started out with the hope of not just discovering abstract laws of human behaviour but also ways of improving people's lives. It's hard for those who are psychologists now to recapture the optimism that Watson and Freud must have felt. Both men believed that greater knowledge would free people to live better and healthier lives. Psychologists who believed that they could mend humankind's destructive ways got their clearest comeuppance in 1939: the previous year, a famous social psychologist, Gardner Murphy, had announced that social psychology would soon find the way to avoid wars. Pity he didn't get the message through to Hitler. However, psychologists didn't give up idealism. In 1950, B. F. Skinner published a description of a behaviourist's utopia called *Walden Two*. There, properly conditioned people led blissful, socially responsible lives.

Psychology Exposed, or The Emperor's New Clothes is the latest work to express profound disenchantment with psychology. It has been written by Paul Kline, a professor at Exeter University, who notes that psychology has actually become 'corrosive' and has failed to provide any insights into human behaviour. He blames all psychologists (including himself) for the parlous state of the discipline. Psychology arouses high hopes and, therefore, risks great disappointment. Kline's book shows that the arguments I have described still persist.

Most introductions end with a plan of the following chapters. My book plan is simple: I start with A and go to Z. However, it is probably worth explaining some of the rules that I have tried to adhere to in compiling *Essential Psychology*.

In the past few years, a number of dictionaries of/companions to psychology have been published. They range from the massive *Oxford Companion to the Mind*, edited by Richard Gregory, to rather bitty works in which every topic listed is given a rather brief definition and that's it. Brief definitions can be elegant but, given the nature of the controversies outlined above, they tend to be inadequate in psychology. The reader needs some sort of critical context.

This is especially true with concepts of schools of thought that have come under much fire. In some entries, such as 'psychoanalysis', 'behaviourism' and 'Piaget', I've tried to indicate both what the concepts have stood for and how others have reacted to them. I have usually attempted to assess the current status of any controversies and to provide up-to-date references both for and against particular positions. Understanding the arguments is a crucial part of understanding psychology.

As a result of this, some entries are a little long. I've tried to provide for this by not aiming to cover every term you might conceivably run into in a book on psychology: some, such as various concepts in Jungian psychology, are very esoteric; others, once vital, are now only of interest to historians. Instead, I have tried in this book to give an outline of the most important terms and ideas that are in use now. I have also given short potted biographies of some of the major thinkers in this discipline.

A to Z

A

Abnormal, literally, what is not >normal. But what is 'normal' is often a matter of convention and social habits.

Until the growth of the anti-psychiatry movement in the 1960s, there was little debate about what was labelled 'abnormal behaviour'. No one disputed that psychiatrists could diagnose it, or that it was a symptom of psychiatric disturbance. But then radical psychiatrists such as Thomas Szasz and >R. D. Laing argued that >psychiatry was a tool of the State, and psychiatrists labelled as *abnormal* those people whose behaviour was inconvenient or challenging. Thus, Ezra Pound, poet turned Fascist, found himself detained in a mental hospital for years because his politics were considered unacceptable. Szasz noted that, in the USSR, dissidents who didn't accept Communism were also diagnosed as abnormal. Laing claimed that many schizophrenics were simply sane people in a mad, destructive world.

Since the 1960s, historians of psychiatry such as >Foucault and Scull have shown that one reason for the development of mental hospitals was the need to curb revolt and dissatisfaction with the Industrial Revolution. Industrial society couldn't cope with eccentric behaviour in the way villages had done. The role of the hospitals was to control such misfits. To justify this action, such people were labelled abnormal.

The anti-psychiatry movement has declined, but it has left a mark. Far more than before, psychologists realize that what is normal is a question of cultural definition. The need to tolerate so-called 'abnormal behaviour' is great, especially if we are to have successful community care.

- R. Banton, P. Clifford, S. Frosh, J. Lousada and J. Rosenthall, *The Politics of Mental Health* (1985); T. Szasz, *Cruel Compassion* (1994).

Accommodation, a process by which the infant's >brain adapts to, and adapts, the information that it receives through >perception and sensation. >Piaget, who devised the concept, argued that, through >assimilation and accommoda-

A

tion, the brain strives for equilibration, which can be roughly understood as balance. *See* Vision.

● J. H. Flavell, *The Developmental Psychology of Jean Piaget* (1962).

Acetylcholine, a >neurotransmitter that smoothes the transmission of electrical impulses from one >neuron to the next across the >synapse. A loss of acetylcholine has been suggested as one possible cause of >Alzheimer's disease. Studies at Edinburgh have shown that it is possible to boost acetylcholine levels in old people by giving them a diet containing a lot of white fish. The fish oils stimulate the production of the neurotransmitter.

Achievement motivation, literally how motivated we are to succeed. Achievement motivation is a function of >nAch, need to achieve. The concept was developed by David McClelland, who claimed initially that it was possible to measure how interested in achievement past cultures were by a >content analysis of their written works. If their literature was full of images that emphasized either striving or success, then it was possible to infer that achievement motivation was high.

McClelland suggested that periods of high achievement – so-called 'golden ages' such as Elizabeth I's England – were preceded by 50 years of much achievement imagery, and that this meant that parents encouraged ambition in their children – 50 years on, the fruits were evident. He extended the notion to studies of different contemporary cultures, and it has also led to the devising of tests of nAch such as the >thematic apperception test (TAT).

The concept and its associated theory is very ambitious. However, there have always been some doubts about how true it is and how effective the measures McClelland used to measure achievement motivation really were.

● David McClelland, *The Achieving Society* (1961).

Action theory, a new approach to the study of >motivation. It rejects both behaviouristic and psychodynamic views that stress how people react. Action theory is about what makes people act, and gives intentions and choices an important role. The most original aspect of the theory is that it accepts that there are different levels of explanations for actions. Some may be biologically driven, but others are highly conscious.

● D. Clarke, *Action Systems* (1985).

Acute, a psychiatric term for when a patient is in crisis, possibly very agitated and even dangerous. Psychiatric illnesses are held to go through different phases, notably acute and >chronic. The acute phase is the most problematic for staff as patients are most demanding then.

Adaptation. *See* Habituation.

4

Addictions. The major addictions are to alcohol, tobacco, illegal drugs (eg heroin) and, increasingly, prescribed drugs such as Valium. The World Health Organization estimates that there are 200 million people worldwide who suffer from alcohol or drug addition. Giving up has been seen as a medical problem since the 19th century, when the writer Thomas de Quincey, in his autobiography *Confessions of an English Opium-Eater* (1822), claimed he couldn't live without opium. Psychiatry became involved in the treatment of addictions in the mid-20th century.

Broadly, there are three different models of addiction which seem to explain why people became addicted – chemical, >psychodynamic and social learning. The chemical school (to which Alcoholics Anonymous belongs) argues that some individuals have a chemical kink in their make-up. They are biologically 'imbalanced' and, as a result, vulnerable to addition. AA sees alcoholism or drug dependence as a sickness due to this biological fault, and the phrase repeated by its members – 'I am an alcoholic' – emphasizes that the person is disabled. Abstinence is the only cure, for one sip is enough to get them hooked again.

The psychodynamic model emphasizes that people become addicts to escape unsatisfactory aspects of their lives: 'I drink or take drugs to avoid facing my personality problems, the fact that my marriage is a bore and that I am terrified of being incompetent at work. When drunk, I feel able to cope with these otherwise overwhelming problems.' As a result, therapy focuses not on the actual addiction but on the underlying causes. Make the addict a whole, competent person, say those who adhere to this model, and he won't need to drink.

A third approach is that of social learning. This claims that addiction is the result of inappropriate learning. 'Problem drinkers' can be retrained to drink sensibly and socially. One programme in Britain called Drinkwatchers would teach groups to sip drinks slowly, always to have a non-alcoholic drink to hand as well, to monitor their weekly intake, and aim for no booze on at least three days a week. Alcoholics Anonymous are vitriolic about the activities of this school: they claim it can't help addicts; those it does help aren't addicts at all.

The strength of addiction is mirrored in the problems people have with withdrawal. Follow-up studies suggest that all these different therapeutic approaches have some merit, though none is sure of success. Much depends on personality and on that once-popular concept 'will'. Addicts who really want to give up seem to be able to do it, but for some, while addiction remains destructive, it continues to have many attractions.

● G. Bennett (ed), *Treating Drug Abusers* (1989).

Adjustment, widely used in ordinary >language to mean getting used to various conditions. *See* Well-adjusted.

Adler, Alfred (1870–1937), Viennese psychoanalyst who joined Freud's circle in about 1904 but set up his own movement of >individual psychology in 1911. Adler stressed that it was wrong to make sex the central driving energy in people's lives; powerlessness seemed key to him. He drew on the work of Nietzsche and Schopenhauer, German philosophers who placed the will and the desire for power at the centre of human actions. Adler argued that human beings

A

tended to have either inferiority or superiority complexes. Individuals compensate for inferiority by seeking power over others. Adler also emphasized what he termed 'masculine protest' in women – their fury at having been born into a sex that is treated unequally. Individual psychology has never managed to achieve the influence of other theories like those propounded by, for example, >Jung and Reich. Nevertheless, Adler's ideas did influence the development of analysis.

● Alfred Adler, *The Practice and Theory of Individual Psychology* (1924).

Adrenalin, a >neurotransmitter and a hormone secreted by the adrenal glands, which helps heighten arousal and is part of the body's response to >stress.

Advertising, American psychologists from 1910 on were employed by advertising agencies to help create campaigns. >John B. Watson, the founder of >behaviourism, went to work for J. Walter Thompson, the advertising agency, after he was forced to resign from Johns Hopkins University as a result of having an affair with a student. Watson brought to Madison Avenue an experimental approach which transformed advertising from the crude tactics of braying that Our Product is Best to sophisticated psychological tactics. Watson found that smokers could hardly recognize the tastes of their favourite brands of cigarettes. He reckoned therefore that what mattered was what he called the selling idea of any product, which we now know as the image. Creating an image was a question of associating it with positive reinforcers. For example, he devised an image for Johnson and Johnson in 1924 that has lasted. Johnson and Johnson products should be white, pure and healthy; good mothers would want to use them. Watson also grasped that some products could be sold through fear and he was instrumental in creating a market for deodorants. Those who didn't use them would suffer social embarrassment. Since then advertisers have used increasingly sophisticated market and consumer research both to test products and to divine whether it is possible to create a demand for a particular new one. V. Packard in *The Hidden Persuaders* (1960) tried to expose some of the devices that advertisers use. The suspicion of advertising has led to a far greater use of humour in campaigns for products such as Guinness and Tennants Bitter, but the basic principles of how to use psychology to get the consumer to fork out have remained much the same.

● D. Cohen, *John B. Watson* (1979).

Affect, a technical term for emotions (*see* Emotion).

Affective disorders, a form of psychiatric illness involving inappropriate emotions (*see* Emotion).

After-images. If you look at an object in bright light and then close your eyes, you will often see an image of the same shape but with light and dark reversed. This is the after-image.

Ageing. We age from the moment we are born. Shakespeare in his famous

'Seven ages of man' speech saw old age as *sans* eyes, *sans* teeth, *sans* everything'. While it is true that our bodies become less agile, our sight may deteriorate somewhat, and a few of us may lose our teeth, ageing nowadays doesn't mean the inevitable chair by the fireside or (worse) the hospital bed it once did.

The neuropsychology of ageing remains mysterious. Brain cells start dying from the age of 40 in normal individuals. Anatomical studies of the ageing >brain suggest that it shrinks in size and that there are growing numbers of tángles and neurofibrillary plaques. Lately, there's been tremendous interest in the causes of >Alzheimer's disease. Recent neurochemical studies suggest that it may be caused by the loss of the cells in the base of the forebrain which produce >acetylcholine, a >neurotransmitter. There, small nuclei form pathways that 'feed' the cortex. This theory raises the possibility that dementia could be prevented, halted or even reversed.

Despite the inevitable decay that age imposes on the brain, there have always been individuals who have managed to retain their faculties well into their late 80s and 90s. Churchill was generally considered to be an effective prime minister until the age of 82 when he had a stroke; Voltaire and Tolstoy both wrote considerable works in their 80s; the artist Georgia O'Keefe was painting in her 90s. Mental 'aerobics' may be a help, for nearly all of these people kept on working. Why some people remain vigorous while others do not remains elusive. Studies suggest that, as we age, various psychological abilities diminish, including perceptual activity, the speed of reflexes and rapidity of coordination. There is also evidence that it's harder for old people to assimilate new information. Welford, Norris and Shock showed, however, that old people compensated for many perceptual and motor defects by using their experience. Their loss of skill is much less than their loss of function. There has been little research on >personality or emotional changes as we grow older. No one knows much, for example, about how people react to growing old. It's an area whose time has come.

It's estimated that, by the year 2000, 8% of the population will be over 75. Moreover, many of these won't be *sans* everything' but will have considerable disposable income and voting power. As a result, it's likely that the social perception of the old – and indeed their own self-perception – will be radically different from that in previous cultures. In the 1960s, youth was at its height. The cult of youth now has competition. Groups such as the Grey Panthers in the US demand rights for the elderly. Previously taboo areas such as 'Is there sex after 70?' have now become areas of debate. Recently, a new form of >therapy – reminiscence therapy – has been developed. It encourages old people to remember their youth, with the aim of stimulating their memory and preventing them becoming too passive. It seems plausible that the next 15 years will see many developments in the psychology of ageing – especially those that focus on how individuals can get the best out of this part of their lives. *See* Senile dementia.

● E. Erikson, J. Erikson, H. Kiunick, *Vital Involvement in Old Age* (1986); A.

A

Welford, A. H. Norris, N. W. Shock, 'Speed and Accuracy of Movement and their Changes with Age' in *Attention and Performance*, ed. W. G. Koster (1969)

Aggression, a very complex concept used in >psychoanalysis, social psychology, >ethology and everyday life. >Freud saw aggression as a central >instinct. Experimental psychologists have focused on it rather less, perhaps because it's not that easy to get subjects to be aggressive in the laboratory. The psychoanalyst Charles Rycroft has pointed out that the word 'aggression' is derived from the Latin *ad gradior*, to move towards. Many definitions of aggression involve positive things such as being assertive, dynamic and having the >drive to do things. Yet, in the psychology literature, aggression is nearly always seen as negative. The attitude is that our biology has left us with a capacity for being aggressive and we have not yet adapted ourselves to behaving more rationally.

There have been studies of the biochemistry of aggression, of the way animals use threat displays out in the wild, of domestic violence and also of the ways in which groups become aggressive towards each other. Attempts to integrate these very different perspectives into a theory of aggression haven't succeeded yet.

Clearly, there is a hormonal link with levels of aggression. Men tend to be more aggressive: certain of their hormones seem to increase this. Certain situations, such as competition for territory or mates, also seem to provoke aggressive behaviour. Konrad Lorenz, the ethologist, noted that human beings are the only species that kills its own kind regularly, and he suggested that one reason for this was that technology made it possible for us to kill at a distance. There's also much research that suggests that, in humans, aggression is also partly a learned behaviour. Aggression, or at least being arrested for fighting by the police, runs in certain groups.

Psychotherapists argue that aggression can be 'cured' because people often resort to it when they can't say what they want to say: teach them social skills, they claim, and they won't have to thump their wives. This has led to some successful programmes in North America for countering domestic violence. Similar attempts to use psychology to curb the so-called aggressive instincts of nations have not done so well. There's no recorded instance of psychologists intervening to negotiate the end of a political conflict, though at times they have very much wanted to do so.

Aggression is a complex form of behaviour, biochemically reasonably well understood. The problem is not to understand its biochemistry but to change our inclination for it.

- J. Groebel and R. Hinde, *Aggression and War* (1989); Konrad Lorenz, *On Aggression* (1966).

Agoraphobia, the fear of open spaces, from the Greek *agora* (market-place) and *phobia* (>fear). This is one of the most common >phobias. Sufferers find it hard to leave their houses, and panic at the thought of being in the street. As a result, they cannot perform the simplest of everyday tasks such as shopping, and are

A

often badly handicapped. Psychoanalysts suggest that its causes include a fear of becoming involved in relationships, with sexual frustration playing a part. Behaviour therapists see it as the result of inappropriate >learning: sufferers may be rewarded by the attention they get for not going out, or staying in may have been strongly reinforced in the past. Behavioural treatments work well, as do >self-help groups in which those who are getting better escort fellow sufferers.

Alcoholism, still the most common >addiction. In Britain, it's estimated that over 3 million people have a drink problem. Not all alcohol problems are identical. At one extreme, there are meths drinkers who tramp the streets and survive on the edge of society; at the other, there is the stressed, successful executive who just about copes with board meetings despite too many cocktails. In addition, an increasing number of housewives now abuse alcohol. As with addiction in general, there is disagreement about the causes of alcoholism. Some blame biology; others the situations that people find themselves in. Social attitudes among the middle class, at least, to alcohol have changed as a result of very deliberate campaigns: few people now boast about drinking and driving; there has been a drop in the consumption of some kinds of alcohol, especially spirits. Rising sales of mineral water and low-alcohol lagers reflect a new health awareness on the part of the public. Treatment for alcoholism ranges from >self-help groups such as AA to >counselling. >Aversion therapy is used occasionally but few experts think it highly effective.

● N. Heather and I. Robertson, *Problem Drinking* (1988).

Alienation, not feeling that one is really oneself; also a sense of distance between oneself and society. This is an important concept in >Marxist psychology, which states that the conditions of >work under capitalism create alienation. The most interesting psychological account of the phenomenon can be found in Herbert Marcuse's *One-Dimensional Man* (1964).

Alzheimer's disease, also known as >senile dementia. Its symptoms are mental confusion and loss of >memory. Some of those affected profoundly by Alzheimer's disease can hardly remember anything other than their own names. The biochemical key to the disease is the loss of >acetylcholine, a >neurotransmitter in the >brain. A diet containing high levels of white fish seems to stimulate the continuing production of acetylcholine and prevents the disease.

Amnesia, loss of >memory, usually due to physical causes such as being concussed. Usually it only affects recent memory, but there are some cases of loss of most of long-term memory. Occasionally, people even forget their names. An unsettling illness that is important for the light it can throw on how memory works.

Anal stage, a stage in >psychosexual development, in which the infant is obsessed with the products of his or her body, such as faeces. The anal stage follows on from the >oral stage. These stages were first formally set out by

A

>Anna Freud.

Clearly, toilet training is an important stage in infancy, so there is some plausibility to >Sigmund Freud's claim that babies go through a period of interest in excretion. But some of his theory is fanciful. It's been claimed that those who remain stuck at the anal stage and, therefore, develop anal personalities are greedy and miserly, hoarding money as they once hoarded their faeces. The proof of this is dubious. Opponents of >psychoanalysis see the anal stage as a bit of a joke – and a fallacy.

Analysis of variance, a statistical technique much used in psychology. Usually, the results of an experiment produce a set of scores which are marked down as scatter points on a traditional graph. The problem for the psychologist is to analyse the reasons for the variability of results and what it can be attributed to. Imagine that the experiment is studying how accurately people shoot. Mathematically, the variance of each point on the scatter is the average squared deviation of the shots from the centre. The mean is the bull's eye. Most shots deviate. The shoot is moved indoors and now the shots fit into a tighter pattern. Outdoors, wind can be said to account for 75% of the variance. Some variance may also stem from the fact that the shooter has an unsteady hand. The gun is mounted. That now brings the shots in further so we can say that unsteadiness accounts for X% of the variance. One way of analysing variance is to plot histograms of scores under different conditions and see where they do, and don't, overlap.

Analytical psychology, the school of >psychoanalysis developed by >Jung in opposition to >Freud. *See* Jung, Carl Gustav.

Anglo-American psychology. Scientific psychology was initially as much German as American or British. The first psychological laboratory was set up in Leipzig in 1879 by >Wundt, who was inspired by the ideas and work of Hermann von Helmholtz (1821–94). Nearly all the great early American psychologists went to study under Wundt. A good description of Wundt's dominance is to be found in the notebooks and letters of James McKeen Cattell, later professor at Columbia University, who noted in 1885 that it was a great honour to have a paper printed in Wundt's *Philosophical Studies*.

Yet very quickly, psychology became dominated by American ideas. One reason was the failure of German >introspection. After the rise of >behaviourism, American psychology believed in empirical experiments as the only way forward. Research focused on >learning, and there was no room for >innate ideas or for strange unprovable concoctions such as the 'soul'. After World War I, there was a huge increase in the number of American universities offering psychology courses. Although the exiles from the Nazis brought over some new ideas, the pattern of American psychology was set: it focused on experiments and the individual.

It was felt that there was little sense in studying how ideology and culture affected groups apart from in studies of >prejudice. There was also a virtual taboo until the 1970s on asking subjects what they felt or thought in case introspection crept back in. Researchers did not understand that there could be different kinds of psychology and different methods for attacking different problems. Instead, vast effort was made to see how rats could learn mazes or, more exotically, whether octopuses could tell a red triangle from a pink ellipse. The exclusion of foreign perspectives in social sciences was not due to just intellectual argument. A fascinating recent study of sociology at Harvard University argues that Talcott Parsons won out in theoretical wars against the Soviet sociologist Sorokin because Sorokin was foreign, didn't understand what he was saying and was apt to give endless, dull lectures. On such turns of intellectual fashion are schools founded.

No one person founded or maintained Anglo-American psychology, but its confidence was nicely caught by Donald Broadbent when he claimed that 'Nobody can grasp the nature of things from an armchair.' He rejected the 'confident dogmatisms' concerning behaviour that editors, teachers and priests revelled in. 'Rather we must be prepared to live with an incomplete knowledge of behaviour but with confidence in that power of objective methods that give us that knowledge some day. These methods have proved themselves in the last 50 years.' The intellectual climate of such an enterprise was best described by Hudson in *The Cult of Fact*, which told of his time in Oxford in the 1950s when success was a question of doing elegant experiments. The subjects might be trivial; the style was superb.

By the 1970s, there were signs of a move against this often arid tradition, with European social psychology gaining new ground. No major centre has rivalled Anglo-American dominance, although in the past 25 years it has itself broadened as psychologists have become more aware of the limitations of a narrow intellectual approach. The consequences for psychology of this setting of the agenda have been profound. Nehemiah Jordan noted in 1968 that 50 years of objective psychology had yielded little live knowledge. Paul Kline, a distinguished experimentalist, has recently published a remarkable lament for the failure of this kind of empirical psychology. The confidence once exuded has turned to self-doubt.

- Donald Broadbent, *Behaviour* (1961); Liam Hudson, *The Cult of the Fact* (1972); Nehemiah Jordan, *Theories in Speculative Psychology* (1968); Paul Kline, *Psychology Exposed* (1989).

Anima and animus, a concept of >Carl Jung. The anima is the female part of the >personality. Men and women both have animas but, in men, the anima is often repressed. Jung argued that it was formed from the image of the mother which was internalized during the resolution of the >Oedipus complex. Unconsciously, the anima influences career and romantic choices, even spiritual ones. With men in therapy, the therapeutic task is to reveal the anima to the client and integrate it into his personality.

Animus is the sibling of the anima concept. This is the thrusting male part of the personality which some women find hard to accept as part of themselves.

For behaviourists, such concepts are seen as mystifying and eccentric. Freud,

A

too, had little that was flattering to say about the animus/anima.

Animal behaviour. *See* Ethology.

Anorexia. Sir William Gull first identified the disease in 1874. He noted that young women refused to eat and yet, despite starving themselves, often had manic energy. Gull recommended not just 'moral treatment' – ie nagging them to eat – but also trips to the Riviera. He caught surprisingly accurately the essence of what has come to be seen as a major modern disease.

Currently, the favoured analysis is that developed by Susie Orbach who argues that girls become anorexic as a reaction against the roles patriarchal society imposes on them, such as being seen as sex objects. Orbach does not deny that anorexia is a serious condition but suggests its root is a rejection of male stereotypes of women – in other words, she sees it as a 'glorious malady', just as >R. D. Laing once saw >schizophrenia. Orbach has argued persuasively that much treatment of anorexics (eg force-feeding) is barbaric and counter-productive. Treatment based on love and care is more effective. More conventional (and usually male) psychiatrists do not see anorexia as a political or sexual protest, but an illness. *See also* Bulimia.

● Susie Orbach, *Fat Is a Feminist Issue* (1979) and *Hunger Strike* (1986).

Antidepressants, drugs which aim to cure >depression by acting on the >central nervous system. Family doctors have tended to prescribe them in situations where it would have been better to counsel patients and discover just what was the matter. As a result, there are groups who have become unnecessarily addicted. *See also* Monoamine oxidase inhibitors.

Anxiety, a concept used initially in >psychoanalysis but then extended more widely. Anxiety can be both an irrational >fear and also a realistic one. In the psychoanalytic literature alone, it's possible to count the following forms: castration anxiety, separation anxiety, depressive anxiety, paranoid anxiety, as well as phobic and objective anxiety. >Freud had three theories of anxiety: initially, he claimed that it was a manifestation of repressed >libido; then that it repeated the birth experience; and finally that it was the response of the >ego to rises in emotional tension.

Other schools of psychology also cover the concept of anxiety. >Eysenck sees the tendency to be anxious as a key part of the trait of >neuroticism. >Learning theorists suggest that people perform best when they experience a modest amount of anxiety.

Much anxiety is irrational, especially that involved in >phobias – the >agoraphobic who won't go out has no reason to be afraid – but there are many situations in which anxiety is perfectly sensible: going to sit an exam, meeting a potential new lover, seeking a job all should arouse anxiety. Psychology, however, has focused on irrational anxiety.

Many therapies (*see* Therapy) attempt to cure anxiety either through getting people to discuss what makes them anxious or through relaxation exercises. Both offer a measure of relief.

Aphasia, a disorder of >language attributed to >lesions of the >brain due to a stroke, head injury or other kinds of damage. Aphasia has fascinated neurologists since 1864; >Freud also wrote on it. Aphasic patients can sometimes speak excessively slowly, sometimes produce a jumble of words (or 'word salad'), and sometimes have quite bizarre difficulties – if you show them a bird, they'll be able to describe it, give names of other flying species (insects, butterflies) but won't be able to say 'Bird'.

There are many different kinds of aphasia. *Wernicke's aphasia* (named after the German physiologist who found patients who had lesions in the brain) is the inability to understand speech or arrange heard sounds into coherent speech. *Broca's aphasia* (after Carl Broca, the French physiologist), also known as motor expressive or non-fluent aphasia, is the inability to produce speech. In *anomic aphasia*, patients can speak but can't name objects.

One reason for the theoretical interest in aphasia is that very specific language problems seem to be the product of very specific brain lesions so that they offer a clue to neurological function of a very exact kind. >CAT scans suggest that Wernicke's aphasia is correlated with damage in the posterior language area, Broca's with damage in the anterior.

Problems linked to aphasia are agraphia (poor writing) and alexia (poor reading).

Apperception, the process of becoming aware of a >perception.

Approach avoidance conflict, a process whereby a person or an animal is torn between wanting to do and wanting to avoid a particular thing. For example, the rat can see that down the T-maze is a piece of cheese. The rat also knows from previous learning that it will get a small electric shock as it crosses the ground. Its behaviour will tend to exhibit a mix of approach-avoidance – going some way down the T-maze and then retreating. In humans, Hamlet is the perfect example: he is always approaching the murder of Claudius and then avoiding it.

Aptitude test, a test of aptitudes. *See* Intelligence testing.

Archetypes. >Carl Jung claimed that the human >mind has certain ancient characters built in that reflect our >collective unconscious. There is no independent empirical evidence of this interesting idea since nearly all the patients who produce archetypes in >dreams or >free associations tend to be Jungian patients who may well be producing the images they believe their analysts want.

● Carl Jung, *Archetypes of the Collective Unconscious* (1934).

Arousal, a state of excitation. It can be caused by both positive stimuli such as sexual attraction and negative stimuli such as a large predator staring at you (*see* Stimulus). Although arousal is a psychological concept, there are physiological means of measuring it especially through the >galvanic skin response. William James suggested that the >perception of emotions is due first to the perception of arousal: 'I first see that I am sweating, then I know I'm afraid.'

Singer and Schachtel (1962) showed that a state of arousal could lead to either positive or negative emotions depending on how subjects saw events. *See also* Emotion.

Art. *See* Creativity.

Artificial intelligence, the attempt to develop robots and computer programs that can mimic human behaviour. There has been considerable success in developing computer programs that can play chess, recognize voices, achieve pattern recognition and carry out high-level computational skills. Nevertheless, Simon's boast in 1960 that within 25 years we would see computers that would be able to perform many human skills has turned out to be false. Artificial intelligence work has been fruitful, however, in making many researchers think about different possible ways in which the >brain might work. After all, if a computer can carry out the kinds of tasks the brain does, the organization of both the former's hardware and software should be comparable to the structures of the brain. This analogy has led to some interesting ideas such as channel theory, >serial processing, parallel processing, Dennett's thought experiments and related projects like the 'Turtle', a learning project in which children use computers. Critics argue that, while the artificial intelligence work may produce valuable new computer programs, there is no reason to suppose that the brain works in similar ways. The sheer numbers of >neurons in the >cortex and the almost infinite number of connections between them make analogies between the brain and computers hard to sustain.

- A. Garnham, *Artificial Intelligence* (1986); H. Simon, 'Cognitive Science: the newest science of the artificial' in *Perspectives of Cognitive Science* (1981), ed. D. A. Norman; R. Penrose, *The Emperor's New Mind* (1989).

Art therapy. The Victorians who built insane >asylums saw that it might be useful for inmates to have a chance to paint, draw and play music, but there was no formal definition of art >therapy until the 1960s. There had long been psychiatric patients who were gifted artists, such as Richard Dadd who was held in the Hospital of St Mary of Bethlehem (commonly known as >Bedlam) in the 19th century. >Freud argued that great artists such as Leonardo used art in order to resolve their unconscious conflicts, and the psychoanalyst's interest in art helped to promote the use of art therapy.

The basic principle is simple. Get patients to 'do art' because by doing so they will be able to express feelings they couldn't otherwise express. Dalley offers a number of case histories in which the discussion of a work of art leads the patient to talk about once untalkable problems. Art therapy offers a way in – much like >play therapy. It is something of a professional battleground because there are arguments about whether it offers a chance to recover, or is just a means of getting patients to pass the time.

- T. Dalley, *Images of Art Therapy* (1987).

Assertiveness training, the acquiring of social skills to learn how not to be intimidated, not to accept what one doesn't want to. A concept developed through >therapy groups and attractive to many feminist psychologists (*see* Feminist psychology).

Assimilation, a concept from >Piaget's theory. In the >sensori-motor stage, the infant takes in – assimilates – all >perceptions. *See also* Accommodation.

Association theory. A theory of the >mind that focuses on how one thought leads to another. Think 'chair' and it is easy (because they are so naturally associated) to think 'table'. Think 'table' and you may well find yourself thinking either '2 x 2' or 'dinner'. Such networks dominate our mental processes and they are born of experience. The theory was first proposed by the English philosopher John Locke and then expanded by David Hume in his *Treatise on Human Nature* (1739–40). Hume argued that one idea leads to another through a number of connections such as frequency and >contiguity. He relied heavily on the work of another Scottish thinker, David Hartley. From about 1750, this theory of how the mind connects disparate thoughts was taken as gospel.

Two things are worth noting. First, such a model was implicitly accepted as true by >Freud and >Jung. They saw, however, that the conscious associations tapped by Hume and others were not the only associations. There was a vast pool of powerful, but repressed, associations censored from our thinking. Thus, '2 x 2' might also evoke dark thoughts of being beaten if you didn't get the sum right, of school and guilty associations of pleasure. Secondly, the principles of association are remarkably similar to those of >learning theory which explains how we acquire knowledge, and was developed much later.

● G. Humphrey, *Thinking* (1951).

Asylums. It is rumoured that the first asylum was in Aleppo, in Syria in about AD 1100. The idea that the mentally ill should be segregated came from religious orders, and was considered an act of charity; in Britain, >Bedlam, the first asylum, was a religious foundation. These high ideals eventually lapsed, and viewing the 'crazies' who were isolated from the rest of society became a spectator sport. In the 18th century, there were a number of private asylums in London in which well-off families incarcerated their embarrassing relatives. Until the French Revolution, the regimes at most asylums were deliberately cruel, with inmates kept in chains.

The French Revolution, with its passion for liberty, led pioneers such as Philippe Pinel to take the chains off patients. Pinel's initiatives were copied in many parts of Europe and triggered a 'moral movement' for decent treatment. Asylums were built in the countryside where the afflicted would recover their wits. At York, Quakers ran the best known of these moral asylums, The Retreat. Patients were given considerable freedom and treated with respect and dignity, and they were led to hope that they might return to normal society. Even Broadmoor, the asylum for the criminally insane, which opened in 1863, was meant to provide decent accommodation, fresh air and artistic pursuits – violin playing would make inmates less violent. However, Scull and Digby have argued that even the idealistic Quakers were apt to treat patients less well than their propaganda would have us think. By the end of the Victorian era, asylums were overcrowded and highly disciplined; warders punished patients who stepped out of line. Broadmoor, for example, had over 800 patients by 1900, and the governor kept them all inside their cells for 23 hours a day. Some therapy!

Asylums tended to be situated on the edges of towns. A few miles from North London, as the comic novelist P. G. Wodehouse observed, one could find a fine collection of nuthouses. Napsbury, Colney Hatch, Shenley and Friern Barnet all competing for the passing lunatic trade. The location wasn't accidental. Patients got the nice country air that the 'moral movement' wanted and society was not burdened with too many patients too close at hand. These huge Victorian 'warehouses' of the mentally ill decayed slowly. Their atmosphere was nicely caught by Dr Stephen MacKeith who went to work in one as part of his medical training: 'It was widely assumed that mental patients, if they were not drooling dements, were liable to be dangerous. Hence all the locked doors and the near panic when a patient absconded.' With such conditions, it wasn't odd that the belief arose that asylums themselves created disease. This trend in the treatment of the mentally ill was copied abroad, including in the United States. After the Second World War, the American journalist Albert Deutsch wrote a seminal book, *The Shame of the States*, in which he alleged that the conditions in huge asylums such as Milledgeville, which had 9000 inmates, were appalling. He wrote: 'The state hospital doctors frankly admit that the animals of nearby piggeries were better fed, housed and treated than many of the patients in their words.'

In 1961, the British MP Enoch Powell, then Minister for Health, denounced these asylums as relics of the Victorian age – fine for their time but in bad need of reform. In addition, it became clear that some patients had been kept in hospital for years even though they had probably never been insane. No one was quite clear why they had been initially admitted. In my own researches, I met one patient who was admitted to Napsbury because she had become pregnant 33 years previously while unmarried, and two old men in Japan who had been incarcerated for more than 25 years but whose diagnoses had been lost.

Such tales of souls lost in asylum systems led to pressure for releasing patients from hospital; asylums were evil and should be closed. Enthusiasts took up this cause as a liberal reform. In fact, reducing the numbers of patients in hospitals suited both radicals and politicians: it would look progressive and save money. The last 20 years have seen most countries in the West reduce drastically their number of patients. In the United States, the number fell from 560,000 in 1955 to under 300,000 today. In Britain, it has fallen from 150,000 to 70,000. In Italy, there has been a move to close all mental hospitals.

Two exceptions stand out. In the Third World, the number of patients is rising, which is probably a good thing since there have been so few facilities; in India, there are under 30,000 hospital beds, for instance. But in some developed and very conformist nations such as Japan, the asylum remains a dumping ground for those who don't conform. Hospitals are private and seek patients, and there has been a growing number of scandals, with patients being abused, even killed.

Releasing patients into the community without proper preparation or facilities now seems a poor policy, too. Many have come to argue that asylums are not evil after all, and that many patients benefit from some of the protection that a mental hospital can offer as long as they don't become institutionalized. This is part of a continuing debate in >psychiatry. Asylums were once the solution; then they became the problem; now they are part of the solution again.

- D. Cohen, *Forgotten Millions* (1988); A. Digby, *Medicine, Madness and Morality* (1986); Andrew Scull, *Museums of Madness* (1980); T. Szasz, *Cruel Compassion* (1994).

Attachment theory, a theory developed by >John Bowlby that draws on psychoanalysis and animal behaviour (>ethology) to explain how we form emotional bonds. *See also* Bonding.

Attitudes, what we think and/or feel about particular issues or groups. Social psychologists began to study attitudes in the 1930s. They argued that attitudes consisted of a combination of three elements: a cognitive element of belief, an emotional element of affects and a conative element of intentions which lead to actions. There was particular interest in >prejudice, especially the attitude of American whites towards black people. The growth of market research has led to more statistical sophistication in measuring attitudes; much money is spent on such things as working out just how the consumer feels about dishwashers or a new brand of soap.

The study of attitudes is bedevilled by many problems. First, how willing are subjects to be truthful? In the 1930s, it was acceptable to be prejudiced against blacks; now it is much less so, so only extremely hostile people will admit to any racial prejudice. Second, even if people honestly express their attitudes, how important are these in affecting their behaviour? Ever more statistically sophisticated tests of attitudes have not resolved these basic dilemmas.

Attribution theory, a theory of social psychology which seeks to explain much social interaction by the qualities we attribute to others. It has been found, for example, that if people are seen as physically attractive, they are also judged to be more competent (*see* Halo effect). Attribution theory stresses the way we explain negative >life events. It has extended work on learned >helplessness and is especially important in >cognitive theory. *See* Locus of control.

Authority and the authoritarian personality. The authoritarian personality type sees the world in a rigid and power-dominated way. The concept emerged out of studies by many psychologists in the 1930s and 1940s, who wanted to discover how it had been possible for the Nazis to succeed. The authoritarian >personality became a key explanatory concept. He was obsequious to superiors, never questioned orders and was brutal to inferiors. Hierarchical social structures tend to attract authoritarian personalities or to turn people into them. Prison warders and regular soldiers were especially authoritarian.

17

As an explanation, the concept always risked being a little circular. Authoritarian personalities behaved in a rigid way. That rigid behaviour proved they were authoritarian. There were controversies, too, about the validity of its basic scale – called the 'F scale', 'F' standing for Fascism. These controversies became heightened after it was found that decent Americans were willing to give electric shocks to subjects who failed to get maths answers right (*see* Introduction). They did so even when the 'shock meter' went past the red danger signal which was embellished with a skull and crossbones and when subjects screamed. Stanley Milgram concluded not so much that we are all authoritarian but that few people could stand up to authority. In a re-analysis of the data, Rom Harré has suggested that the setting of the experiment makes Milgram's conclusions dubious: did those delivering the shocks really think that respectable Yale University, pillar of the Ivy League, would play host to a study in which real harm came to people? No, they were just going along with the experiment.

Autism, a condition in which an individual doesn't speak and often refuses to communicate even in a non-verbal way. Initially, autism was attributed to brain damage but increasingly research suggests that sufferers are refusing to participate in normal social life. The great ethologist, Niko Tinbergen, suggested that much of their behaviour resembled >shyness.

More recently, Uta Frith has claimed that autistic children are unable to pretend in their playing. This inability may be at the root of their disability.

● Uta Frith, *Autism* (1989).

Autonomic function. The autonomic >nervous system serves the many visceral structures that are concerned with basic processes of life such as the heart, the blood vessels, the digestive system. Usually we do not feel conscious of, or in control of, how these functions operate. Much interest exists because it seems that we can, through >biofeedback, learn to control some of these areas. Blood pressure, for example, can be lowered by many people if they are given constant feedback on the state of their blood pressure. *See* Nervous system.

Auxiliary egos. *See* Drama therapy.

Aversion therapy, a form of >therapy which tries to condition patients to give up a habit by associating it with pain. Some forms involve giving patients a drug which makes them violently ill if they smoke or drink. This does discourage smoking and/or drinking but only for a limited period. Other types of aversion therapy have included showing particular pictures (eg photographs of children to pederasts) and accompanying this with mild electric shocks.

Aversive stimulus, an event or >stimulus which is unpleasant and makes the organism withdraw.

Avoidance learning, training by negative >reinforcement, so that a person or animal does whatever it has to to avoid an >aversive stimulus. If the right response is learned, the 'bad' event doesn't happen. This learning is very difficult to alter.

B

Babinski reflex, one of the reflexes of newborn children. If the soles of the feet of a newborn are stroked from heel to toes, the baby will spread its small toes and raise its big ones. The evolutionary history of this >reflex is linked to that of the monkeys. The reflex disappears after six months.

Balint, Michael (1896–1970), Hungarian psychoanalyst who settled in Britain. He studied interactions between GPs and patients and found that the average GP consultation lasts six minutes. This is often inadequate as many problems raised are emotional, psychological and social, and patients treated so quickly feel abandoned. Balint alerted the medical profession to the fact that its conventional skills were not the only ones needed. The lesson that GPs need psychological training has been slow to filter through to medical schools in the UK, however.

Bartlett, Sir Frederic (1886–1969), one of the fathers of British experimental psychology. He helped set up the department of psychology at Cambridge University and is now best known for his work on >memory which suggested that we organize our recollections around >schemas. His book *Remembering: A Study in Experimental and Social Psychology* (1932) remains a minor classic.

Bedlam, a corruption of the Hospital of St Mary of Bethlehem which was the name of the first psychiatric hospital in the British Isles. Set up originally in 1247, it was turned over to the care of the insane in 1402. Bedlam was a very cruel and public madhouse. Spectators could come and gawp at the insane in chains. Like many psychiatric institutions, it was reformed in the 19th century when the moral movement in >asylums became influential, arguing that patients needed to be humanely treated. The Bethlem Royal Hospital still exists, in Beckenham outside London.

Behaviourism, one of the major schools of psychology from 1913 to about 1970, which influenced the development of scientific psychology enormously. The key behaviourist idea is that thoughts, feelings, intentions – in fact, all mental

B

processes – don't determine behaviour. We are biological machines. We don't act of our own free >will but rather we react to stimuli (*see* Stimulus) according to the ways in which we have been conditioned. If I have been conditioned to fear rats, then show me a rat and, whatever I may think, however much I might will myself not to care, I'll be afraid of the rat.

Behaviourism was created and promoted by >J. B. Watson, in reaction against the introspective psychology (*see* Introspection) of the German school. Watson argued in 1913 that psychology could do without the concept of >consciousness, and that human beings could be studied as objectively as animals. We do not have inaccessible souls or minds; psychology ought to study what human beings did, rather than to try to guess what was going on inside their heads. Behaviourism claimed that it was possible to observe behaviour scientifically. Two well-trained observers ought to be able to agree on how fast a man added up or learned to type. For Watson, the prediction and control of behaviour was the goal of psychology.

He also used the ideas of >Pavlov and argued that the behaviour of animals and human beings was determined by their conditioned >reflexes. He promoted the study of infants to trace the full >conditioning history of individuals: if you could log the complete history of the rewards and punishments that a child had experienced, Watson said, you could predict every one of his or her actions or reactions. In practice, however, no behaviourist ever managed to give a detailed history of this sort for any organism, so it remained a theoretical ideal.

With their emphasis on >learning, behaviourists had little time for >innate ideas or abilities. According to them, babies were born without >instincts or genetically given skills. Watson echoed the Jesuits when he said that if he were given the education of a child until he or she was seven, he could shape that child's future as he wanted. Learning was all.

For all his concern about making psychology scientific, Watson also wanted to root it in real life. Behaviourists would study the complexities of behaviour in the office, the factory, the maternity clinic and even the bedroom. It wasn't to be a discipline based in the laboratory. But after a divorce scandal in 1920, Watson was forced to leave academic psychology, and behaviourism became much more of a laboratory science and concentrated on detailed experiments of minute segments of behaviour. Its subsequent giants, >B. F. Skinner and Clark Hull, focused on animal studies. They were not as interested in human behaviour, although Skinner would eventually write essentially philosophical works about how behaviourism could better the human lot. *Walden Two*, his behaviourist utopia, and *Beyond Freedom and Dignity* offer visions of a world in which people are conditioned to be socially responsible. However, neither Skinner nor Hull did the detailed human experimental work in the real world that Watson pioneered. Writers such as George Orwell and Aldous Huxley feared the power that behaviourist social engineering would give governments. Both in *1984* and *Brave New World*, behaviourist techniques are employed for evil ends by an omnipotent state.

Skinner did develop some important concepts in behaviourism. The best known are >operant conditioning and >shaping behaviour.

Behaviourism was an approach of a particular time. Critics claim it has failed. Current psychology emphasizes much that it regarded as either *passé* or taboo. Consciousness is no longer a dirty word. Excluding all mental causes was certainly extremist, but it had some point. The fervour of the early behaviourists was necessary as so much psychology was bogged down in unproductive introspective experiments. Psychologists quibbled about whether A's introspections were truer than B's, a quarrel no one could resolve. The value of studying behaviour objectively is today recognized even by those who argue that it can never give the full story. For example, >Anna Freud the psychoanalyst noted that everyone was a behaviourist in the 1960s – to some extent at least. The child analyst could gain many insights by studying how a child ate meals, played with toys or responded to various tests.

Like many psychological theories, behaviourism was imperfect and incomplete, but it played an important role in shaping psychological thought. It remains, together with >psychoanalysis, perhaps the most important influence on psychology for the first 60 years of this century. *See* Latent learning.

- R. Boakes, *Animal Behaviour from Darwin* (1986); D. F. Broadbent, *Behaviour* (1961); B.F. Skinner, *Beyond Freedom and Dignity* (1972).

Behaviour modification, a technique based on >learning theory as used in >behaviourism, to modify or alter behaviour. Behaviourism hoped to change people: if a man is handicapped by the fact that he sweats every time he meets an attractive girl, he could learn, or be conditioned, to perspire less (*see* Conditioning). >Watson claimed that individuals could use the lessons of behaviourism to perfect themselves. Our perspiring lover could learn to control his sweating, the worried executive could learn to be calm and decisive. Freudians argue that the technique deals with superficial symptoms only and that they will reappear in some different disturbance. Left-wing critics claim that it is the State and capitalism that would use behaviour modification in order to ensure conformity.

In practice, however, behaviour modification hasn't achieved much more than curing >phobias, although, to a small extent, it has been used in penal reform. Here, programmes of token economies encourage less antisocial behaviour. Given the hopes that Watson had for behaviour modification, it's been disappointing. However, the use of video has injected new energy into this technique; it is now possible for individuals to see how they behave and to remodel themselves, to be more socially skilled.

- G. Martin and J. Pear, *Behaviour Modification* (1983).

Behaviour therapy, a special variant of >behaviour modification aimed at those with clinical problems. >Watson established and then eradicated, or cured, a boy known as Little Albert of his fear of rats. As Watson described it, he banged a steel bar very loudly behind Albert when Albert was playing with the rat. Result: fear. A slow re-introduction of the rat when Albert felt safe was the cure. There have been ethical and historical doubts about the Little Albert

B

study. Curiously, from 1920 to 1950, although Little Albert was much discussed in textbooks, the ideas of the study were not applied; then it became a model for behaviour therapy.

>Eysenck argued, for example, that psychoanalysts got much better results when they had phobic patients relax at the end of an analytic session and walk towards the door. Wolpe and Rachmen then developed the idea of relaxation while either having patients imagine what they feared most or putting them in the presence of the object that provokes the >phobia. A second form of behaviour therapy is flooding, when people are exposed to massive amounts of the >stimulus that frightens them. Behaviour therapy techniques work well with phobias and in variants developed by Masters and Johnson in sexual dysfunction (*see* Sex therapy). Psychoanalysts claim that these methods cure symptoms, not the real problems that led to them.

● S. Fairbairn and G. Fairbairn, *Psychology, Ethics and Change* (1987).

Benzodiazepines, a class of >tranquillizers of which Valium (diazepam) is the best known. They work by encouraging the function of (gamma) Y-aminobutyric acid called GABA. They make the >receptors more responsive to GABA.

Bereavement. *See* Loss.

Bergson, Henri (1859–1941), French philosopher best known for his ideas on creative evolution. His literary and philosophical study of >laughter, in which is claimed that we laugh when human beings act as machines, remains one of the central texts for psychologists interested in the subject. Bergson seems to have modelled his theory on French farces, and, because of this, it is very partial and inadequate.

Berkeley, George, Bishop of Cloyne (1685–1763), Irish philosopher who did some pioneering work on the psychology of >vision. He anticipated some modern ideas by working out that our judgement of distance is crucially dependent on the fact that we have two eyes and that they converge on far off objects. Berkeley was also puzzled by – but did not solve – one of the perennial visual illusions, the moon illusion. The moon looks small when it is high up in the heaven and large when close to the horizon. Why? Berkeley's philosophical ideas, however, remain largely irrelevant for psychology today.

● George Berkeley, *A New Theory of Vision* (1910).

Bettelheim, Bruno (1903–), a psychoanalyst who survived Auschwitz and wrote one of the first books about surviving the Holocaust. Bettelheim argued that, even under such dire conditions, individuals could manage to retain a basic humanity. The lessons he learned in the camps inspired him to specialize in remedial education. He started a school in Chicago for delinquent children and developed a systematic method of helping them. He also analysed, in his book *The Children of the Dream* (1960), the effects of being brought up in a kibbutz system, concluding that the radical experiment of not having a permanent

B

parent didn't work well – either for parents or for children. Professional carers just didn't do as well when they were looking after a whole group. He showed that kibbutz children became both aggressive and dependent. Bettelheim has also analysed our passion for fairy tales. An eclectic and important thinker.

● B. Bettelheim, *The Informed Heart* (1987).

Bias. *See* Prejudice; Response bias.

Binet, Alfred (1857–1911), French psychologist who created the >intelligence test which was to become the >Stanford-Binet test. Binet wanted to establish norms for intellectual abilities at different ages. Once norms for verbal, spatial and mathematical problems were established, it was possible to work out if a child scored above or below average. If a child could solve 12 problems when the average for his age was 10, >intelligence quotient (IQ) would be 12/10 or, as it came to be expressed, 120. Binet helped put psychological tests on a scientific footing, and the subsequent politics of testing would have dismayed him. Testing, Binet hoped, would improve the education of the mentally handicapped by diagnosing the problems of individual children. He did not foresee it would cause children to be separated into the intellectually worthy and the less worthy. Binet died with little sense of the controversies his methods would cause.

Biofeedback, a technique which allows subjects to know how their bodies are reacting to stimuli (*see* Stimulus) and to alter those reactions. Studies show we can exercise far more control over the >autonomic functions of our bodies – that is, those which normally occur automatically without conscious thought – than was once believed. Using biofeedback, in which electrodes are attached to the body to measure such things as >galvanic skin response, subjects have learned to control their heart rate, blood pressure and brain waves. This can be therapeutic when used to teach subjects how to relax, say, to control >pain or reduce the chances of a heart attack recurring.

Bion, Wilfred (1897–1979), a psychoanalyst who more or less invented group analysis or >group therapy which flourishes today in many forms. Bion did pioneering work on >group dynamics as a result of his appointment, during World War II, to a military psychiatric hospital. His theory covers the unconscious mechanisms underlying the behaviour of people in small and large groups. Although Bion's theory is extremely complex, it has implications for every kind of group in everyday life – from the family to the nation.

Bion divided groups into two kinds: the 'basic assumption' group with no specific purpose; and the 'sophisticated' or 'work' group which was supposed to fulfil a specific aim. Within the 'basic assumption' group, a number of unconscious mechanisms inevitably come into play: fight/flight (opening the window, moving your chair); pairing; dependency (on a leader); schism. To let these mechanisms develop, Bion was non-directive with groups.

Bion remains an important source for understanding groups and is rather undeservedly out of fashion. *See* Klein, Melanie.

B

- Wilfred Bion, *Experiences in Groups* (1961) and *The Long Weekend* (1987).

Bipolar scale, a scale which offers those who respond a choice of answers from the extremely positive to the extremely negative. Generally the use of such a scale is better than a simple 'Yes' or 'No'. The problem remains knowing whether what is rated extremely negative for one person is the same as for someone else.

Birth order. To suggest that first-born children do better in life sounds like an old wives' tale, but there is some evidence for it. >Freud noted that he always felt like a conquistador because he had been first in his mother's love. First-born children do seem to be more intelligent and to have greater emotional stability. Freud attributed this to the security they felt because they are first to get their parents', and especially their mothers', love. Other writers attribute the luck of the first born to the fact that they get a period of undivided attention. There is no evidence that second children do better than third children, or that the youngest children in large families do best. The statistical advantages of being the first born are real enough but not that large. Plenty of second and third children have had brilliant careers and happy lives.

Birth trauma. The psychoanalyst Otto Rank argued that we never got over the >trauma of being born. Ejection from the womb was the first rejection. It was no accident that babies came screaming out into the world; they had lost security and comfort. >Freud was critical of the concept, but it managed to take root. Some therapy groups get members to relive what is presumed to be the agony of birth. The best known of these approaches is that of Arthur Janov, who says that adults need to re-experience birth and rescream the primal scream that punctuates birth in order to get their lives in focus. Follow-up studies on Janov's ideas have been very thorough and find little evidence for their validity. The birth trauma may be one of those analytic ideas which has some poetic or symbolic truth but whose scientific status is doubtful.

- Arthur Janov, *The Primal Scream* (1970); Otto Rank, *The Birth Trauma* (1929).

Bisexuality, being physically attracted to people of both sexes. Studies of individuals who are practising bisexuals are rare largely because the homosexual attachments are often hidden. The AIDS situation has reinforced this.

There is also a less erotic definition: >Freud and >Jung both claimed that in every >personality there are elements of both the feminine and the masculine. In this, they echoed Plato's famous *Symposium*. Jung called these parts >anima and animus. One of the tasks of >therapy is to integrate these warring elements of the personality to make the person whole. The concept was revived by Sandra Bem in her studies of >psychological androgyny: she claimed that people who scored high on both masculine and feminine traits – ie they weren't limited to the stereotype of one sex – were the most successful and best adjusted. Bem's research was highly influential in the 1970s when it fitted the ideas of feminism, but there have been some doubts as to whether she interpreted her data correctly. High masculine scores have been said to account for most of the positive effects.

B

Black box theories, theories which see the internal physical workings of either animals or human beings as psychologically irrelevant. The >stimulus enters the 'black box' and out comes a response. The task of the psychologist is to specify the relationship between the ingoing stimulus and the outcoming response. The mysteries of how this occurs biologically, of what happens inside the mind or body, do not matter. Some behaviourists adopted this view either pragmatically or with a certain grand defiance, as if to say they didn't care about physiology. *See* Skinner, B. F.

Blinking, the most commonly used >reflex. Blinking keeps dirt and dust out of the eyes. It can be rather surprisingly conditioned, just like other reflexes.

Blood phobia, fear of the sight of blood, especially human blood. Sufferers often faint at the sight of it. The phobia was recognized but little was known about it until 1988 when Isaac Marks estimated that perhaps 1 per cent of the population may suffer from it. Marks suggested that fainting may have survival value in that it confuses aggressors. He also said that it may be a phenomenon similar to animals playing dead or playing possum.

Body image, what we think, and feel, our bodies look like to ourselves and to others. This is a key component of our sense of personal identity. People who have been involved in accidents often feel that their body image is badly damaged. This appears to lead to a variety of traumatic after-effects including >depression and loss of self-confidence. Anorexics (*see* Anorexia) also suffer distortions of body image believing their emaciated bodies are fat. There is some evidence that >counselling can make up for some of this. Some primate studies have tried to discover whether apes have some form of body image. *See* Self-image.

• Seymour Fisher, *Development and Structure of the Body Image* (1986).

Body language. What can be learned from body posture and gestures is very revealing both in terms of who has power over whom and who is sexually attracted to whom. The man who sits while others stand, for example, is generally considered to be more powerful and if two people lean towards each other, it suggests that the individuals might feel sympathetic to one another. Studies have also revealed that certain postures, such as having the arms crossed, are 'hostile'. As more people knew the tricks of body >language, it became easier to manipulate it so one could use one's knowledge of body language to give the impression one wished to give. *See* Facial expressions; Non-verbal communication.

• Michael Argyle, *Bodily Communication* (1985).

Bonding, a concept initially developed by >Konrad Lorenz to explain how young animals became attached to their parents. Bonding is the basis for >love. Lorenz bonded a number of geese to him, which acted as if he was either their parent

25

B

or their mate. The importance of physical touch in establishing bonding in mammals was demonstrated by the Harlows (American animal psychologists) in their studies of infant monkeys; those that didn't get to cuddle anything became less and less able to manage or to learn how to handle their own offspring. >John Bowlby adapted these ideas to human behaviour and his theories of how we need attachments.

Bowlby, John (1908–), British doctor and psychoanalyst. He set out to make >psychoanalysis scientific, and his great contribution to human understanding has been to relate human behaviour to animal behaviour which can be seen to have evolved because of its survival value. Bowlby drew on >ethology and the work of >Konrad Lorenz and >imprinting (or 'sensitive periods' as it is now known); of Robert Hinde and his studies of cats, kittens and primates; of the Harlows and their work with primates.

Bowlby himself is one of the group of British psychoanalysts whose work was given a great boost by the War. He was scooped up by the War Office – along with >Wilfred Bion and Jock Sutherland, first chairman of the Tavistock Institute, a centre for developing analytic ideas – and set to work devising intelligence and other tests for use with military personnel (*see* Intelligence testing). Bowlby's first major study of 44 juvenile thieves suggested that >maternal deprivation led them to delinquency. From then, he moved on to analyse how infants form bonds. His work on attachment and loss shows how, to be emotionally healthy, we need to take the risk of making (and, therefore, losing) relationships. His stress on the need for a child to be mothered angered many feminists who saw Bowlby's ideas as reactionary. Bowlby slowly came to accept that fathers could also provide 'mothering', at least to some extent.

One of the great discoveries he made during his investigations was that friendship – hetero- or homosexual – was not necessarily an aspect of sexual or reproductive behaviour, but related to 'protection from predators', a valid survival phenomenon on its own.

- John Bowlby, *Attachment and Loss* (1972).

Brain. The human brain, divided into two hemispheres, looks like a very wrinkled cauliflower with a great vent in the middle. The hemispheres are linked by a bundle of nerves, the >*corpus callosum*. The brain is studied by many disciplines and, within psychology, different groups. >Neuropsychologists are close to psychologists in how they view the brain, trying to pin down the precise role of its various structures.

The brain is organized hierarchically – that is, from most complex to least – the major anatomical divisions being:

- *forebrain*: telencephalon, cerebral hemispheres, basal ganglia, amygdala, hippocampus, septum pelucidum

- *diencephalon*: thalamus, hypothalamus

- *midbrain*

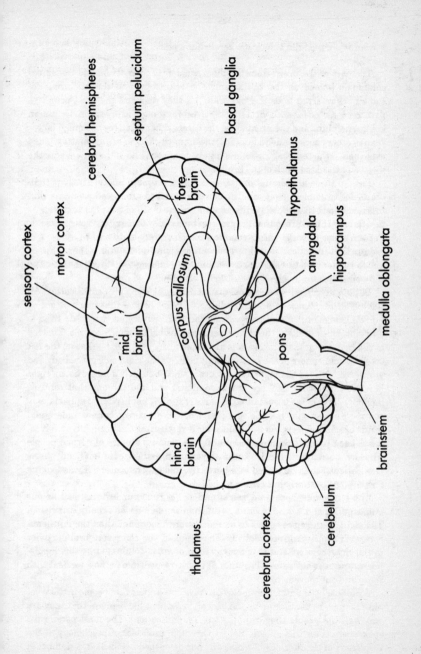

B

● *hindbrain*: medulla oblongata, cerebellum, pons

The part of the brain from the diencephalon to the entrance to the spinal column is known as the brainstem. The brainstem and the midbrain are sometimes referred to as the 'old brain', as they comprise the most primitive part, responsible for such vital functions as breathing and digestion. In human beings, dolphins and the great apes, the cerebral hemispheres are much larger than in other species, and in humans, the 3mm-thick layer of grey matter folded over them – the cerebral cortex – is highly developed and is the area where the most sophisticated work of the brain is done.

Each of these anatomical divisions is only the first of many. The hypothalamus, for example, has a number of *nuclei*, packed groups of >neurons that function together. And, while the anatomy of the brain may be hierarchical, its functioning is not: areas that are far apart may 'ally' to carry out specific tasks. For example, to walk, using complex movement of joints and muscles, will require the sensory cortex (concerned with receiving information), the thalamus and the motor cortex (which deals with outgoing information) to collaborate. The cerebellum is also involved since it helps coordinate balance.

In human beings, what is most distinctive is the sheer size of the cortex. All the higher functions – thinking, talking, 'relating', etc. – that mark us out as human beings are located there. From the 19th century on, scientists tried to pinpoint which areas of the cortex were responsible for which actions. This led to the realization that the brain is asymmetrically organized – that is, the left cerebral hemisphere of the brain usually controls the right side of the body and vice versa. This led to the further discovery that, in most humans who are right handed, the left hemisphere is the dominant one and the one that controls language. If damage is sustained to parts of the left hemisphere >aphasia may occur – ie speech may become very jumbled, and the person cannot understand words or name objects. As techniques for investigating the brain have evolved, it has been possible to make fascinating and minute studies of normal people who have been injected with sodium amytal to anaesthetize the left hemisphere. One patient, when he looked at a butterfly, told experimenters, 'I was looking for the word butterfly but couldn't find it.'

The left hemisphere analyses situations. It runs our logic as well as our language. Since we tend to think so much in words, this isn't really surprising. The right hemisphere seems to be much more 'emotional' then the left hemisphere. If a one-month-old baby listens to music, you can record brain activity in the right hemisphere. Our appreciation of art is dominated by this hemisphere, and so is our sense of rhythm. It is also responsible for how we deal with space and our movements.

A number of American psychologists have now argued that people in the West have become so dominated by the logical, verbal left hemisphere that they are only half the people they could be (*see* Lateralization). The most persuasive spokesperson for this view is Robert Ornstein, professor of psychology at the University of Southern California, who has developed his ideas in a number of books on the psychology of >consciousness. He argues that we have become slaves to one half of our brain.

There is nothing wrong, of course, in being logical and in relying on language, but Ornstein claims that we are suppressing the more creative and the more joyful part of our selves. It also means that we look at every new problem in much the same way. We have to make the world fit the world that our left hemisphere imposes; we become limited. There are ways of freeing ourselves, according to Ornstein, and he thinks such a dash for liberty is well worthwhile.

In order to suppress the verbal left hemisphere, you have to learn to think without words. You have to learn to loosen the stranglehold of logic. In some cultures, Ornstein says, this is done automatically – in the East, for example, where even prime ministers spend some time each day meditating. In this way, you can release the more creative, emotional right hemisphere. The rhythms that are involved in chanting also help free the right hemisphere so that it can enjoy most of our attention. You don't have to become a Buddhist or start doing Gregorian chants in order to suppress the left hemisphere. Just sitting quietly and trying to think in pictures rather than in words will serve.

Ornstein believes that if we all dabbled a little and stopped being nothing but left-hemisphere people, we would be more complete and happy. He says that if you give the right hemisphere the opportunity, it will allow you to do and to be much more than you are now. Some scientists dispute Ornstein's claim that the left hemisphere actually suppresses the right hemisphere, and almost all point out that you cannot really make do with only one. (At one time, scientists asked why we needed the right hemisphere at all.) However, Ornstein's ideas are provocative and offer a new way of looking at ourselves. On a less theoretical level, the study of the brain remains one of the greatest scientific challenges of the next 50 years. *See* Language areas.

• Floyd Bloom and Arlyne Lazenson, *Brain, Mind and Behaviour* (1988); D. Dennett, *Consciousness Explained* (1993); Robert Ornstein, *Multimind* (1987); J. Z. Young, *Philosophy and the Brain* (1988).

Brain development. There has been much interest recently in charting how the >brain grows and how well formed it is at birth. What is most astonishing is that, after birth, no new >neurons are created.

At 20 days after conception, a primitive neural plate can be discerned in the embryo. As early as this, certain parts of the plate are programmed to form particular areas of the brain. By the second month, there are the first signs of eye development. Different parts of the brain emerge at different times. The first to do so are the olfactory (smell) regions of the brain and the hippocampus. Then the walls of the forebrain become thicker; this part of the brain is crucial in integrating sensory input. Finally, the cerebral cortex develops; this is responsible for the higher functions. The surface area of the cortex is so large – it contains 70 per cent of the billions of neurons that make up the brain – that it has to be arranged in folds, which is what gives the brain its characteristic look. At one point, 250,000 cells are being created every minute.

B

At birth, the human brain weighs an average of 25 per cent of its adult weight. By six months, it reaches half its adult size, and 75 per cent of it by the age of two. Since no new neurons are created after birth, the increase in weight is accounted for by the increase in the size of neurons and in the number of connections they make.

Brainstorming, a technique to produce a stream of ideas without any critical inhibition. In a brainstorming session, participants are asked to come up with any idea however odd or daft. Anything that might solve a problem should be contributed. Brainstorming is used in advertising and in some American-style management practices. It owes a great deal to the vogue for divergent thinking and for >lateral thinking which both claim that normal 'convergent' intelligent problem solving isn't creative. New ideas will emerge best when no one is frightened that they might look foolish. Brainstorming enthusiasts argue that ideas produced this way can be analysed critically later on. Brainstorming sessions certainly succeed in producing hundreds of ideas but how effective they are at producing useful solutions remains controversial.

Brainwashing, the term originated in the Korean war when North Koreans made American GIs renounce the glories of capitalism and declare that they now believed in Communism. In the 1950s, these apparent conversions had a tremendous effect on American morale. The CIA believed that the Koreans had a magic sinister drug which affected the mind. The CIA tried to discover what the drug was and, in the process, inflicted a great deal of psychological damage on unwitting human 'guinea pigs'. There was no magic drug, of course. The North Koreans realized that if they deprived prisoners of >sleep, allowed them no rest, bombarded them with information and kept them under severe emotional stress, they could make them infinitely malleable. About 4% of those suffered long-term psychological damage leading usually to >depression. In popular fantasies, brainwashing was a powerful tool. In reality, most attempts merely damaged people so that they would be useless to their new controllers. Much British work went into this area and recently there have been court cases in which, 25 years later, the guinea pigs used by the CIA have secured substantial damages for the suffering inflicted on them. *See* Sensory deprivation.

● W. Sargant, *Battle for the Mind* (1957); G. Thomas, *Journey into Madness* (1989).

Brainwaves, the electrical activity of the >brain which can be measured by electrodes placed on the scalp. There seem to be different amplitudes which distinguish conscious activity, drowsiness, light sleep and deep sleep.

Broca's aphasia. *See* Aphasia.

Bulimia, an eating disorder characterized by the person eating too much and then inducing vomiting or abusing laxatives. There has been much controversy about whether bulimia is caused by similar factors to >anorexia. The most vocal advocate of this view is Susie Orbach, who suggests that both diseases are a rebellion on the part of women who refuse to play the roles that patriarchal society has allotted to them.

Burnout, a syndrome in which professional individuals feel that they are too tired, exhausted and emotionally stressed to continue with their work. A lack of appreciation for their efforts makes symptoms worse. Groups who have complained of burnout include doctors working in casualty departments (too much work), nurses in terminal wards (too much death causing too much despair), and dentists – yes, dentists. With dentists, the problem isn't a surfeit of cavities but the fact that no one tells them that they have done a good job and are truly worthwhile human beings. Dentists need constant fillings of love.

There is no doubt that there is some validity to the concept, but it can also be included in that group of 'cute concepts' invented in the late 1970s which could be said to reflect the very narcissistic concerns of that time. *See also* Post-traumatic stress.

Burt, Sir Cyril (1883–1971), British educational psychologist who is likely to be remembered for having perpetuated one of the greatest frauds in psychology. The chief educational psychologist for the London County Council, Burt was one of the first psychologists to use the tests devised by >Binet in order to assess children's >intelligence. He believed in streaming children according to their abilities and argued that intelligence was largely inherited. He reported a series of test studies of identical twins who had been raised apart. He claimed that, because they had virtually identical IQs, intellectual ability must be genetically determined. These correlations were the highest ever found, and suspicion about their authenticity first surfaced in 1973, two years after Burt's death, when Leon Kamin argued that they were too high to be true. A medical journalist, Dr Oliver Gillie, then tried to find the co-authors listed and could not trace them. Even supporters of Burt's theoretical position, such as >Hans Eysenck, came to accept that he had invented data and faked results, and his not insubstantial achievements were dwarfed by the scandal. The fact that Burt managed to hoodwink so many colleagues reflects the fact that psychologists very rarely see each other's raw data. Robert Joynson recently alleged that Burt has been unfairly discredited – a view that seems, however, hard to maintain.

- L. Hearnshaw, *Cyril Burt* (1980); Leon Kamin, *The Science and Politics of IQ* (1974); Robert Joynson, *The Burt Affair* (1989).

Bystander apathy, people tend to refuse to help others in emergencies – they watch accidents, muggings and attacks without intervening. In Cinncinnati, psychologists once arranged for a number of people to collapse on trains at an identical moment. Generally, the only people to offer to help were off-duty nurses. Social psychologists argue this proves that altruism is a myth – the good Samaritan no longer exists. However, bystanders may not be so much apathetic as afraid. Media coverage shows that cities, especially in the USA, are dangerous. Those who intervene may pay a heavy price for doing good.

B

31

C

Caring professions, a term that came into use in the late 1970s to describe professions involved in helping others. They include psychologists, social workers, therapists, nurses and doctors. Increasingly, those who work in these professions have come to ask who cares for the carers. Studies have revealed that carers risk >burnout, not simply because they have got fed up with being kind, understanding and compassionate, but because they often have to make critical decisions that affect people's lives. In the United States and Western Europe since 1965, there has been a huge increase in the numbers of those who do such work. Doctors have been studied at some length, and they appear to have specially high rates of >alcoholism, drug abuse, attempted and 'full' >suicide and >depression. As more people join the caring professions (which are a booming business), expect more attention on the agonies of caring.

● Glin Bennett, *The Wound and the Doctor* (1987).

Case studies, a method which involves in-depth analysis of particular individual cases. *See* Idiographic.

Castration anxiety. >Freud introduced the idea that most boys are frightened that their penises will be cut off. In Freud's time, and much later, it was common for parents to threaten boys who touched their genitals. However, psychoanalysts also suggested that castration >anxiety was the result of less obvious guilt: the child who desired his mother unconsciously (ie had an >Oedipus complex) knew that really he deserved to be castrated.

Catastrophe theory, a mathematical theory which deals with sudden 'catastrophic' changes that often cannot be undone. It has also been applied to marital rows, >phobias and reversals of the >Necker cube, but its use in psychology has not been validated.

Catharsis, a Greek word initially used by Aristotle to describe the purging or cleansing that came from the release of emotional tension on seeing dramatized tragedy. >Freud adopted the term to describe the relief that follows a discharge of psychic energy or tension. He also spoke of *cathexis* (noun) and *cathexed* (verb) when referring to such discharges.

CAT scan, computerized axial tomography; also known as CT scan. An X-ray procedure in which computers draw a map from the measured densities of the body. One of the reasons why this is more useful than conventional X-rays is that it gives a 3D representation of the body, and has allowed the emergence of a far more detailed and dynamic picture of how the >brain works.

Causes in psychology. In most sciences, it is relatively clear when the cause of a particular event has been established. We know, for example, the precise way that the moon affects the tides on earth. The pioneers of psychology hoped to discover equally precise causes of complex human behaviour. The French social psychologist, Gustave Le Bon, argued in the 1890s that it should be possible to predict the behaviour of crowds just as meticulously as the behaviour of atoms. >Freud wanted a scientifically based >psychoanalysis, and in his book *The Project for a Scientific Psychology* he suggested some basic brain mechanisms for it. >Watson and the behaviourists also believed in the possibility of establishing definite causes for definite behaviours, especially after they had absorbed >Pavlov's work on >conditioning.

In fact, however, it has proved very difficult to establish the causes of particular actions or behaviour. There are a number of reasons for this. First, most studies extrapolate – ie they use data from specific laboratory experiments or from paper-and-pencil personality tests – and it remains contentious how well you can generalize these results to real life. Second, many psychological questions deal with probabilities, rather than absolutes. They reveal that there is, for example, a 1 in 100 probability that a particular trend (say a link between unemployment and rates of suicide) was due to pure chance. This doesn't quite explain why older men are more likely, if unemployed, to attempt suicide, let alone why a particular individual has made an attempt. At best, the trend establishes a correlation, not a cause.

Finally, even in areas where it might seem possible to establish a definite cause, there are problems. A patient who has a brain >lesion in a specific area may suffer speech impairment, but just what has the lesion caused? It might have damaged the >brain's capacity to retrieve words or to control the muscles that produce speech or even to attend to the cues that are part of speaking. Specifying precise causes is especially hampered when so much data are based on correlations: a correlation between A and B doesn't prove that A *causes* B.

The statistical techniques that are used in psychology have become something of a replacement for attacking issues of causation as energetically as they might be. The growing complexity of the discipline doesn't help. Many entries in this book reflect the changes that have occurred in psychology over the last 15 years as >reductionist theories failed to provide convincing answers and new data to do with >consciousness, feelings and motives have come back into >empirical psychology. This has made psychologists aware of the problem of relating varying types of terminology.

33

C

Part of the problem is that there are many different kinds of causes that psychologists have to juggle with. It is possible to discover a physiological reason why I see a particular car as red, but some questions require different answers. The reasons behind why I am falling in love with Julia or why I persist in not buying a new vacuum cleaner when my partner says we obviously need one can't be simple. In social psychology, establishing causes is hard in the laboratory and even harder out of it. With the discipline fragmented, few psychologists (with the notable exception of Rom Harré) attempt to look at different kinds of causes that need to be analysed. Clarifying the levels of causation remains an urgent problem for psychology.

- David Clarke, *Action Systems* (1985); Rom Harré, David Clarke and Nicola De Carlo, *Motives and Mechanisms* (1985); Liam Hudson, *The Cult of the Fact* (1972); Howard Kendler, *Psychology, A Science in Conflict* (1982).

Central nervous system (CNS), the network of >neurons, cells and fibres which make up the >brain and spinal cord. The CNS regulates the major functions of the body.

Cerebellum, the area at the base of the >brain which is important for balance and the control of voluntary movements. It helps coordinate small units of 'action' into sequences of behaviour.

Cerebral blood flow, the blood flow round the >brain. Loss of cerebral blood flow usually causes serious brain damage and consequent loss of function because blood carries oxygen into the brain. Cerebral blood flow must not be confused with cerebro-spinal fluid, which is a colourless solution of sodium chloride and other salts that fills the ventricles (spaces) inside the brain and circulates around it and may help in the excretion of metabolic wastes from the brain.

Normally, there is an even pattern in the way that cerebral blood flows in both hemispheres of the brain. >CAT scan techniques now make it possible to monitor cerebral blood flow with minute accuracy and to link abnormalities with disease. Reimann *et al* concentrated on areas of the brain which are known to have links with emotional behaviour since they reasoned that the brain structures responsible for panic would lie there. Among the structures that they looked at were the hippocampus, the parahippocampul gyrus, inferior parietal lobule, the hypothalamus and the amygdala in the part of the forebrain known as the >limbic system. They compared the blood flow in the left and the right hemispheres.

They found that in one of these structures (the parahippocampal gyrus) there was a significant asymmetry – that is, there was a difference in the blood flow in the left and right hemispheres. They argue that this is one of the first times that a brain abnormality with such a clear location has been linked to patients with a distinct psychiatric disorder. Locating a 'kink' in the blood flow in one area made Reimann's results exciting. It may be that this asymmetry in the blood flow between the two cerebral hemispheres is another indication of their different specializations.

- E. M. Reiman *et al*, 'A Focal Brain Abnormality', *Nature*, vol 310, p. 683.

C

Cerebral cortex. *See* Cortex.

Cerebral hemispheres. The two hemispheres of the >cortex.

Chance. Almost all psychological experiments depend on the concept of chance. Statistical tests compare the actual findings in an experiment with what would be expected to happen by chance. Findings are reckoned significant if they are likely to have occurred by chance less than 1 time in 20 or 1 time in 100.

Underlying this methodology is the assumption that chance works randomly. If you spin a coin 100 times, it will fall 50 times on heads and 50 times on tails. In fact, empirical studies of such chance events show that chance doesn't quite work according to chance; there are mysterious kinks in the process. One study claimed that, during a run of 1 million digits, a random number generator produced an excess of 8s. Is this deeply meaningful? Or is it just one of those kinks of chance?

Few psychologists question the mathematical assumptions that underlie the statistics they use and so they tend to accept that chance and probability operate as crude theories. Common sense suggests they should. There are, however, serious risks in this.

- Alistair Hardy, Arthur Koestler, *The Challenge of Chance* (1968).

Child abuse, the neglect of children, violence against them or sexual assaults. It is impossible to know how widespread the problem is; the NSPCC claims that perhaps one child in ten is abused though, of course, the severity of abuse differs widely. US government figures claim that in 1983, 1.5 million children were abused in the USA. Psychologists have suggested a number of factors which lead to child abuse, especially a history of violence in the family, poverty, the powerful Id-driven loves between parents and children and, increasingly, the number of families with stepparents. There is some evidence to suggest that children from violent families will tend to be violent to their own children. It's learned behaviour, partly. Child abuse doesn't just cause suffering, but also cognitive problems, including difficulties with language learning.

>Freud showed long ago that many of his patients had memories of seduction and abuse by their parents. He came to believe that these memories were secret wishes, not real recollections. According to Jeffrey Masson, a Sanskrit scholar, analyst and critic of analysis, Freud suppressed his seduction theory in order to make psychoanalysts respectable. To suggest parents regularly abused children in late-Victorian Vienna would have ensured Freud was seen as mad. However, Freud's ideas highlight how parents can seek to seduce children. The current anxiety about the extent of child abuse would make theoretical sense to him. The rise in the number of step-families means that children live closely with adults who are not blood relatives and who may either want to exploit them or

35

C

hate them. The child of a previous marriage/relationship can seem like a constant source of irritation and jealousy. Some of the most horrendous recent cases of child abuse have concerned stepparents or partners. Psychologists can contribute not just to an understanding of the problem but can help to change behaviour by teaching about parenting skills and encouraging parents at risk to deal with their feelings. This does not, however, offer much of a solution. It seems strange that, given the outcry child abuse causes, there is little legislation in the UK to protect the child. In the Netherlands and Sweden, for example, it is illegal for parents to use violence on their children as part of ordinary discipline.

- J. Masson, *The Assault on Truth* (1982); J. Masson, *Against Therapy* (1989); Violence Against Children Study Group, *Child Abuse* (1989).

Child development, the study of how children grow up, a minefield of theoretical conflict but also very lively.

>J. B. Watson said in 1916 that the essential task of psychology was to map out the way that children developed. Between 1916 and 1970, studies of child development tended to focus on a number of different areas: intellectual development; >psychosexual development; and >language development. There was little interaction between specialists in these different areas. >Jean Piaget, for example, said that he found only one instance – in 50 years of study – in which Freudian ideas had been of any value. (>Sigmund Freud was never known to quote Piaget.) Theories of child development, therefore, developed in some hostile isolation.

Piaget stressed the ability of the child to think. He claimed that there were a number of stages of intellectual development, and eventually the child would graduate to formal operations and would be a master of logic. For Piaget, social and emotional development was secondary. Freud's theory was nearly as one sided: he emphasized emotional and psychosexual development. Other psychologists were less theoretical and developed a rather less exciting but useful base of information about what language skills children might be expected to have at various stages.

By the 1970s, the limitations of these approaches to child development were becoming apparent. It also became clear that there was an unexpected link between Freud and Piaget. Both held to the idea of development by stages: a child had to pass through stage A before he could get to stage B. These stages were all rather grand; Piaget's involved the ability of a child to grasp >symbols, for example, or to understand that other people had different points of view from him or her. The psychologists' task was to find out what these different stages were and to explain how getting stuck at one stage would affect adult life. So, children who remained fixated at the >anal stage, which Freud postulated, would be misers. The concept of stages is, however, very much a 19th-century concept. Piaget and Freud were giants but with one-track theories.

It was slowly realized that development need not proceed according to stages, and the stage model came to be seen as rather inflexible. Children did develop differently. Psychologists preferred to adopt a skills mode: the child acquired cognitive (eg reasoning) skills, >social skills and emotional skills. Obviously, you could discern a general progression, but the skill model had some advantages, especially the fact that it allowed for a more flexible pattern of growth. It can deal with real children with real differences – for example, the child who is intellectually mature but emotionally immature.

C

According to Piaget, neither parents nor teachers influenced the evolution of the child, and he always mocked American psychologists for their mania for seeing if they could speed up the development of children. Freud left it unclear what parents could do for their children. He praised the love they gave them but gave few precise recommendations on how to get little George over his >Oedipus complex. This lack of a role for parents meant that neither theory highlighted what has come to be seen as adequate. Neither deals with the reality that children are social beings and develop through interaction with 'significant others' (*see* Mother/child interaction).

By the 1970s, psychologists had become interested in how that interaction worked. From the outset, they made two sorts of findings. The first was that very young children were more skilled than we had believed. Tom Bower, for example, found that babies only a few days old can imitate facial actions: if you stick your tongue out at them, they poke it back at you. This new line of research also highlighted the fact that some assumptions about the failures of children were mistaken. In 1972, Peter Bryant showed that often what appeared to be intellectual mistakes were due to the fact that the children had misunderstood the question. Then the Harvard psychologist Jerome Bruner investigated the interaction between mothers and children and >play, and claimed that, through this, children learned social rules. Studies of development have used interesting tools, ranging from diaries to video.

As a result, the general view of the child has changed radically from that of Freud and Piaget's time. The child is no longer seen as someone who progresses through fixed stages but as a person who learns skills through playing, fighting and imagining. This change has been fairly remarkable, perhaps most so in the growth of work on how children are active (not passive) recipients of learning, how they develop socially, and how they create for themselves a theory of mind. But there are also warning voices. In 1985, M. M. Kaye stressed that we mustn't, as the pendulum swings, go too far and see the baby born as a master of social skills.

What is extraordinary is the length of time that it has taken psychology to return to what would seem to be the obvious – that the social relationships of children are crucial to their development and that empirical science ought to attend to this. Throughout his long life, Freud only observed a few children directly; Piaget excluded enormously important areas largely because they didn't fit his theoretical preconceptions. Developmental psychology has become a very lively field. *See* Bowlby, John; Freud, Anna; Klein, Melanie.

- T. G. R. Bower, *The Rational Infant* (1989); John S. Bruner, *Beyond the Information Given* (1974); G. Butterworth and P. Bryant, *Causes of Develop-*

C

ment (1992); J. Dunn, *The Growth of Social Understanding* (1989); J. H. Flavell, *The Developmental Psychology of Jean Piaget* (1963); Henry Wellman, 'First Steps in the Child's Theorising About the Mind' in *Developing Theories of Mind* (1989) edited by Janet Astingon, Paul Harris and David Olson.

Child sexuality. The study of sexuality has always been problematic. First, Christianity has always had its doubts about sex – children were innocent, hence they could not have any interest in sex. Until >Freud's work, it was believed that children did not have sexual feelings. Freud found that they did, even if admitting this fact makes adults uncomfortable. For Freud, many of these feelings and >fantasies were unconscious, but there is also much observable evidence of children's curiosity about sex: they often touch their genitals; they often ask questions about where they come from. Freud pointed out some of these things but found himself denounced as immoral. He postulated a number of >psychosexual stages in the development of children – the oral, anal, and genital stages – each reflected by interest in the particular part of the body.

Freud initially argued that many of the experiences of childhood sexual activity that his adult patients remembered were true, but when so many recalled being seduced by relatives and parents, he eventually concluded that these were fantasies. This was what the children had wanted, he said, and this 'evidence' reinforced his views on child sexuality. But was Freud right to back away from what could very well have been the truth? Jeffrey Masson claimed in 1985 that Freud changed his mind and stated that these were wish-fulfilling fantasies because he was afraid of the social scandal that would follow; to suggest that Vienna was full of child molesters would put >psychoanalysis beyond the pale. Masson is probably wrong in attributing such craven motives to Freud, but the growing evidence of >child abuse makes it hard to accept that what the latter's patients told him was not the truth.

Freud's interest in child sexuality inspired even those psychologists who were hostile to much else in his theories. >J. B. Watson welcomed the honesty about sex that Freud seemed to have recommended, and he advocated being honest with young children and giving them sex education from a very early age.

The reports of Margaret Mead and other anthropologists on the sexual freedom of the young in far-off places went uncriticized because these young were 'savages' who hadn't had the benefits of Western civilization. It was much harder for Western psychologists to investigate such activity in developed countries. There was outrage in 1948 and 1953 when the two >Kinsey Reports were published in the United States and in the 1960s when Michael Schofield reported on the >sexual behaviour of teenagers in Britain. For example, Kinsey shocked a large majority of people by discovering that about 30 per cent of girls had lost their virginity before marriage. Eventually, however, these attitudes faded, but empirical evidence about the sexual development of children, their fantasies, their fears and their behaviour is still lacking. Goldman and Goldman, in a 1952 study of children's sexual thinking, noted that 'children are still largely regarded as asexual creatures, in thought and behaviour, and childhood remains characterized as the age of innocence unaffected by an interest in sex'. They found that children in morally 'free' areas of the world such as Scandinavia knew much more about sex than those in the UK.

C

Chlorpromazine. An anti-psychotic drug (trade name Largactil) which has a sedative effect. It achieves this by blocking >neurotransmitters, >adrenalin and >noradrenalin. It's one of the phenoziathines. *See* Tranquillizers.

Choice experiments. Forced choice experiments are those in which animals have to choose one of usually two alternative routes.

Chomsky, Noam (1928–), linguist who argued that the capacity all humans have to speak a >language shows that we are 'wired' into the >deep structure. The particular form of language a child learns to speak depends on the language he or she is exposed to, of course, but language is a distinguishing characteristic of being human. Chomsky became embroiled in a controversy with >B. F. Skinner who said that language was 'verbal behaviour'. There was nothing innate in the >mind, Skinner argued, that made children speak. Chomsky has won the argument over the last 25 years. His ideas are recognized as changing our view of human nature. Chomsky has also argued recently that one consequence of the innate structure of the mind is that the mind may not be able to know itself. It may be beyond the mind's ability to understand how it works. He remains one of the most formidable thinkers in psychological theory.

- J. Lyons, *Chomsky* (1975).

Chronic, the opposite of acute; long-lasting (condition).

Clairvoyance, the ability to foresee events which couldn't be foreseen in other ways. Many experiments in >parapsychology have tried to establish whether clairvoyance really does exist. There is much less evidence for this than for other skills of >extra-sensory perception (ESP) such as >telepathy.

Claustrophobia, >fear of closed spaces; one of the most common >phobias. Psychoanalysts claim it has sexual fear as its root, but behaviour therapists see this as unnecessary mystification.

Clever Hans, the name of a horse that apparently could spell and do calculations by tapping one of its hooves. Hailed initially as a miracle, it became clear after meticulous study that the horse responded to tiny signals that its trainer Pfeffer made unconsciously. When the horse had tapped out enough, Pfeffer relaxed and that gave the horse the signal that it needed to stop. The case alerted students of animal behaviour to the dangers of making excessive claims about what animals could achieve.

Client-centred therapy, a form of >therapy devised by Carl Rogers. Its aim was initially to demystify some of the techniques of >psychoanalysis and give the client very obvious, direct support. Instead of lying down on a couch with the therapist out of view, the client sat opposite as an equal. The therapist wasn't to give deep, clever interpretations of >dreams or word >associations but should

C

focus, face to face, on the client and his immediate problems and offer 'warm, positive regard'. Rogers claimed that this form of therapy was far more practical than psychoanalysis because it was quicker and more accessible, although he accepted that therapists sometimes had to be directive (ie telling the client what to do).

● Carl Rogers, *A Way of Being* (1980).

Clinical interview, interviews that are designed to help diagnose what is wrong with a patient and later become part of treatment. They should be warm, helpful and empathetic.

Clinical psychology, the brand of psychology which deals with abnormal behaviours. Most clinical psychologists work with psychiatrists, using tests that assess the mental state and ability of psychiatric patients.

Cognitive behaviour therapy, a form of >behaviour therapy which relies on the patient using statements about himself or herself as crucial >stimuli. The aim is to get new, better responses to statements like 'I am bound to fail'. The approach involves patients using both techniques like relaxation to combat stress and self-created help manuals. It has some links with >cognitive therapy. *See* Rational emotive therapy.

Cognitive neuropsychology, a sub-discipline of >cognitive psychology which essentially studies how the >brain works when we are engaged in various intellectual tasks.

Cognitive psychology, not a school but an approach which highlights some areas crucial to psychology. The most central is cognition, or thought. The new-style cognitive psychologist seeks to avoid the >introspective muddles which were so damaging at the turn of the century. The first sign of new interest in thinking came in 1956 with the publication of Bruner, Goodnow and Austin's *A Study in Thinking*, which tried to use experimental methods to discover how people solved problems. The experiments were designed so that people had to demonstrate openly their >problem-solving strategies. The book's success showed that thinking was no longer a taboo subject. Studies of brain >lateralization also aroused interest and it became less and less possible to stick to >black box theories where psychologists disdained investigation into what happens inside the head. Finally, the rise of new technology made it fashionable to compare the >brain to a computer; working out what kind of programs might be running in the brain seemed valid (*see* Mechanistic models). In 1976, the psychologist Ulric Neisser brought together a range of work on attention, mental >imagery, problem solving and >memory under the heading 'cognitive psychology'. He maintained that experimental psychology, which had once insisted on excluding >consciousness, could no longer do so. For example, those studying mental imagery who would once have asked subjects to introspect now asked them questions about their subjective experience that were similar to those they would have asked about 'objective' experiences; for example, subjects would be

C

asked to describe mental images in detail. Were the various objects they saw in their minds close or far, vivid or dull? Cognitive psychology has succeeded in bringing back important areas into psychology with sufficient methodological skill to avoid the pitfalls and confusions of former times. Critics such as Paul Kline argue, however, that all too often cognitive psychology redefines processes in scientific >language rather than explain them. *See* Neo-behaviourism.

- G. Claxton, *Cognitive Psychology* (1986); P. Kline, *Psychology Exposed* (1989); U. Neisser, *Cognitive Psychology* (1976); N. Singley and John Anderson, *The Transfer of Cognitive Skill* (1989).

Cognitive science, the branch of psychology that studies >thinking, reasoning and >problem solving. Throughout the history of psychology, there has been interest in how we think. Some seminal books such as *A Study of Thinking* (1956) showed how people adopted different problem solving strategies. The influence of >Piaget had meant that most psychologists assumed that teenagers finally matured to logical thinking. Given much human behaviour this always seemed optimistic. Since the 1970s, there has been logical confirmation of how hard most of us find it to think logically. Studies with undergraduates by Johnson Laird and Wason have shown that we tend to find it hard to solve some problems using negatives. We are very used to confirming beliefs and conclusions. We over-value evidence that points to what we already believe. Leon Festinger in his famous studies of cognitive dissonance showed how we could be swayed by and cling to beliefs despite evidence that proved them wrong. It was generally assumed that intellectuals were above being so illogical. No sooner had Johnson Laird and Wason pointed to the struggles that undergraduates have with logic than Simonton argued that scientific geniuses aren't much more logical. He claimed that Einstein, Poincaré, Newton – all physicists – were all inclined to follow hunches and refuse to see evidence that falsified their ideas. If great physicists are so illogical, what hope for psychologists? Indeed, can cognitive science itself be logical? The whole field is interesting, often paradoxical, and emphasizes an area of psychology that was long neglected during the heyday of behaviourism.

- J. S. Bruner, J. Goodnow and G. A. Austin, *A Study of Thinking* (1956); Leon Festinger, *Cognitive Dissonance* (1957); P. N. Johnson Laird and P. Wason, *Thinking: Readings in Cognitive Science* (1977); K. Simonton, *Scientific Genius* (1989).

Cognitive styles, different ways of thinking. The best-described styles are *convergent* and *divergent*. J. P. Guildford argued that convergers tend to be good at problems which had one correct answer, while divergers were more creative, recognizing a variety of possible solutions. The easy division of thinkers into logical convergers and creative divergers hasn't stood up to examination. Liam Hudson has shown that some convergers were highly creative, and has suggested that, among clever schoolchildren, the study of different subjects led to different cognitive styles.

C

- J. P. Guilford, 'Traits of Creativity' in *Creativity and its Cultivation* (1959); L. Hudson, *Contrary Imaginations* (1966).

Cognitive therapy, a form of >behaviour therapy which relies on changing patients' cognitions (thoughts) and beliefs about the things that cause them to be anxious. Beck argued that cognitions affect behaviour and that, initially, the therapist and the patient have to analyse together the latter's behaviour. Changing the patient's ideas has to coincide with reconditioning the patient's behaviour. >Eysenck and Wolpe, traditional behaviour therapists, have criticized Beck's position as illogical, partly, of course, because he assumes that the way people perceive both themselves and their problems may well be an important factor in their difficulties. Beck's technique is, in fact, much closer to >rational emotive therapy than to classical behaviour therapy.

- Aaron Beck, *Cognitive Therapy and the Emotional Disorder* (1989).

Collective unconscious, the >dreams, >fantasies, >imagery, that are common to all the human race. In a famous dream, >Jung saw himself going down into a cellar where he found layers of skulls and a throne – all powerful >symbols. He claimed that the cellar stood for the collective >unconscious, the deepest layers of the mind. >Freud did not believe in it, and it's not clear how it would pass from one person to another. Jung envisaged it rather poetically as being part of biological heredity. Yet it's an idea that has exercised a considerable fascination. *See also* Archetypes.

- Carl Jung, *Archetypes and the Collective Unconscious* (1934).

Colour vision. *See* Vision.

Community psychology, a new branch of psychology which involves putting psychologists in the community to see how they can affect local services and conditions. The community psychologist liaises with health workers, with social workers, with those responsible for the local environment and tries to help people get these agencies to respond better to local needs. The area is rather vague and, in the UK at least, community psychologists tend to work in those local authorities which have a high profile left-wing stance. It's arguable that community psychology isn't a discipline at all. Rather, it's one of those amorphous areas like community development work which is well intentioned but whose results are rather vague.

- M. Binder, *Community Psychology* (1979).

Complex, a term used by >Freud to describe emotionally charged feelings and peculiarities of behaviour, as in >Oedipus complex.

Compulsion, a need to carry out a particular action, often many times a day, which seems to have no meaning or purpose. *See* Obsessional neurosis; Repetition compulsion.

C

Computers in therapy. Since the 1970s, computers have been increasingly used in medicine. Now, it seems, they are about to establish themselves in psychiatry as well. Dr Tony Carr, a psychiatrist at the Royal Maudsley Hospital in London, has succeeded in developing new programs which allow a computer to take the social history of a patient, to diagnose >depression and even to treat >phobias. Dr Carr does not want to make psychiatrists redundant but he does want to reduce their workload.

If a patient agrees to have his history taken by a computer, he is installed in front of a console, and shown how to use it. Once he gets an idea of what to do, the doctor disappears, and the patient can then work at his own pace without feeling guilty about holding up a busy doctor. Patients have to respond to two kinds of question – ones with a yes/no answer and multiple-choice ones. For example, a patient will be asked if he is in trouble with the police: if he answers 'Yes', there will be a subset of 'police' questions; if he answers 'No', the program skips these and goes to the next topic.

Each question and its possible answers stay on the screen until the patient has finished answering. This is an important benefit, claims Dr Carr: 'Confused patients often do not follow what a psychiatrist is saying, but with the computer, the question is always there. The patient cannot forget being asked.'

Patients seem to enjoy what is still a novel procedure. They feel that they can take their time and that they are under less pressure. Ninety-five per cent say to the computer what they meant to say. Ninety-two per cent of the answers would have been acceptable to any psychiatrist who may have interviewed them.

Curiously, the computer makes a good confessional. In a number of cases, Dr Carr found that the computer was told more than the GP or the 'real' psychiatrist had been.

In a study of 125 depressed patients, Dr Carr found that none dropped out of the programme. Even in an acute state, patients usually managed to operate the computer. The main problem was illiteracy: 7 per cent of the patients could not read what was on the screen. And a few patients, of course, remained mute: they refused to speak to the psychiatrist, and they refused to consort with the computer. From the psychiatrist's point of view, the main benefit is the time this procedure saves, time that is then devoted to treatment.

The most startling development has been computer programs for treating phobias. These have been devised to provide a step-by-step method that patients can use to >condition themselves out of phobias. There was a time, in the enthusiastic heyday of >behaviour therapy, when therapists often went out with their patients. If a man was terrified of, say, Alsatians, he would be exposed to a pack of them after he had been relaxed at length. Now such therapeutic derring-do is rare. Therapists ask patients to imagine anxiety-provoking situations, tell them to relax and get them to expose themselves (without the therapist) to those situations in real life; the patient reports back on progress. There is no reason why a computer cannot do this as well as flesh-and-blood therapists. In practice, the computer works out a hierarchy of what makes the patient most anxious. If the patient cannot go shopping in crowded places, the computer says, 'Well, why not go to the supermarket at a quiet time like a

C

Monday afternoon.' When the patient reports back, the computer prints out its verdict: 'EXCELLENT'. If he had only gone to the supermarket on two days, the computer will ask why and prompt him to do better.

So far, the results seem to suggest that being given this kind of behaviour therapy by a computer is not too different from being given it by a therapist. A proportion of patients drop out – but a majority return and improve. One study found again that patients liked the procedure, and Dr Carr believes that some patients who have 'ridiculous' phobias may find it easier to confess to a computer.

Computer models of the mind. *See* Artificial intelligence.

Concept formation, the process by which concepts are developed. Research into this predated the fashion for >cognitive psychology.

Concrete operations, the third stage of >Piaget's stages of cognitive development. Children are now thought to be able to handle logical relationships as long as they do not have to deal with abstract theories.

Concurrent validity. *See* Validity.

Conditioning, a process by which a new response becomes associated with an existing >stimulus. It was first developed experimentally by >Pavlov in his work with dogs. This 'classical conditioning' became a key concept in early 20th-century psychology and was used to explain many forms of >learning. The behaviourists argued that conditioned reflexes were the basic elements out of which all behaviour is built up. >Skinner modified Pavlov's ideas and demonstrated the existence of >'operant conditioning'.

● W. Hill, *Theories of Learning* (1988).

Conflict resolution, more of an aim than a technique. Social psychologists often argue that they have particular insights into the causes of conflict which allow these to be resolved. The evidence for this is ambivalent.

Connectionism, a theory from >artificial intelligence which argues that knowledge is represented in the >brain in a particular way. The theory explains how the brain can handle problems quickly. It starts from the view that the brain is a parallel machine. It can carry out a number of operations at the same time as opposed to a serial machine which can only perform one operation. Connectionism assumes that information is stored as a series of connections or associations between neuron-like elements. Some connectionist models assume local information networks in one part of the brain, others widely distribute links between different areas. The theory is an attempt to respond to the fact that the brain can work so fast.

● A. Garnham, *Artificial Intelligence* (1986).

Consciousness. For human beings, to be is to be conscious. It is hard to imagine what an unconscious existence would be like. We are conscious throughout our

44

waking lives, although, of course, we regularly do rather more than we are conscious of. For example, as I jog along the pavement, I may not be aware of the cars on the road or the flowers in the municipal gardens; I am more likely to be fretting about my boss who is pestering me to finish a particular job. Despite my worries, my >brain – 'on automatic' – keeps me out of the traffic and stops me trampling on the roses. I can only bask in my conscious thought because many vital functions work well without my being aware of them. I am not conscious of breathing or of placing one foot in front of the other. If I had to think of these things and let them become conscious problems, I would probably be very unwell.

Consciousness appears, therefore, to be both central to our lives and yet superfluous. When psychology first became a scientific discipline, William James argued that we experienced continuous thoughts, and coined the phrase 'stream of consciousness'. 'Consciousness,' he wrote 'feels continuous.' Even if there is a time gap such as sleep, 'the consciousness after it feels as if it belonged together with the consciousness before it, as part of the same self'. Changes in the quality of consciousness were never totally abrupt. James claimed: 'Consciousness thus does not appear to itself chopped up in bits. Such words as Chain or train do not describe it fitly . . . It is nothing jointed; it flows. A river or stream are the metaphors by which it is most naturally described.'

Experimenters did much work on consciousness, using >introspection. This required subjects to be aware of everything that was going on in their minds when earnest psychologists flashed five dots, a loud tick or some other >stimulus in front of them. The aim was to tease out the basic elements of consciousness. Just as physicists had managed to discover the fundamental atoms of matter, psychologists hoped to be able to reveal the fundamental elements of >mind. The exercise collapsed, however, when different psychologists reported totally different results.

The years since the mid-1970s have seen what has been called a 'rediscovery' of consciousness. A number of factors have contributed to this: some remarkable biochemical and neurological discoveries about the brain; 'computer passion' which has fuelled speculation on the kind of computer that the human brain might be (*see* Artificial intelligence); and also a realization that one cannot hope to understand how human beings work without taking into account the fact that they are conscious and, even more complicated, conscious of being conscious. Even the smartest ape is not that.

The new interest in consciousness, however, has made scientists more aware than ever before of the mysteries of the brain. In the 1940s a number of epileptic patients requiring brain surgery were operated on in a remarkable way. The brain has no touch receptors at all so it is not always necessary for patients undergoing brain surgery to have a total anaesthetic. A Canadian neurologist, Wilder Penfield, pioneered the use of local anaesthetics and a series of operations on epileptics. He removed the tops of their skulls, rather like slicing the top of a well-boiled egg; then, using an electrode, he applied tiny bursts of electricity to various parts of the exposed >cortex. Penfield, who was aiming to find the right place at which to perform a rather delicate procedure, was very surprised when the patients responded by producing a stream of memories. For example, one woman said: 'They are yelling at me for doing something wrong – everybody is yelling.' Apparently those yelling included her brothers and sisters; the scene was quite vivid and the patient tightly gripped a bar near the operating table. Penfield seemed to have shown that areas of the cortex could have memories prodded out of them.

It was against this background that some neurologists in California in the mid-1950s saw a number of patients whose >epilepsy was so disabling that it seemed necessary to sever the *corpus callosum* – the connection between the right and left hemispheres of the brain. That way, if they had an epileptic fit, it would be contained on one side. When the psychological after-effects of these operations were studied, they revealed an extraordinary pattern. Superficially, the patients seemed to be coping quite well. They did not bump into doors or suffer memory lapses or great personality changes; they seemed much as they had been before. So what did the operation do?

Detailed analysis revealed surprising changes. Each cerebral hemisphere seemed to have a life, and personality, of its own, and it began to look as if there were two different people locked in every skull. The physiology is complicated, but it is hard to understand the experiments without some sense of it. The left cerebral hemisphere controls the right hand, right leg and the right-hand side of the body; the right hemisphere controls all the left. With >vision, the situation is more complicated. Each retina (the light-sensitive layer at the back of the eye) has a left visual half-field and a right visual half-field. The left visual half-field is linked to the right hemisphere and vice versa. As a result, if you want to test what the left hemisphere thinks of an object it sees, you have to be very careful to present that stimulus to the right visual field on, say, the right eye.

When Roger Sperry and his Californian colleagues studied patients who had the *corpus callosum* cut, they found that the left side of the brain did not know what the right brain was doing. When the left cerebral hemisphere was shown a picture of a fork, the subject would say 'fork'; when this was shown to the right hemisphere, the subject – though he knew what it was since he would pick it up and move it towards his mouth – could not name it (*see* Split-brain studies). Psychologists contrasted the logical and verbal role of the left hemisphere with the emotional and musical role of the right hemisphere. Many seized on this research to suggest that 'Western man' was too dominated by his left hemisphere and overly conscious. Various meditation techniques promised to get people 'in touch with their right hemispheres'. And, in the United States, Barbara Evans' *Drawing on the Right Side of Your Brain*, a book that offered to teach people to draw by using their right brain, hit the bestseller lists. Psychologists who had so long ignored consciousness began to see it as a vital area of enquiry. The interest in mood-altering drugs in the 1960s also contributed to this change in outlook, downgrading logic in favour of emotion.

Throughout history, human beings have been interested in using drugs – from the time of the secret rituals of the Elysian mysteries in Greece 2500 years ago right up to the present. In the end, what has proved far more interesting are experiments which seem to show that the mind can affect the body. The fashion for Eastern mysticism which led to such praise for the right hemisphere of the brain also led some scientists to research the claims of yoga experts. Some, like the much-garlanded Maharishi, the Beatles' guru, claimed that >meditation could reduce one's pulse rate, heart rate and general level of >stress. At the Maharishi's British headquarters at Mentmore, there is even a psychology department which carries out research that appears to back his ideas.

There seems little doubt that those who learn to meditate can, by altering their consciousness, alter the state of their body. The meditation does not have to have any religious element. Bruce Cuthbert of the University of Wisconsin, for example, used agnostics and found that subjects could reduce their heart rate even better if they meditated by chanting the neutral word *One* rather than the Buddhist *Om*. Three researchers from the Harvard Medical School reported in the journal *Nature* that the three Tibetan monks that they studied could, while meditating, increase the temperature of their fingers and toes by about 7–8°C – a remarkable warm-up. Nor are these isolated results. On average, it has been shown that, during meditation, subjects can increase their peripheral blood flow by about 40 per cent. These discoveries have led to new therapeutic techniques for the control of high blood pressure (*see also* Biofeedback). These interesting results have revealed, again, unsuspected aspects of consciousness, but it is hard to see how they pave the way for anything like a general explanation of its functioning.

There have been two recent developments in consciousness studies. John O'Keefe has felt it legitimate to analyse the complicated mix of determination, thought and feeling involved in writing. He noted that he could remain aware of the fact that his sentence didn't quite catch his meaning. A nose itch, a snatch of Elgar, a determination to write better and awareness of the noise of builders outside all invaded his mind and demanded attention.

Then, too, models of computers have contributed to the debate. Paradoxically, the most significant effect of computers on research has been to highlight the complexities of consciousness that machines cannot match. We think, we think about ourselves, we think about how our thoughts will affect others, we realize that (but do not know quite how) our feelings affect our thoughts. Books such as *Godel, Escher, Bach* pointed up how convoluted our consciousness is, loving patterns and puzzles like Escher's drawings. None of this resolved any problems about consciousness, but it alerted scientists to how hard it would be to build a computer which did more than mimic some of our basic cognitive skills. And being conscious involves rather more than that. Computers have not solved any problems about how human minds work – so far, the traffic has been all the other way!

I have necessarily had to leave out much research in this short survey. For example, we have not considered the claims of >parapsychologists who believe that their work on >telepathy and >clairvoyance shows that some human minds have >extrasensory perception. Equally, I have not touched on the series of experiments in which psychologists have learned that people have, and can use, mental imagery. Daniel Dennett, professor of philosophy at Tufts University in Massachusetts, and author of *Brainstorms*, a book on the philosophy of the mind,

C

argues that there should be more research of that sort into the concepts of consciousness. Dennett is certainly aware of the possible pitfalls. Introspection was first ridiculed because of the battles of different descriptions between different schools. The return to the study of consciousness is new, but there has been more work on describing and analysing some of the contents of consciousness than on seeking to explain it. No one has really attended to the problem of how consciousness arose (was it to do with language?) or whether consciousness has changed – in 1979, Julian Jaynes suggested that primitive peoples were not as conscious as we are – or what the survival value of consciousness is. Psychologists are beginning to accept that any account of human beings, a theory of humankind, must have consciousness at its centre, but our thinking about it is far from clear. Dennett has suggested that the confusion may indicate that we are asking the wrong questions.

- P. M. Churchland, *Matter and Consciousness* (1988); P. M. Churchland and T. Sejenowski, *The Computational Brain* (1993); D. Dennett, *Content and Consciousness* (1969) and *Brainstorms* (1986); D. Hofstadter, *Godel, Escher, Bach* (1981).

Conservation. In psychology, this has nothing to do with preserving old buildings. >Piaget introduced the term when he came to examine how well children could judge that the quantity of a substance remained identical even if it was presented in a different shape. His most cited story is one in which children saw a liquid being poured from a tall glass into a fat, small one. Typically, children under the age of seven did not 'conserve': they were misled by the tallness of the glass and usually said that the taller the glass, the more liquid was in it. Subsequent studies have shown, however, that under some circumstances young children can master these tasks, but they have to be clearly explained or demonstrated beforehand. Piaget may have phrased the task rather badly so that the children were not at all clear as to what was being asked of them. The results reflected their confusion rather than their conceptual lack. There are also conservation experiments dealing with number, length, etc. These studies were central to Piaget's ideas on the stages through which >intelligence develops.

- P. Bryant, *Perception and Understanding in Young Children* (1972).

Constancy, seeing an object as stable and the same.

Construct validity. *See* Validity.

Consumer behaviour describes how people react in a buying or selling situation. The models developed by economists classically have been very theoretical, not studying how people actually behave but centring on figures. For many years, psychologists didn't really concern themselves too much with consumer behaviour, but the increasing awareness of the fact that we live in a consumer society forced them into it. Some interesting trends have been identified. For example, in grocery shopping, men tend to be much more interested in value for money than quality; one class of shopper will always want to buy the latest gadget as soon as it appears. Much consumer behaviour research is unpublished since it is commissioned by corporations to decide how to tweak particular products in order to sell them.

Content analysis, a technique that involves counting the number of times a word or a theme appears in a particular text. It has been used to reveal how concerned subjects are with particular issues, and is much employed in >achievement motivation.

Contiguity, a concept in >learning theory. Two stimuli (see *Stimulus*) are contiguous if they appear next to each other.

Control group, a group of subjects randomly chosen who are compared with an experimental group. The control group goes through the identical process as the experimental group but it is not exposed to the independent variable. Any difference between the control and experimental groups is, in theory, due to this independent >variable. This is easy to demand, hard to be sure of in practice.

Convergent. *See* Cognitive styles.

Corpus callosum, a mass of nearly 2 million nerve fibres which links the two hemispheres of the >brain. Severing it may help in >epilepsy because it isolates the areas in which nervous activity arises and prevents this activity from spreading. This procedure has led to insights into how the different hemispheres of the brain operate. *See also* Lateralization; Split brain studies.

Correlations in psychology. Most findings in psychology depend on correlations (interdependence) between two variables. It is difficult to translate this statistical relationship into a form of words that can be part of a theory of causation (*see* Causes in psychology), and it requires a mixture of mathematical skill and common sense. *See also* Oblique rotation; Orthogonal factors; Statistical significance.

Cortex. The top layer of the >brain; from the Greek word for 'bark'. The cerebral cortex consists of 'grey matter'; the rest of the cerebrum is 'white matter'. It controls all the higher functions such as >language.

The cortex is divided into two hemispheres, and each of these is in turn divided into four lobes: the frontal, temporal, occipital and parietal lobes. The two cerebral hemispheres are linked by the >*corpus callosum*. The cortex is protected first by the skull, then by three delicate membranes known as the *meninges*. In humans, the cortex can have an area of up to 2500 sq. cm, but it is only 1.5 to 3 mm thick. Nature's solution to the problem of how to get such a large surface area within a space small enough to pass through the birth canal is to fold the cortex over and over into many convolutions known as *gyri*. The cortex contains something like 10,000 million brain cells. It is believed to be the last area of the brain to evolve.

Usually injuries to the cortex lead to major impairment of >language, >thinking or >vision. However, there are intriguing exceptions, such as Phineas Gage who lived with a pick axe through his skull. Studies at Sheffield University

C

showed that individuals with much of their cortex destroyed could still do very well at university and even, in one case, get a first-class degree in mathematics. Such oddities make one ask an apparently bizarre question: how vital the cortex is. It seems to be crucial to intelligent life yet the odd dramatic case history suggests that we can rely on older structures in the brain for some aspects of complex behaviour.

In the 1960s, it was discovered that the left and right hemispheres specialize in different functions: the right in emotional/creative functions; the left in language and logic. *See* Lateralization.

Counselling, literally, to give advice. The term now covers a wide range of therapeutic and pseudo-therapeutic activities. There are counsellors who deal with traditional psychological problems such as alcohol abuse but increasingly there are specialists who offer a similar service in areas where psychology might seem irrelevant such as job loss (*see* Unemployment).

What usually distinguishes counselling from therapy proper is that it is shorter and more informal, and there should be no bar on the counsellor directly giving advice, suggestions, even orders to the person they are seeing. In addition, counsellors do not have to be medically or even psychologically trained.

Counter-transference, a term found in >psychoanalysis. If >transference is the process by which the client risks becoming too emotionally involved with the therapist, counter-transference is the attachment the other way round: the therapist, either flattered, seduced or needy in his/her own way, becomes too attached to the client. Revelations that there has been far more sexual contact between clients and therapists than had been dreamed of suggests how potent these forces can be. >Freud warned that counter-transference is potentially highly damaging.

Creativity, a faculty that is difficult both to define and to explain. Psychologists have studied creativity in two ways. First, they have tried to analyse what has made successful artists succeed, ranging from >Freud's study of Leonardo da Vinci to a number of studies of famous architects and physicists. A second approach has examined >problem solving to see what kinds of 'ordinary' individuals provide creative solutions.

One difficulty of this latter approach has been the definition of 'creative' – all too often, quantity rather than quality is meant. This has come about because 'divergent >thinking' has been equated with 'creativity'. To be creative in the 'Uses of' test, for example, you have to find as many uses of an object as possible. The person who can think of 56 uses of a brick is, therefore, supposed to be very creative – but is this really creative?

The data on successful artists suggest that there are no clear factors that make someone creative. For instance, Freud argued that great artists sublimate, converting their sexual energy into artistic energy. It's an interesting notion which is true for some and untrue for others. There have certainly been some immensely creative personages – Leonardo da Vinci, T. S. Eliot, Isaac Newton – who seem to have suppressed their sexuality. However, others have

C

flaunted theirs and revelled in sensuality: the French novelist Gustave Flaubert logged the number of women he had slept with, noting during one trip to Beirut that he had made love to three before lunch and one after dessert; W. H. Auden kept a log of the boys with whom he had slept while he lived in Berlin. And many great artists have had perfectly normal sex lives. >Sublimation is no guarantee of creativity.

The Romantic poets from 1790 onwards also suggested that there was a link between madness and creativity as well as between suicide and creativity. The madness/creativity link has recently been taken to an extreme by E. Hare, who has claimed in the *British Medical Journal* that all great artists have been manic-depressives (*see* Mania). However, if this theory were true, now that there are drugs for manic-depression, we can expect to see an end to great art. Equally odd is the alleged link between suicide and creativity. There certainly were some great artists who committed suicide such as Vincent Van Gogh and Sylvia Plath, but most successful poets have lived to a ripe old age – Tennyson died when he was 83 and Browning when he was 77. The attempt to fit definite personality characteristics to creative people seems to be inherently flawed, although it remains perennially fascinating as the search for a formula for creativeness continues.

In experimental work, creativity has been defined as the ability to make unexpected connections between stimuli (see Stimulus). Hence the 'Uses of' test and also the 'Remote Associates Test' which asks subjects to discover such things as the link between 'rat', 'blue' and 'Dutch'. (It's cheese.) Liam Hudson has shown, however, that very creative schoolchildren are often convergent (*see* Cognitive styles), the key influence on them being the subjects they are taking. The scientifically creative will tend to convergent thinking; the arts specialists to divergent thinking. Creativity itself remains elusive. Partly this is because the creative solution to a problem is never a set one. To expect creative people to conform to a nice, neat formula is perhaps a contradiction in terms.

- Sigmund Freud, *Leonardo* (1979); E. Hare, 'The Key to Genius', *British Medical Journal*, vol. 297, p. 1275 (1988); L. Hudson and B. Jacot, *The Way Men Think* (1992); A. Storr, *The Dynamics of Creation* (1974).

Critical period, a concept that straddles both >child development and >ethology. >Konrad Lorenz argued that there was a period when a baby animal learned which species it belonged to. >Bowlby claimed that there is a similar critical period for the forming of deep-rooted emotional bonds in humans. It's here that such basic attitudes as warmth or hostility, trust or anxiety are developed in a baby.

- K. Lorenz, *King Solomon's Ring* (1952); J. Bowlby, *A Secure Base* (1988).

Cross-modal transfer, a transfer of information from one sense to another. If one learns to separate the figure from the ground (*see* Figure/ ground) simply by touch then, when one actually sees the >stimulus, it will be easier to see that separation.

C

- M. K. Singley and John R. Anderson, *The Transfer of Cognitive Skill* (1989).

Crowd behaviour. Fifteen years' study, especially of football crowds, has led to little real understanding. Crowds are susceptible to rumour and panic, but the hopes of nineteenth-century psychologists like Gustave Le Bon who believed that it was possible to predict their behaviour mathematically have turned out to be false. Not all crowds become violent or mob like. The evidence of disasters like Heysel and Hillsborough shows that it is small gangs within crowds who behave like a mob.

- Gustave Le Bon, *The Crowd* (1911); David Canter *et al, Football in its Place* (1989).

Cry for help, an expression popularized by Erwin Stengel in his studies of attempted >suicide. Stengel established that those who actually committed suicide ('true suicides') and those who attempted suicides ('parasuicides') were very different. Many more older men succeeded at suicide than any other group; with attempted suicide, the major group was young women. Stengel argued that many a suicide attempt was not supposed to end in death but was a 'cry for help', a desperate attempt to make those close to the person see that something is terribly wrong. From Stengel's original idea, the phrase has been extended so that now those in the >caring professions often employ it as a kind of shorthand, as in 'His drinking is a cry for help'.

- Erwin Stengel, *Suicide and Attempted Suicide* (1961).

CT scan. *See* CAT scan.

Culture-free and culture-fair tests. During the row over race and IQ (*see* Intelligence testing; Jensen controversy) there was much argument about whether existing IQ tests were equally difficult for whites, blacks and Hispanics. Many items seemed to assume familiarity with Western culture and therefore couldn't be called 'culture-free'. Researchers suggested that some tests, such as Ravens' *Matrices* were more 'culture-fair' – that is, in doing their own, members of one culture didn't have an unfair advantage over members of another.

D

Dark adaptation, the process by which the eyes become used to the dark and better able to see in low light or at night. It takes about 15 minutes for the eyes to be fully adapted to the dark. During this time period, the rods in the retina (*see* Vision) become full of unbleached rhodopsin and, therefore, highly sensitive.

Darwin, Charles (1809–82), author of the *Origin of Species* and of the theory of evolution. Darwin has affected psychology profoundly. The theory of evolution required continuity in the animal kingdom. According to the theory, humans were, at best, only the kings of the beasts. As such, they could be studied as animals were; there was no need to worry about the soul or other spiritual mysteries. However, it took surprisingly long for this lesson to filter through.

Darwin also pioneered the study of emotions in animals and humans. He became interested in gathering anecdotes of animal behaviour, and in *Emotional Expressions among Animals and Men*, he traced links between human and animal behaviour. Some of Darwin's insights remain provocative more than a century later – for example, his views on >laughter and smiling.

- Robert Boakes, *Animals and the Origins of Behaviourism* (1986); Robert Richards, *Darwin and the Emergence of Evolutionary Theories of Mind and Behaviour* (1988).

Daydreaming, dreaming while awake. It's hard to be sure that daydreaming means anything other than >imagining or >fantasizing. Many people report that they daydream every day, but the process seems significantly different from >dreaming while asleep.

Death instinct. In *Beyond the Pleasure Principle*, >Freud argued that there were two kinds of instinct – those which promoted life and those which sought to return all living matter to a state of death. It is important to distinguish between the destructive instincts – ie the wish to kill others – from the death instinct, which is the wish to die or to annihilate oneself. There is no biological evidence to support the existence of such an instinct, although, as with much in psycho-analytic theory, it has passed into the general culture – for example, we speak of a 'death wish'. It seems likely that Freud, like many thinkers, was profoundly affected by the carnage of the First World War, and he postulated this death instinct to explain how the millions of deaths had been allowed to happen and, to some extent, had been accepted.

● Sigmund Freud, *Beyond the Pleasure Principle* (1920).

Deductive reasoning, a skill of logic which involves drawing conclusions from a set of premises. There is evidence from both >cognitive psychology and developmental psychology (*see* Child development) of the difficulties that this causes even fairly intelligent individuals. Logic often defeats us.

>Piaget showed that it is only at the age of 13 or 14 that teenagers begin to master the formal operations of logic. He never quite accounted for the fact that many never totally succeed with such problems. In a study by Johnson Laird and Wason, even university students, who should have been capable of solving such things, were very poor at coping with some deductive problems – especially those involving negative inferences. It is easy to be misled when trying to plot the logical consequences of propositions like 'X is not a mineral' and 'minerals are not vegetables'. People easily assume that, therefore, X is a vegetable. That is illogical. K. Simonton has also found that even great scientists often prefer to confirm their hypotheses by finding examples that support them rather than seek to test them by looking for contradictory evidence.

● Jean Piaget, *The Psychology of Intelligence* (1947); P. N. Johnson Laird and P. Wason, *Thinking: Readings in Cognitive Science* (1977); K. Simonton, *Scientific Genius* (1989).

Deep structure, a term used in linguistic theory. The 'deep structure' is the meaning of an utterance. >Noam Chomsky has argued that, in the >brain, sentences are represented not in terms of their grammatical structure – ie >surface structure – but in terms of their meaning. The speaker then has to transform this, through the rules of the particular >language being used, into surface structure. Chomsky says that the deep structure of a sentence could be set out in terms of its fundamental meanings.

Others have proposed that deep structure is 'wired' into the 'hardware' of the brain so that children, for example, are set to learn whatever language they are exposed to. *See* Language.

● J. Greene, *Language Understanding* (1986).

Defence mechanisms, a term from psychoanalytic theory. According to >Freud, these are techniques the >ego uses to defend itself when it is in conflict. The ego needs protection both from realistic threats and from the demands of the >superego (conscience) and against increases in instinctual tension. Freud analysed a series of defence mechanisms that achieved these ends, including

D

>repression, >protection, >denial, >regression and >splitting. Defence mechanisms are supposed to help the ego, but they may well themselves create >neurosis if they do not deal with the realties a person has to face.

The concept has made its way into common parlance: for we speak of 'defensive reactions', 'being defensive' or 'being well defended' which basically means ignoring some of our feelings. *See also* Perceptual defence; Psychoanalysis.

Déjà vu experience, the feeling of having seen a particular sight or having been in a particular place before. It's one of the most puzzling of psychological experiences. Gopal, an Indian boy about four years old, for example, told his parents that he had already been to a town some 100 miles away. They had never taken him there before, and were apparently amazed by his local knowledge, including details of a recent murder in the town. Such experiences have been used as proof of reincarnation.

Stevenson has argued that the only valid *déjà vu* experiences are those of children: if a child says that he feels he has been somewhere before, then it is unlikely that he is fooling himself. However, Stevenson's own apparently meticulous account of 12 childhood cases fails to banish scepticism, partly because it incorporates too many coincidences to convince those who are not disposed to believe.

● I. Stevenson, *Children Who Remember Lost Lives* (1988).

Delayed gratification, being willing to wait for one's rewards. There are both personality and class differences among individuals as to how long they are willing to wait for these rewards.

Dementia, gradual loss of intellectual function due to decay of the >brain. *See* Alzheimer's disease; Presenile dementia; Senile dementia.

Dementia praecox, term that was used to describe >schizophrenia in the nineteenth and early twentieth centuries. Assumed obsolete, but Healy has argued that it was a useful diagnostic term.

● D. Healy, *The Suspended Revolution* (1990).

Denial. The mechanism of denial is one of the >defence mechanisms used by the >ego to protect itself. When faced with a traumatic >life event such as death in the family or divorce, people often act initially as if it has not happened – they *deny* the existence of the crisis. It is now accepted that this is a normal stage in the process of coping with >loss. The healthy reaction is then to move on to the next stages of what has come to be known as the process of adjusting to loss – especially anger, grief and, finally, acceptance. Some people, however, never manage to accept whatever the tragedy was and either crudely or subtly continue to deny it. An obvious example is divorced people who try to act as though nothing has happened and attempt to pretend they still have a relationship.

D

Dependency, a state in which a person relies, usually too much, either on another individual or on an institution.

Depersonalization, the process of losing one's identity. This can happen to people under conditions of extreme stress, generally through torture or detention in a concentration camp. The experience doesn't affect everyone in the same way. *See also* Brainwashing.

Depression, one of the most common forms of mental illness. It has been estimated that 1 in 9 men and 1 in 6 women will become clinically depressed at some time in their lives.

There are many different forms of depression, but the most important distinction is between reactive and endogenous depression. *Reactive depression* is an extreme but not illogical response to problems of living. If my marriage splits up, or if I lose my job, I have good reasons to be depressed. It is likely that most people who become depressed as a result of such a >life event will work through it without too much medical or psychological attention – a new job, a new romance or even just the passage of time will do the trick. However, there has been a tendency for doctors to treat such a normal, if profound, reaction as an illness and to prescribe tranquillizers and >antidepressants, even though such drugs will do nothing but suppress the real and (arguably) appropriate feelings that people experience at such times. This medicalization of ordinary misery led, in the late 1970s and early 1980s, to great problems as vulnerable people became dependent on drugs such as Valium. Doctors found it easier to write a prescription rather than listen at length to someone's woes. The situation has improved as some doctors now perceive the dangers of drug dependency.

Endogenous depression is very different. It appears not to be the result of anything in a person's life. Rather, its cause seems to be almost wholly biochemical, and it tends to occur slightly more often at certain times of the year. However, its biochemistry is far from being well understood.

There are two elegant theories of the causes of depression, both of which go beyond the obvious. M. E. P. Seligman, a psychologist, has argued that much depression is learned >helplessness. First, he gave electric shocks to animals when they could not escape from the cage they were in; they tried to but found that their way out was barred. As a result, they began to show the lethargy and listlessness characteristic of depression. Seligman then gave them shocks but with the cage door open. It was now easy for them to escape, yet they did not. They had learned to be helpless, and Seligman noted that, in terms of behaviour, they seemed very depressed. His analysis has been extended to human beings, and it is now claimed that depression is the result of failing to act on your environment. Aaron Beck has outlined a cognitive approach to treating depression which gets patients to re-evaluate what they say, and thus think, of themselves.

A different theory by sociologists George Brown and Tirrill Harris which has also been influential states that there are some underlying conditions that make it easier for a crisis to trigger a depression. The three most apt to do this were losing your mother before the age of eleven, the lack of a confiding relationship, and poor housing. The two theories are not incompatible.

Psychologists have tried to develop questionnaires to measure how depressed people actually are. These include the Beck and the Hamilton depression inventories, which ask people to tick if they have a variety of symptoms such as waking early in the morning, feeling listless, not being interested in work or in sex.

There are no easy cures for many types of depression but one useful recent development has been the >self-help group. In these, depressed people can help each other by giving members the opportunity to talk and sometimes become less depressed in the process. *See also* Antidepressants; Electro-convulsive therapy; Mania; Postnatal depression.

- Aaron Beck, *Cognitive Therapy and the Emotional Disorders* (1989); George Brown and Tirrill Harris, *The Social Origins of Depression* (1975); M. E. P. Seligman, *Helplessness* (1975).

Deprivation. *See* Maternal deprivation.

Depth perception, the ability to see distance and to see in three dimensions. The eyes use both binocular and monocular cues to tell how far away things are.

The main binocular cues are convergence and retinal disparity. In convergence, if something is close, both eyes turn inwards to see it; if it is far away, they look nearly straight ahead. The >brain controls the extraocular muscles so it knows the angle at which the sightlines from the eyes converge. The second factor is retinal disparity: images at different distances fall on different areas of the retina in each eye.

There are also monocular cues. These include perspective and texture, information from head movement, and 'good form', or >Gestalt. For example, we 'fill in' gaps in stimuli (*see* Stimulus) by imagining things that should be there. *See also* Vision.

Depth theories, a global term that encompasses >psychodynamic and psycho-analytic theories (*see* Psychoanalysis). Such theories stress the emotional and unconscious causes of behaviour. The phrase *depth theory* is, of course, biased. Technically, it refers to the fact that these theories handle deep material which wells up out of the unconscious. However, it also has a polemic edge: the phrase implies that rival theories are not deep but shallow and superficial. *See also* Psychotherapy.

Determinism, the notion that human behaviour is not a matter of free >will but is determined, or caused, by factors outside the control of the subject. Both >behaviourism and >psychoanalysis are essentially deterministic theories. Neither believes that a person can really choose his actions freely. Very crudely, psychoanalysis claims that childhood experiences and unconscious factors cause behaviour. Behaviourists argue that the history of >reinforcements determines the next actions a person will take. Determinism is the complete opposite of free will.

D

- J. Sabini and M. Silver, *Moralities of Everyday Life* (1982).

Developmental psychology. *See* Child development.

Diagnostic and Statistical Manual, a manual produced by the American Psychiatric Association which lists all psychiatric conditions and criteria for diagnosis. New editions reflect changes in social attitudes. For example, homosexuality, which was once listed as a disease, is no longer so listed.

Dichotic listening, experiments in which subjects listen through headphones to different messages in each ear. The extent to which they both are processed – that is, how much of each the subject takes in – reveals much about the workings of >perception.

Diminished responsibility, a legal concept that depends crucially on psychological criteria, and first articulated in 1841 in the McNaughten Rules in the UK. The judge then held that if people didn't know what they were doing when they committed a crime, then their responsibility for the criminal act was diminished, and they couldn't be found guilty because they could not have fully intended to carry out the crime.

The problem is how to ascertain whether someone knows an act is right or wrong. Society leaves this decision to psychiatrists, but most psychiatrists acknowledge that such a judgement is desperately difficult to make even if the 'criminal' is being honest. It may well be, for example, that a person was very depressed and yet knew it was wrong to pull the trigger. Often, too, people pretend to have diminished responsibility in order to evade punishment, especially in countries which still have the death sentence.

The concept does not always help the accused, however, as it can lead to longer terms of detention. In the UK, many people have been detained longer in high-security psychiatric hospitals than they would have been in prison for comparable offences if they had just been found guilty. In the Soviet Union, many political dissidents were declared insane and not responsible for their actions; their fate was to be held for long years in prison-like mental hospitals without knowing when they would get out. Ordinary prisoners know that they will be freed when they have served their sentence; those who have been judged 'insane' only get out when the doctors say they are cured. For all its imperfections, however, the concept of diminished responsibility continues to be used in legal practice.

- S. Bloch and P. Reddaway, *Russia's Political Hospitals* (1977); A. Clare, *Psychiatry in Dissent* (1976); H. Toch and K. Adams, *The Disturbed Violent Offender* (1989).

Displacement, a concept used in >psychoanalysis. It is the process by which energy from one mental image is transferred to another. Therefore, in >dreams, displacement makes it possible for one image to stand for another.

Displacement activity, a concept used in >ethology. A displacement activity is

D

a behaviour that an animal performs to discharge aggressive or sexual energy, and often occurs when instinctual energy is pushing an animal in two different directions. Thus, a bird who wishes to mate but also sees that it might be in danger will engage in a third form of behaviour which includes parts of both the other types of behaviour, such as hopping (sexual display) and pecking (aggression). Some displacement activities, however, appear absolutely inane, such as the ostrich burying its head in the sand.

● N. Tinbergen, *The Social Behaviour of Animals* (1966).

Divergent. *See* Cognitive styles.

Dopamine, a >neurotransmitter released by some >neurons in the >brain. Dopamine seems important for the treatment and understanding of Parkinsonism for if it fails then neural messages get blocked or confused.

● O. Sacks, *Awakenings* (1984).

Double bind, a form of destructive interaction in families in which conflicting messages are given. A typical message would be: 'I love you but you are disgusting.' The person who receives such a message is 'in a bind' because the elements within it are so conflicting. >R. D. Laing argued that such messages were crucial in causing >schizophrenia.

Double blind, a methodological procedure, particularly necessary in the testing of drugs. If I want to test the effect of a drug, I will not personally give the drugs but get a third party to do so. That way, neither I, nor the subject taking the drug, can be influenced by my expectations. This is an important safeguard in drug testing, when the >placebo effect can come strongly into play and alter results dramatically.

Down's syndrome, a form of mental handicap due to the presence of an extra chromosome. Down's children used to be known as mongols because of their slightly bloated, Asiatic-looking faces. Genetic screening now makes it possible for parents to know if the child in the womb is a Down's syndrome child. Typically the IQ of Down's children is below 80 but they can be trained to care for themselves fairly well. Their life expectancy is shorter than that of normal people.

Dramatherapy, the use of dramatic techniques in >therapy to reveal and work through particular problems. The best-known form is >psychodrama as developed by >Jacob Moreno. In dramatherapy, the past with its agonies is re-enacted in the present here and now. The patients, or clients, play parts, assuming what Moreno called 'auxiliary egos'. Playing a part – taking on another ego – allows patients both to explore their conflicts without total risk and can, if they play people with whom they have had difficulties, give them insights into how others see them. In the past 20 years, with the advent of >social skills groups and >assertiveness training, many less rigorous approaches have made some use of dramatherapy techniques.

59

- P. Holmes and M. Kays (eds), *Psychodrama: Inspiration and Technique* (1990); I. Yablonsky, *Psychodrama* (1976).

Dreams, a key topic in the development both of >psychoanalysis and >neurology.

Until 1953, it was not possible to study dreams directly, only what people remembered of their dreams. The only dreams that Freud was able to study directly were his own. At best, the psychologist could ask his subject in the morning what he had dreamed the night before; there was no way of distinguishing between the memory and the dream. Strictly what 'I dreamed' means is 'When I woke up, I remembered a dream.' In the interval between dreaming and waking, the dream could be elaborated or changed slightly or completely distorted.

The discovery of external signs of dreaming opened up new areas of research. In 1953, William Dement and N. Kleitman found that if they woke subjects in the middle of a period of REM (>rapid eye movement) sleep, they were usually able to remember a very vivid, just fading dream. This REM period seemed to correspond with dreaming. It was a plausible view: when we move our eyes when we are dreaming, we are scanning some image, as if we are in our own private cinema. When the period of REM sleep starts, the pattern of brain waves (as measured by an electroencephalograph) changes abruptly from the slow, deep waves characteristic of deep sleep, to short sharp waves much like those of >consciousness. It also became possible to measure physiological variables, such as heart rate, without waking subjects, and scientists could begin to ask if our bodies' responses in dreams were more like those of sleep or of wakefulness.

Animals also have periods of REM sleep. The French neurophysiologist, Michel Jouvet, christened animal dreaming sleep 'paradoxical sleep' because the cats he worked with had brain waves typical of animals that were awake and active even though they appeared to be in a deep sleep, relaxed and often flopping over into a ball. It was much harder to rouse them than from normal sleep; sometimes only very drastic methods would work – such as dipping their heads in cold water so that they had to wake up or drown.

Jouvet discovered that, during paradoxical sleep, a powerful inhibition is imposed on the muscles of the body: they are virtually paralysed. He identified the particular structure in the >brain responsible for this brake as the >pons, which releases large quantities of the hormone >serotonin at the start of dreaming. This seems to play a part in inducing the inhibition, leaving mainly only the eye muscles free to move.

When they dream, many people experience a feeling of not being able to move. This is particularly common in nightmares. One person gave the following account:

> It is a solely physiological sensation. Happens infrequently but is consistent when manifested. It has no ascertainable cause. It cannot be associated with any traumatic experience in the day or preceding days. The feeling is one of being throttled, although one is aware that there is no one else present.

Whole body feels rigid. There is a tightness at joints so the feeling is not that of being weak-kneed. Some shaking and also some sweating are present. One feels complete powerlessness over one's bodily sensations, inability to move even though one is constantly trying to 'will' it – ie moving to other side of the bed. When you eventually manage to move, you have the feeling you have torn yourself away from the throttling agent.

This is clearly an intense and frightening feeling. The person quoted above was conscious of it lasting for about two minutes. It used to be thought that subjects who reported such experiences were deluding themselves, especially as they were reporting drowsy, semi-conscious experiences. In fact, dreamers who said they felt paralysed were giving strictly accurate descriptions of the state of their bodies.

There are some other movements possible, including facial twitches. In a series of experiments in the 1960s, J. Baldridge attached a strain gauge to the eyes, throat, wrist and ankle of each of his subjects, and found there were fine movements – tiny and quick, especially of the wrist – at the same time as rapid eye movements. Sometimes, though, he noticed a complete absence of any movement whatsoever for periods of up to 30 minutes. He argued that these fine movements could be attempts on the part of the dreamer to follow the action of the dream. This is a more attractive hypothesis than two alternative ones: that these movements themselves provide material and sensations to the brain out of which it fashions dreams; or that these movements have no connection at all with dreaming. If the dreamer is trying physically to follow the action of his dream, it supports the view that he is like a person in a cinema reacting to the images – the content of the dream causes his reaction.

The 'cinema' analogy has important implications. In >psychoanalysis, it is the content of the dream that matters. Freud said that the dream was the 'road royal to the unconsciousness'. Dreams reveal our unconscious wishes, if only you know the code by which to read them. In his book *The Interpretation of Dreams*, Freud provided that code because, he claimed, dreams used all kinds of symbolism to hide obscene and guilt-ridden desires. Freud's book remains the best guide, from an analytic view, to the minutiae of dreams. Classical psychoanalysis has made us see the dream as the outcome of psychic forces.

Freud would have perhaps been amused that science finally permitted a study of the penis during dreams. The penis is certainly not inactive at these times. In 1944, the German physiologist Ohlmeyer reported that, while subjects slept, they usually had an erection every 84 minutes, which lasted an average of 25 minutes. It occurred to Dr Charles Fisher of the Mount Sinai Hospital, New York, that the interval between erections was much the same as that between periods of dreaming sleep, and he wanted to see whether there was any connection between dreaming sleep and erections. He found there was. The main pattern discerned from hundreds of studies of heart rate, pulse rate, blood pressure, breathing rate and even kidney function while we dream is that they all fluctuate a great deal in sleep.

We can now usefully pursue our analogy of the dreamer as a man at the

D

cinema. Imagine you are seeing quite a good film. At certain points, you become really involved; at others, the action drags and you notice that ice cream is on sale and that the man in front of you is bald – you are no longer involved. At tense moments in the film, your heart rate quickens, so does your pulse, and you may even hold your breath. Your whole system might show the kind of arousal that is sometimes found in dreamers. At other times, your responses would be more sluggish and relaxed. This irregularity of autonomic function could be caused by what we cream – in fact, it would be surprising if our bodies did not react to our dreams. This is consistent with Baldridge's idea that the dreamer tries to follow the action of the dream by his movements. To test this hypothesis, however, appears to be impossible. It would require the dreamer to give an instant, blow-by-blow description of what he is dreaming. Even if such a procedure became possible, giving a commentary on one's dream would be likely to alter the physiological reactions of the dreamer.

Dreaming has been a lively topic in recent psychological debate. Christopher Evans dismissed Freud's ideas as mere wishful thinking, and began his explanation of why we dream by looking at the work of Michel Jouvet. Jouvet found the brainstem structure which inhibited movement in REM sleep. He cut it. Then he found that dreaming cats, still asleep, exhibited a frenzy of stereotyped acts of aggression in which cats savaged mice and, from time to time, cowered from fierce dogs. Jouvet concluded that REM sleep allows the animal to rehearse or 'see' its basic instinctual repertoire. Evans here made a logical leap. Cats need to kill mice to survive, but humans are more subtle and need social skills to survive. Evans argued that, in dreaming, all the brain programs that we need in order to function are being updated. Tomorrow you may need to be nice to the boss and may want to make a pass at that attractive biochemist – better run through the game plan in the dream box during the night! This may be why babies need to dream more: they have more to remember and learn.

All this seems rather pat but it is actually philosophically rather dim. Just who is sitting in the >cortex during the night getting the benefit of this clever social planning? Social life has conscious and instinctive aspects, but our plans and reflections surely need conscious attention to be of any use. Evans does not see this as a problem, preferring the neat answer – dreams help you cope. He also ignores >daydreaming and the fact that we often consciously imagine how we will behave in certain situations. Is this like dreaming or is it something utterly different? *See also* Displacement.

● J. Allan Hobson, *The Dreaming Brain* (1988); J. Empson, *Sleep and Dreaming* (1989); C. Evans and P. Evans, *Landscapes of the Night* (1984); Sigmund Freud, *The Interpretation of Dreams* (1911); L. Hudson, *Nightlife* (1985).

Drive, a term used both in >psychoanalysis and in >learning theory. In psychoanalytic terms, a drive is the same as an >instinct: an innate, biologically determined push to action. In learning theory, the main drives are also biologically determined – especially hunger, thirst and the need for sexual contact. >Freud and Clark Hull, a leading behaviourist, both claimed that drive reduc-

D

tion was the primary model of >motivation: when an animal is hungry or thirsty, it will do much in order to satisfy or reduce that drive.

This model was tremendously influential and for about 40 years seemed entirely correct. However, it has become very evident that, at best, the drive reduction hypothesis offers only a partial account of what 'drives' us to do things. For instance, not all drives have to be reduced. It's much more problematical to speak of reducing the sex drive because, unlike hunger, it has often to be specifically aroused. Many human beings only become sexually aroused in special circumstances, and they actively seek, not a reduction of sexual tension, but initially an increase of sexual tension. We don't have a built-in sexual 'clock' like our other body clocks, requiring frequent attention – it's not a question of finding that at six o'clock one wants dinner and nookie. Even more inconvenient for drive reduction theory are drives such as curiosity. Both rats and people will do much to get the chance to explore new environments in relative safety, but then it doesn't make sense to speak of reducing one's curiosity.

Drive remains a vital concept, but drives are more variable than early theorists have allowed.

Drug dependency, *See* Addiction.

Dualism, the theory that suggests that >mind and body are dual entities existing on different planes. The >brain is matter and the mind is, well, mind. Most psychologists ignore the philosophical implications of this theory. *See* Behaviourism; Psychoanalysis.

Dyslexia, a form of difficulty in >learning to read. It tends to afflict middle-class children. Much controversy centres on whether dyslexia is due to perceptual problems or whether it is simply a label which middle-class parents use to conceal the fact that their children have reading problems. Some recent work shows that the way dyslexic children scan texts is deficient. Their looks are too quick and go too wide, which reinforces the notion that, initially at least, it is a perceptual problem.

- Max Coltheart, K. Patterson and J. C. Marshall (eds), *Deep Dyslexia* (1987).

E

Eating. >Hunger was seen as a major >drive and so, in many theories, eating became a key reward used in many learning experiments. Behaviourist Clark Hull tried to calculate the strength of the hunger drive by calculating the time that an animal had gone without eating. Usually very hungry animals were used in experiments. However, food that is not essential to maintain the body can also be a reward.

The pattern of how we eat has little to do with physiological need and much to do with habit and culture. Our pattern of three meals a day is almost a convention, stemming from the fact that most of us are used to eating before work, at work and after work. In the last 20 years, the eating habits of developed nations have changed: middle-class people now tend to eat less red meat, fewer dairy products and more fruit and pulses. Hunger may be a basic drive, but what we eat is very much a product of malleable social habits.

Psychologists have also helped unravel the >brain mechanisms that control eating. This is controlled by an area in the hypothalamus, and >lesions in this can lead either to massive overeating or to a refusal to eat. Many interesting psychological problems remain, however, such as how personality affects eating patterns, what makes people overeat or starve themselves (*see* Anorexia; Bulimia). >Freud suggested that overeaters were seeking oral gratification, and there is good evidence that some people 'comfort-eat'. The subjective meaning of eating remains a fascinating area.

Eating disorders. *See* Anorexia; Bulimia.

Ebbinghaus, Hermann (1850–1909), German psychologist who pioneered the study of >memory, by investigating how people, including himself, remembered lists of syllables. He discovered certain important effects of memory, including the >recency effect and the >position effect. His studies were among the first sophisticated experiments in psychology.

Eclectic therapy, a form of >therapy which is not linked to any one school of psychology. Rather the eclectic therapist employs theories, practices and ideas from any therapy if they seem useful. The eclectic nature of eclectic therapy means that it doesn't tend to have zealots.

ECT. *See* Electro-convulsive therapy.

E

Educational psychology, that branch of psychology which looks at how children learn and how they behave in schools. Some of the topics it covers include learning, the best ways of organizing and how to maintain discipline in schools. Human beings have long wanted to get their children to do well. The philosopher John Locke in *Some Arguments Concerning Education* (1692) already had a number of ideas on how to persuade children to learn the alphabet. Later thinkers like the French philosopher Jean Jacques Rousseau warned of the damage learning by rote could cause. In the last 100 years there has been tension between those educationalists who believed in the innate beauty of the child's mind and its ability to flower and the less romantic who hoped to find new ways and technological methods to ram knowledge in. Idealistic thinkers argue that education's first task is not to harm the child by blighting the natural processes of development.

One of the most important early educational theorists, Maria Montessori, was the first woman in Italy to qualify as a doctor. Her complex system required teachers to be alert to critical moments in each child's development when he, or she, might be open to learning particular skills. Montessori's ideas spawned a whole philosophy of nursery schooling. A modern form of the technology of learning was programmed learning which seeks to break down the information a student has to acquire into manageable chunks and to reward the student for each chunk mastered. In theory, there should be a close link between educational psychology and theories of >child development. In Britain, educational practice was badly affected by a misunderstanding of the Swiss psychologist Jean Piaget's ideas. Piaget argued that children pass through set stages of development, that children under the age of about 7 are egocentric and that it is only later that they are able to master logical relationships. Teachers assumed that what Piaget meant was that they shouldn't expect too much of young children. They couldn't be expected to master too much. In fact Piaget made no such assertion. Rather, he claimed that what teachers actually contribute is not crucial, for the child will develop alone through natural interaction with the environment and biological maturation. According to Piaget, the idea of using psychology to accelerate development is misguided. He saw that as a typically American fallacy. But the bulk of American educational psychology has either been aimed at accelerating children's development, or remedying deficiencies.

- M. Donaldson, *Children's Minds* (1978); A. D. Pellegrini (ed.), *Psychological Bases for Early Education* (1988); J. H. Flavell, *The Developmental Psychology of Jean Piaget* (1962).

EEG. Electroencephalograph. *See* Brainwaves.

Effect, Law of, a law which states that the behaviour that 'gets a result', or

E

produces the desired effect, is likely to be repeated. >Thorndike hit upon this law in the early years of this century through his work with cats. He put cats in cages which had latches, and the hungry cats had to work the latch in order to get out; once out, they could eat food placed in a dish. Thorndike observed that the cats were very active and that, after a while, they usually opened the latch by accident. They became increasingly efficient until they could work the latch the moment they got into the cage. Thorndike called this 'learning by trial and accidental success'. Responses that had a pleasant outcome tend to be repeated. This led Thorndike to postulate that 'any act which is rewarding in a given situation, if the situation reoccurs, the act is likely to recur also'. Thorndike's law was much used in early >behaviourism and anticipated the concept of >reinforcement.

● E. Thorndike, *Educational Psychology* (1905).

Ego, the Latin word for 'I'; a term popularized by >Freud. In his book *The Ego and the Id*, the ego is the realistic part of the mind that faces the world. It does its best to handle external reality while dealing with the competing demands of the other two parts of Freud's inner trinity: the wild, pleasure seeking >id and the stern, puritanical >superego. In a memorable quote, Don Bannister, a psychologist and novelist, described the ego as the 'referee between a puritanical old spinster and a sex-crazed monkey'. 'Ego' is a word that has passed into Western culture. There are some related uses, such as ego-ideal. *See also* Dramatherapy.

Egocentricity, a term used by >Piaget to describe the inability of young children to see any event from any point of view other than their own. He argued that this stage in development marked both the >sensori-motor stage and much of the pre-operational one. Piaget arrived at the concept of egocentricity through studies at a play school, but the record of his observations can be interpreted differently. From 1975, psychologists have shown that children can actually be trained to overcome their egocentricity – especially by being asked to imagine, for example, what dolls in a different pattern would see or hear.

● M. Donaldson, *Children's Minds* (1978).

Ego psychology. This has two senses: the psychology of the >ego; or the psychoanalytic theory which stemmed from >Sigmund Freud's *The Ego and the Id* and >Anna Freud's *The Ego and Mechanisms of Defence*. Ego psychology stresses the strength of the ego and its ability to use its contact with reality. It contrasts with >instinct theory in its emphasis on the ego's ability to impose a measure of control over our sexual and aggressive urges.

● H. Hartmann, *Ego Psychology and the Problem of Adaptation* (1958).

Eidetic imagery, if a child is shown a picture and then looks at a grey surface, a memory image is sometimes projected so accurately that the child can literally count the number of spokes on a wheel or even read the letters in a strange word.

The child can move his eyes, as in real >vision, examining what he sees. How these images arise remains unknown.

Electra complex, the >Oedipus complex as applied to girls. The term is little used now and was even rejected by >Freud.

E

Electro-convulsive therapy (ECT). This was first given in 1938 by the Italian psychiatrist Ugo Cerletti, to a Milan railway engineer. The engineer protested but the psychiatrist carried on regardless, a start that was appropriate as ECT has always been controversial, arousing anxieties about patients' rights. Some doctors argue that it is a very effective treatment for >depression and, even, in some schizophrenias. Yet many patients have complained that it is almost a form of torture, called by some 'the electric hammer'.

In ECT, a small electrical current is passed through the >brain, via electrodes attached to the patient's scalp. Recommended treatment in the West insists that patients be given a muscle relaxant and a short-acting general anaesthetic beforehand to eliminate pain and reduce the risk of physical injury. In the past, patients were often rocketed up into the air by the electric shock; bones were broken and patients regularly complained of headache.

ECT does seem to lift depression; a range of studies has shown significant improvement in about 70 per cent of patients. The disadvantages are the side-effects, including loss of >memory and, over long courses, confusion. These can be so pronounced that, in the United States, it is a legal requirement to tell patients in some detail of the risks of ECT and have to get their 'informed consent' before it is administered. In California it is banned.

These arguments leave one mystery: why does ECT work? No one is even close to the answer. The many controversies it has engendered led in 1980 the Royal College of Psychiatry in Britain to commission a report on the use and efficacy of ECT. It concluded that ECT did help but that it was poorly administered, with patients not knowing what was going to happen or being aware of the side-effects.

Different attitudes to ECT often indicate the level of political awareness of patients' rights groups. In the Third World, unlike the US, few safeguards exist. Recent controversy also centres on whether ECT is effective in the treatment of >schizophrenia. Evidence exists of some improvement in small samples.

● John Pippard and Les Ellam, *ECT in Great Britain* (1981).

Embarrassment. Psychologists have become increasingly interested in embarrassment and shyness, and in finding ways of teaching those who suffer from them the skills they need to overcome them.

Emotion. It is difficult to define what an emotion is. We usually experience emotions as feelings. We say that we feel angry, we feel happy, we feel frightened, we feel in love. We also say, however, that we feel annoyed, we feel cheerful and we feel sick. Feeling sick is obviously not an emotion, and neither are annoyance nor cheerfulness.

Generally, only strong feelings are seen as emotions. Psychologists have

E

certainly spent most of their time studying fear, anger and passion rather than less extreme feelings. Consider the phrase 'I feel emotional': this would be a very odd phrase to use to describe how you felt if you had just missed the bus and felt annoyed. If you discovered that you had a rival for your loved one, however, to feel angry or jealous would be apt.

The classification of emotions is an ancient art. Generally, three kinds are identifiable. First, there are 'fear' emotions. These usually provoke a flight response in animals. People, however, flee usually only when they are in exceptionally threatening circumstances such as fire or in a lion's cage, but they are often placed in circumstances where their inability to flee causes great distress. Take the classic farce scene where the lover is about to be caught with his pants down by the jealous husband who is also a good shot. The lover dives into the nearest cupboard where he sweats, fidgets and virtually faints with anxiety. Fainting, he falls out of the cupboard and then totally panics as he tumbles out on the cuckolded marksman.

Second, there are 'anger' emotions: continuing the farce, the husband flies into a towering rage. Third, there are the 'pleasure' emotions such as happiness and joy. It used to be argued that pleasure was nothing but relief from tension. This idea came from studies of sexual drives and sexual activity, where the discharge of pleasure at orgasm was taken to be the model for all other types of pleasure. However, research has shown this to be untrue about sex, and other pleasures also do not fit this model well.

In an 'emotional state' such as fear or anger, the body is highly aroused. Various physiological changes occur: salivation stops so the mouth feels dry; digestion slows down; the colon and bladder don't empty as easily as usual, except in some cases where fear causes defecation and urination; the heart beats faster, and more blood is directed to the >brain and muscles, the pupils of the eyes dilate; sweating increases to get rid of the heat generated by all the extra muscle activity; the adrenal gland secrets considerable amounts of >adrenalin and >noradrenalin. Crudely, the body is preparing for action. It is surprising how fast you can move if you find yourself in the path of an oncoming bus.

So much happens to the body in an emotional state that the American psychologist William James argued that it is our awareness of these bodily changes that gives rise to emotion. He wrote: 'We do not run because we are afraid: we are afraid because we run. And because I become conscious of my running.' This theory has been very attractive especially to those who want to deny any major role in psychology to conscious intentions or feelings. You are not afraid because there is something special about the state of your consciousness inaccessible to all others; you notice your heart is thumping like mad – which anyone else could hear if they pressed their ear to your chest – and when you feel that, you become afraid.

However, this theory has proved impossible to sustain for a number of reasons, especially Jerome Singer and Stanley Schachtel's work in 1962 which showed that we pin a particular label on a state of arousal depending on the context: someone flirts with me, and I feel happy; someone quarrels with me, and I am angry. This has led to increased interest in the effect of cognitions

E

(thoughts) and emotions on each other. Much of this research shows how our thoughts are affected by our feelings and by emotionally laden impressions. It appears that feelings undermine reason, but there's much less evidence to suggest that thought and rationality affect feelings. As Pascal observed, '*Le cœur a des raisons que la raison ne connaît pas.*' The >limbic system has been seen as central to the brain's processing of emotions.

In modern Western civilizations, we are taught from an early age to control our emotions. Only babies are excluded: when they cry, they are fed, cuddled or changed. By the time the child is three years old his parents will usually have tried to make it clear that every whim cannot be gratified, and he learns that he will not always get what he wants. This makes him very angry but if he expresses that anger – by hitting his parents or by hitting himself – he will usually be punished. It is only under special circumstances that we allow ourselves or our children to become emotional. A death in the family is one such occasion; then grief is acceptable, but only to a certain extent (*see* Loss).

>Freud argued that civilization depended on the repression both of sexual feelings and of emotions. Humans managed to repress sexual and emotional energy and use it to build cities, farm and create works of art, even though they would rather have remained perpetual sex maniacs in a less developed environment. Herbert Marcuse (*see* Alienation) has said that society uses >surplus repression to maintain its level of functioning. Experiments have shown that emotions affect efficiency. If you are too highly aroused, you are less good at such laboratory tasks as spotting signals, unravelling difficult messages or even keeping a pencil fixed on a moving disc. Pupils who are too anxious about examinations often do poorly. To perform well on a task, you have to be motivated but not too much. Too high a >motivation often impairs performance (*see* Yerkes Dodson law).

A great deal of recent psychology has argued that we have gone too far in repressing our emotions. Many therapy groups spend their time learning how to express suppressed emotions, usually through a good deal of physical contact such as hugging, which is rare in our society (we usually only hug lovers). Men often – and especially in Western cultures – have been conditioned not to say or show how they feel, especially when such feelings are negative. It is a 'bad show' for police officers, executives and tough manual workers to cry; tears in the boardroom or on the building site are not impressive. A favourite way of dismissing an argument is to denounce it as 'emotional', which suggests that it is cheap and illogical.

- Paul Harris, *Children and Emotions* (1989); C. Izzard, J. Kagen and R. Zajone, *Emotions, Cognition and Behaviour* (1984).

Empathy, a skill that allows one to know what someone else is feeling and makes it possible to identify with them. It's an important ability. One of the best ways of getting people to talk, to rid themselves of tension, is to make them feel that you know what they are feeling. The >caring professions depend on such skills. There is evidence that the benefits of >psychotherapy depend on the match of

E

therapist and client which, in turn, depends on empathy. Philosophically, empathy is also important because it is one of the best proofs of the existence of other minds. The mysteries are why only some people have the ability and what we can do to develop it.

Empirical approach, an approach to psychology based on the scientific method. It depends on framing hypotheses, devising experiments that will test them and a careful analysis of results to see if the hypotheses have been confirmed. The empirical approach to psychology can be traced back to Hume, Hartley and the Scottish associationalists (*see* Association theory). Traditionally, empiricists are suspicious of >intuition, >insight and grand theories, especially when these are devised by self-important armchair thinkers.

Two of the most successful of post-war British psychologists, Donald Broadbent and >Hans Eysenck, have said that, whenever they have relied on their intuition, they have tended to be wrong, and that only those who are lazy and vain would suggest that they could solve psychological problems without recourse to experiments. Both contrasted the sanity and success of the empirical approach with other 'methods' that were full of profound-seeming theorizing but rather short on proven facts. Broadbent warned that the rise of interest in various therapies and >encounter groups was wishful thinking and led to all kinds of mistaken values.

The empirical approach tends to be rather dry, and its followers believe that psychology must not be over-ambitious. It can't easily help people lead happier lives. The empirical approach has certain rigidities, too, for it has tended to see only one kind of experimental approach as being acceptable. However, some questions can't be asked, let alone solved, if one sticks too firmly to empiricism.

● Donald Broadbent, *In Defence of Empirical Psychology* (1974).

Employment. Once, utopians fantasized about a world without work in which, with lovely leisure, we could all develop our creativity and personality. That image was shown to be romantic bunk in the 1970s when, increasingly, studies showed that >unemployment had a psychologically damaging effect. It was at first assumed that this was due to money problems and loss of >status, but it has become clear that employment (without its crude rewards) is psychologically beneficial. Marie Jahoda has argued that people need to be employed: it gives their daily life a pattern and a structure; it also gives meaning to their lives, for Western societies see personal identity as closely linked to the work one does. Finally, work helps pass the time and reduces the extent to which people rely on the family group as the only group which provides support.

● Marie Jahoda, *Employment and Unemployment* (1981); P. Wair, *The Psychology of Work* (1979).

Encoding, how the >brain encodes >perceptions and memories. It is a growth area due to computer analogies of the mind. *See* Learning; Memory.

70

Encounter groups, groups of people brought together for the purpose of exploring feelings and dealing with problems. Encounter groups grew out of >group therapy, and were popularized in California by Esalen, a sort of therapy centre cum commune.

A historian may well conclude that the enthusiasm for encounter groups can be linked to various movements which sought to perfect human beings. It's quite easy to see antecedents in the free-love groups of 16th-century Europe and in the 19th-century radical groups. The conventional norms of society fetter our feelings, say all these groups; create a new organization and freedom and happiness will follow. In many ways, encounter groups were idealistic and utopian. The belief was that a group of people could explore feelings, anger and frustrations and come out of the experience happier and 'more together'. In their heyday, you could join an encounter group on a one-off basis or attend regular weekly sessions at therapy centres such as Esalen in California and Quaesitor in London. Later, a number of Indian gurus took over some encounter group techniques, most notably the Bhagwan. How useful encounter groups were, and for whom, has remained controversial.

Studies were done to discover who actually sought out encounter groups and what these encounter groups achieved. The encounter movement turned out to consist largely of a small number of people, most of whom were neurotic and tended to try many different brands of >therapy. The achievements of the groups were more complex. Just what did people hope for? Few of those who went to encounter groups were seriously disturbed, although they were often emotionally needy and hoped that the groups would mend their marred lives. Psychology hasn't yet solved the issue of how to judge whether such therapy works because the criteria for success are so vague. Whose judgement matters? The person who goes to the group? His family and friends outside? The group itself? And how many changes do there have to be for the experience to rate as success?

From the outset, there were ethical worries. First, some organizations seemed to be making lots of money – most notably the Bhagwan who acquired 80 Rolls-Royces and preached the highly original gospel that the richer he was, the more insight he had. Leaders of groups had particular power; there were rumours of violence and illicit sex. One Austrian commune required its members to sleep with everyone else in the group. Encounter groups still exist, but today there is much less enthusiasm for them.

● A. Clare and S. Thomson, *Let's Talk about Me* (1979); Norman Cohn, *The Pursuit of the Millenium* (1965).

Endocrine system. Essentially the biochemical systems of the body. It is important in psychology because the endocrine glands release hormones which have consequences in growth and emotions. Key endocrine glands are the pituitary, the thyroid and the andrenal glands.

Endogenous depression. *See* Depression.

Endorphins, a group of >neurotransmitters which also include the encephalins; substances produced by the >brain with effects that resemble those of morphine.

They are released by the brain at times of stress – eg in response to pain, anxiety, fear or even hard exercise. The 'high' that sometimes occurs during a long run has been attributed by some to the release of endorphins. Unlike drugs such as morphine, however, endorphins are quickly degraded by the body and so there is no risk of physical addiction.

Environmental psychology. Long before the Green movement became flavour of the month, psychologists were interested in examining how the design of buildings could be made more 'user friendly'. In the UK, the pioneer in this field has been David Canter. He has found that the design of modern offices, complete with air conditioning and computer systems, can lead to headaches and other vague symptoms. The use of environmental psychology to help design environments has spread to other areas such as hospitals and prisons. Studies have analysed how people use space and this feeds back into the design process to produce, in theory, more worker-friendly environments.

● David Canter, *Psychology in Practice* (1987).

Epilepsy, a form of illness in which the person is subject to epileptic fits. The fits seem to be triggered by what seems like 'a storm in the >brain'. Fits can be very frightening. The person falls down, loses control and can be in danger of biting his or her tongue. Epilepsy used to be taken as a sign of divine grace. It has two major forms – *petit mal* and *grand mal*. *Petit mal* means that the patient is subject to small seizures. Usually, lying down and keeping quiet is enough to make them pass. *Grand mal* are the frightening fits described above. Some stimuli (*see* Stimulus) like strobe lights can trigger epileptic fits. Drugs now control epilepsy to some degree but epileptics argue that, like many other groups, they are discriminated against. Psychologists have long been interested in epilepsy because of the light it throws on normal brain function. The >split brain studies arose out of treatment for epileptics.

Epiphenomenoma, literally 'additional phenomena', used to mean trivial phenomena. In psychology, the term refers to >consciousness that is merely a by-product of >brain activity, and neither a cause nor a result of anything. The concept is important because it exemplifies crucial theoretical differences.

We feel we are free and yet (according to many theories) our behaviour is determined. When I decide to get a divorce of apply for a job, I think I am acting freely. However, is this real freedom? Not according to >behaviourists such as >B. F. Skinner. He has argued that we are deluded about the importance of our feelings and intentions. They are, like all mental states, mere epiphenomena. A real phenomenon causes behaviour or other effects, but epiphenomena don't cause anything. Skinner attributed the real cause of behaviour to >reinforcement. This doesn't explain why our biology makes us feel that our intentions and feelings matter and appear to affect our actions.

The most poignant example of epiphenomena is Skinner's own extended biography. In this, he describes how he had originally wanted to be a writer, but he decided to become a psychologist, he says, once he realized that he did not have the talent to succeed as a writer. Yet he blithely argues that his feelings of disappointment in no way caused such actions as his going to Harvard to study psychology. This is a curious illustration of the paradox that many psychologists find themselves in when their biographies contradict their own theories.

● B. F. Skinner, *Particulars of My Life* (1976).

E

Equilibration, in >Piaget's theory, the process by which >schemas are developed to take account of new information. Equilibration is the result of both >accommodation and >assimilation.

Ergonomics, the study of how work can best be arranged or organized for the psychological and physical well-being of people. The organization of work has been a concern of psychology since the 1920s when an early kind of consultancy called the Psychological Corporation started to offer advice to businesses. The idea that psychology could develop the perfect worker stemmed from F. W. Taylor's work on >time and motion, and as early as 1910 there were tomes such as Pillsbury's *Industrial Psychology*. Psychologists came to realize that it wasn't just a question of motivating workers but also of providing a good environment in which to work. Ergonomically inclined psychologists have analysed the design of office and office equipment. They've found, for example, that there are risks involved in using visual display units (VDUs) in offices – not only the chances of developing the well-documented repetitive strain injuries (RSI) and other aches and pains but also the isolation and stress typical of this type of work. Ergonomists have been instrumental in the redesign of both VDUs and work stations – an example of a successful practical use of psychology.

Erikson, Erik (1902–94), one of the wise elders of the psychoanalytical movement (*see* Psychoanalysis). He came from Germany to Boston in 1933 – where he worked at the Harvard Medical School. His early studies were of children's drawings and play. His long descriptions of play and the use of toys suggest that play is a way of developing mastery.

In 1959 he published a theory which suggested, unlike those of >Freud and >Piaget, that the stages of development don't end in the late teens: we don't become fixed at about the age of 20 into an adult persona that lasts until death; we keep evolving. Erikson postulated eight stages of development. At each one, there is a crisis and a choice between different attitudes and behaviour. The stages are: infancy, whose crisis is basic trust and basic mistrust; early childhood, whose crisis is autonomy and shame; play age, whose crisis is initiative and guilt; school age, whose crisis is industry and inferiority; adolescence, whose crisis is identity and role confusion; young adulthood, whose crisis is intimacy and isolation; maturity, whose crisis is generativity and stagnation; and old age, whose crisis is ego integration and despair. Each stage offered a crucial chance to turn *towards* life or *against* life.

Erikson, like many psychoanalysts, believed that therapeutic insights could tell us a good deal about political figures, and he wrote famous psychobiographies of the young Martin Luther (who suffered from chronic constipation)

E

and of Gandhi. Erikson was also part of a secret American government committee that drew up guidelines for the interrogation of Nazis. Given his background
these guidelines are noteworthy for their genuine human concern: Erikson
argued that it was important not to assume that all Germans were inhuman,
Nazi monsters; they had rights too. *See* Lifespan development.

- Robert Coles, *Erik Erikson* (1973); Erik Erikson, *Young Man Luther* (1958)
  and *Gandhi's Truth* (1970).

Errors. *See* Psychopathology of everyday life.

Error sampling. Essentially mistakes made in gathering together the sample
on which a survey or an experiment will be conducted. The sample may be biased
because the two groups (the >control group and experimental group) aren't
different enough or are not different in the way that the study presumes. Take,
for example, a study of sexual behaviour in women, the aim of which is to tease
out whether or not they become more sexually active with age. If the experimenter contrasts the sexual behaviour of a group of nuns aged 30 with a
group of married women of the same age, he would be guilty of vast error
sampling.

A famous historical error was that of the American *Literary Gazette* which in
1936 predicted that Franklin Roosevelt would lose the presidential election in
a landslide. The magazine had polled car owners and those who had telephones.
This had worked in the 1920s, but in the 1930s, the great Depression had forced
many of the former middle class to give up their cars and phones. The magazine
had just been sampling the rich, who, not surprisingly, were against Roosevelt.
One frequent sampling error is to rely too much on a group of undergraduates
and extrapolate from their behaviour that of the rest of humankind.

ESP. *See* Extrasensory perception.

Ethology, the study of animal behaviour in the wild. The discipline owes a great
deal to >Darwin's pioneering work. However, throughout the early years of this
century, while there was some observation of animals in the wild, this was not
seen as having any particular relevance to psychology. Psychologists did study
animal behaviour but they tended to do so in very controlled conditions. Thus,
>Thorndike got his cats to work his puzzle box (*see* Effect, Law of) and J. B.
Watson studied how rats behaved in a maze, although he did briefly study the
behaviour of monkeys and birds on Key West, Florida and noted now much more
interesting they were in the wild. Even later on, Wolfgang Kohler, who studied
chimpanzees in the relative freedom of the Azores, didn't try to discover how
they behaved normally but concentrated on whether they could solve a variety
of puzzles to see whether they had particular >insights

There was a real division between animal behaviourists and psychologists
until >Konrad Lorenz and Nikolaas Tinbergen insisted on linking the study of
animal behaviour with psychological experimentation. They and other ethologists argue that >instincts are important and that much animal behaviour can
be explained as the unfolding of a behavioural repertoire which has been 'wired'

into the animal. Tinbergen believed in the value of bringing into the lab for detailed investigation sequences of behaviour seen in the wild. This made it possible to show how improbable events could disrupt the animals' behaviour, such as having geese become imprinted to people (*see* Imprinting).

Ethological work has led to the development of some very interesting concepts, including >displacement activity, imprinting and >territoriality. Tinbergen found, for example, that a stickleback's behaviour would alter dramatically depending on whether it was in its own territory or not. Lorenz used his ethological observations to write on >aggression and embellish key differences between animals and humans. Animals rarely kill their own species, and kill 'hand to hand'; they always see what they are doing, and this means that they fight with terror and pity. Humans, on the other hand, prefer to kill at a distance, and are capable of distancing themselves emotionally from the act.

It seems to be a human characteristic to like having the animal, the beast in urban man, in us discovered. The scientific success of ethology has led to a series of bestsellers in which authors have explored the ways in which we behave like other species. The most famous of these books is Desmond Morris's *The Naked Ape* in which he claims that we are still very much like apes but have learned to dress up.

- I. Eibl-Eibesfeldt, *Human Ethnology* (1989); Konrad Lorenz, *King Solomon's Ring* (1952); Desmond Morris, *The Naked Ape* (1965); Nikolaas Tinbergen, *The Social Behaviour of Animals* (1960).

Evoked potentials, a measure of brain activity that is 'evoked' when a >stimulus is presented. Often the stimulus is repeated a number of times so that an average measurement can be obtained. *See* Brain.

Excitation, the >on/off law states that a nerve either is or is not in a state of excitation.

Existentialism, a school of philosophy owing much to Jean-Paul Sartre and Simone de Beauvoir. They argued that there was no such thing as essential human nature, but that our personalities are formed by the choices we make as we live – hence, existence makes us. Some psychiatrists such as >R. D. Laing were influenced by Sartre's ideas, especially those which examined 'authentic' behaviour that revealed what a person was really like. In some mental illnesses, people assume crazy-seeming behaviour to protect that true self.

- M. Warnock, *Existentialism* (1970).

Experimental method, a method of investigation that is based on formulating a hypothesis and designing experiments which will, at the very least, eliminate one potential answer. It depends heavily on work in the laboratory. *See* Empirical approach.

- Morawski, *The Rise of Experimentation in American Psychology* (1989).

E

Experimental neurosis, a form of >neurosis deliberately created in the laboratory.

Experimenter effect, a curious anomaly where subjects produce (without knowing it beforehand) the result that the experimenter wants. The mechanism by which experimenters influence subjects has never been properly identified. Presumably it is akin to the hidden messages that >Clever Hans, the mathematical horse, got from his trainer. In order to avoid the experimenter effect, techniques such as >double blind tests were developed.

Expert systems, a term used in >artificial intelligence. An expert system is a computer that has absorbed the knowledge of experts. This expertise can be used to design a program that can perform tasks normally undertaken by humans. Computer programs that attempt to perform medical diagnosis are an instance of an expert system. Basically, the program draws together research in the field together with the expertise that exists in order to provide a probabilistic way of judging whether a person is suffering a particular illness and what its causes might be. The organization of the program will include such logic as: if symptom A exists, then the person is suffering that illness. In many areas, research suggests that the precious and expensive time of human experts is wasted doing work which a program can do, although their design can be difficult because they do have to interact with humans. Architecture and medicine are so far the fields in which they seem to have been most used. A. Garnham alleges that expert systems have something of a bad name because in some fields of expertise they have been used to make a fast buck.

● A. Garnham, *Artificial Intelligence* (1986).

Exploration. This was accepted as a >drive which could motivate behaviour after work by F. D. Sheffield *et al.* in the 1940s. In terms of psychological theory, this was very important because it showed up the inadequacies of the drive reduction model of >motivation. For 50 years, psychologists had managed to ignore the obvious fact that babies like to explore their environment and to handle new objects. Exploration has clear survival value as it helps organisms adapt to new environments and maximize their potential. When Sheffield's work was published, it came as a revelation that rats (as long as they weren't hungry) would actually prefer the chance to explore an interesting environment to a food reward.

Child psychologists have worked out the situations in which children are most comfortable exploring, usually when they can see or are in close contact with their mothers. The explorer needs confidence.

● D. Berlyne and K. B. Madsen, *Pleasure, Reward, Preference* (1973).

Expressed emotion, a recently developed concept. It distinguishes between emotions people feel but do not reveal and emotions they let out, even flaunt — or *express*. High expressed emotions are when individuals let out all their feelings. When these are intense, it tends to trigger new episodes of >schizo-phrenia.

External validity, the measures used in a psychological test – especially a questionnaire – may be wholly meaningless because they may not apply to the real 'external' world. For example, a paper and pencil test of how good a basketball team player you are (and such a test does exist) is rather useless if you can't catch. External validity is a test of how realistic a questionnaire is and is, in practice, linked to predictive validity. *See also* Validity.

Extinction, a term used in >learning theory. A habit is extinguished when the >stimulus that used to evoke it no longer does so. Extinction happens either when a habit hasn't been rewarded for too long or when a new, contradictory habit is learned more strongly.

Extrasensory perception (ESP), >perception which doesn't depend on the usual senses. Studies tend to focus on >telepathy and >clairvoyance. It has been suggested that some people have special ESP skills. *See also* Paranormal phenomena.

Extraversion/introversion, one of the best established >personality dimensions, first postulated by >Jung and elaborated by >Eysenck, who argued that it ranged from the extravert at one end to the completely withdrawn introvert at the other. Eysenck developed the EPQ (Eysenck Personality Questionnaire) which includes such questions as 'Do you like going to parties?' This offers a quick, generally reliable method of assessing this particular dimension of personality. The extravert tends to be outgoing, easily bored and likes new stimuli (*see* Stimulus). The introvert is nervous, shy, withdrawn and doesn't like going out. Extraverts respond better to punishment and introverts to praise since the latter are anxious of their performance. Eysenck argues that the difference is due to variation in the organization of the >cortex of the >brain. Despite the controversies about >personality tests, the dimension has been generally accepted. For Eysenck, this was only one of a number which could be precisely quantified – a first step towards an >empirical theory of personality.

• H. J. Eysenck, *The Structure of Human Personality* (1970) and *Sense and Nonsense in Psychology* (1958).

Eye contact, looking someone else directly in the eyes. Eye contact seems to indicate sexual attraction and honesty. Not looking (ie avoiding eye contact) is interpreted as being shifty. Those who don't know when to engage or break off eye contact are often labelled as or are really strange or mad. It has been noted, however, that some individuals are Machiavellian: they produce perfectly sin-cere seeming eye contact while lying through their teeth (or should it be through their eyes!).

• M. Argyle, *Bodily Communication* (1985).

Eysenck, Hans Jurgen (1916–), psychologist whose most lasting contribution

E

is in the area of personality measurement (*see* Extraversion/ introversion). Eysenck started a controversial career with a damning attack on the efficacy of >psychoanalysis. His original paper in 1952 alerted many to the need to prove that psychoanalysis was effective, and it helped create a climate in which psychologists asked how to test the efficiency of any >therapy. Eysenck was extreme – and witty – in his attacks on >Freud, noting that what Freud had said that was new wasn't true and what had been true wasn't new.

In the 1960s, Eysenck again was in the centre of controversy when he argued that >IQ was largely the product of heredity and supported >Jensen in the controversy on race and IQ, claiming that IQ analyses suggested that it was factually true that black people scored less well on >intelligence tests. He also said that Oriental races were superior to Caucasians. As a result, he was attacked as a racist even though he himself had been a victim of Hitler. There is much wrong with IQ tests, but the allegations of racism aimed against Eysenck seemed misplaced.

- David Cohen, interview with Eysenck in *Psychologists on Psychology* (1977), H. J. Eysenck, *The Rise and Fall of the Freudian Empire* (1986).

F

Face validity. *See* Validity.

Facial expressions. >Darwin pioneered the study of emotional expressions. Later researchers identified a series of typical 'freeze-frames' of facial expressions showing emotion. In most cultures, similar looks mean anger, happiness, joy, threat. In the 1970s, Paul Ekman found a surprising degree of unanimity and went on to look at the intensity of emotional expressions on different sides of the face. An early summary of these results led to predictable wisdom: emotional expression was asymmetrical, with less intensity on the logical right side of the face (controlled by the linguistic left hemisphere of the >brain), and more intensity on the left side (controlled by the right hemisphere) (*see* Lateralization). Ekman has recently questioned whether this is a real finding or merely an artifact. Most research employs photographs for which people have been asked to pose with a particular expression on their faces. Asked to assume a happy look, perhaps their faces froze in an asymmetrical, and atypical, look. Under less artificial conditions, the whole face might reflect total, rounded emotions.

In one study, people were observed in a restaurant. It was found that there were twice as many emotional expressions on the left side of the face. In an attempt to replicate this result, Warren Dopson and others studied 14 female and 9 male undergraduates. The subjects were made to sit in an armchair with a specially designed head rest. First each subject listened to a relaxation tape. Then they were made to listen to a 'sad' tape full of depressing sentences such as 'I am very discouraged,' 'I feel dejected.' They were also asked to listen to a 'happy' tape with sentences such as 'I feel exhilarated.' The subjects were asked to do their best to identify with these expressed feelings, and while they did so, four pictures were taken without them knowing. New photographic techniques made it possible to test Ekman's doubts; photographs of faces could now be split and then reprocessed so that a full face was made out of doubling one side of the face. So, for example, Face A is divided into two half faces, B and C, and both

F

are reversed so that one gets two full faces. Face D is, therefore, a full face which only has the emotional expression shown on the right side of Face A; Face E is a full face which only has the emotional expression of the left side of Face A. A quite different set of undergraduates, blind to the hypothesis under study, then rated these photographs for (1) head tilt, (2) clarity and (3) emotional expressiveness. The ratings for emotional expressiveness were far higher for faces made by doubling the left side of the face, and Dopson and his colleagues concluded that, in a natural setting, the left side of the face does reflect greater >emotion.

A second issue concerns how fast we respond to faces – and to different kinds of faces. Peter Duda and Julie Brown of the University of Guelph in Canada photographed three men and three women each in three poses – sad, happy and neutral – a total of 18 pictures. They then showed these to 20 male and 20 female undergraduates and logged how fast people identified the emotions on the faces. They found that their female subjects responded faster than the men, and that both responded more quickly to happy faces and to male faces. This was especially true when subjects were made to use their left visual field which is linked to the right cerebral hemisphere. There were no differences in response between the left visual field and the right visual field in speed of response to sad faces. This suggests to the researchers that the right hemisphere may be specially suited to identifying that happy grin on your face.

Combined together, these two studies point to the fact that Ekman may well have been wrong to question the validity of the accepted wisdom in facial research. The left side of the face does exhibit more emotion and the right side of the brain is better attuned to picking up signs of emotion or, at least, positive emotions.

Factor analysis, a statistical technique which tries to extract from a series of correlations the particular factors that account for most of the variation in data. For example, a study of road accidents might reveal various factors such as (i) weather conditions, (ii) traffic conditions, (iii) driving skill, (iv) drinking of each driver. Factor analysis could tease out the contribution of each part.

Fainting. *See* Blood phobia.

Family dynamics, the relationships within a family and, especially, their ebb and flow. *See* Psychodynamic theories.

Family therapy, a form of >therapy which involves treating the whole family. It rejects the idea that one person is sick but instead suggests that there is one family member who is acting out the sickness of the whole group. Family therapy tends to stress, and to try to unravel, the mixed messages of >family dynamics. In the 1960s, following studies of families of schizophrenics (*see* Schizophrenia), >R. D. Laing, Esterson and Bateson argued that so-called schizophrenics were in a >double bind emotionally. Typically, a mother would tell her daughter that she loved her but also that she was a slut and couldn't be trusted to go out with a boy. Laing never developed these ideas >empirically but published some astute poems in a book called *Knots*, which were all about the tangles involved in relationships. The most intensive work done on family therapy has been done in Italy, where what is known as the Milan School has developed systemic family therapy.

Family therapy has become technically sophisticated. Some clinics have a therapist in the room with the family and a second therapist watching from outside who comments (by telephone!) on what is going on. The idea is that the flow of family dynamics – the shifts, changes and twists – are so complex that the therapist working with the family would be unable to grasp all the subtleties. There are some practical problems with family therapy – for example, sometimes not all the members of the family are willing to attend. Patients who have gone through family therapy report very different experiences, but follow-up studies suggest that it has a reasonable rate of success.

- John B. Burnham, *Family Therapy* (1986); J. Haley, L. Hoffman, *Techniques of Family Therapy* (1967); R. D. Laing, *Knots* (1968); R. D. Laing and A. Esterson, *Families of Schizophrenics* (1968).

Fantasies. The ability of children to create and respond to fantasy as part of >play has been widely studied. It seems that from the age of two, children can fantasize quite competently. They can play roles such as Batman and they seem able to tell what is a true story and what is fantasy. >Jean Piaget noted, too, that some children created, around the age of three, imaginary friends, creatures of fantasy, who would play a very important part in their lives for a few years. Paul McGhee has suggested that certain kinds of personality traits tend to accompany the ability to fantasize and that, in children's groups, the child with a good 'fantasizing' ability is often a leader. Henry Wellman has argued that studies of how children learn to handle the >language of fantasy offers a way of understanding the theory of >mind.

This image of the competent child who fantasizes is very much at odds with how we view adults who fantasize – that is, they are usually seen as inadequate. This reflects the fact that, as we grow up, we are supposed to stop playing. Studies of adult fantasy stem from >Freud's view that >dreams were wish-fulfilments and especially sexual wish-fulfilment. For Freud, fantasies were private and struggled to escape past >repression. He would have been surprised by how public fantasies have become in consumer societies; few people are now ashamed of indulging them. Mills & Boon purvey romantic fantasies; porn magazines purvey sexual fantasies; and the growing number of paramilitary magazines purvey macho fantasies.

Early studies of fantasy concentrated on discovering the kinds of sexual fantasies people had. >Kinsey claimed, for example, that Americans had many fantasies of infidelity. Later surveys were even more remarkable, with Maurice Yaffe claiming that up to 30 per cent of the UK population fantasized about taking part in orgies – and a sizeable number in orgies with animals! Recently, psychologists have done some work on discovering what proportion of every day people spend fantasizing, and they found that 8 per cent of each day was spent in fantasy, although there were wide individual differences.

F

Traditionally, to fantasize, to be off in dreamland, has suggested that a person can't face life's realities, but the ability may not be a sign of inadequacy for everyone. Some people can turn their fantasies into millions and, apart from such super-stars, it seems obvious that the ability to fantasize is closely linked to the >imagination. Those who can use their fantasy skills without letting them dominate their lives can be very effective and creative in their work.

Psychologists have not researched the imagination very imaginatively so far. But it's becoming more possible.

- David Cohen, *The Development of Play* (1987); Sigmund Freud, *Leonardo* (1979); Paul McGhee, *Children's Humour* (1981); Jean Piaget, *Play, Dreams and Imitation in Childhood* (1952).

Fasting. *See* Anorexia.

Fatigue. The effects of fatigue on performance show up as slower reaction times, a failure to persist and a growing inability to spot errors. These effects become apparent in tasks after 10 hours of steady work or in general if a person tries to tackle them after about one night's lack of sleep. Nevertheless, the >brain is able to compensate if the person is well motivated or if he or she is under threat.

Fear, a normal emotional reaction to threatening stimuli (*see* Stimulus). Our understanding of fear comes from studies of emotions that are not quite fear, such as >anxiety in humans and flight in animals. It's clear that fear has enormous survival value for it prepares the organism to be ready for action and especially to run away. *See also* Emotions.

Feedback, a process by which information about efferent action (the actions of limbs) is relayed back to the >brain very quickly through privileged pathways. When the brain instructs the parts of a body to move, it needs a signal to tell it that its orders have been executed so that it can stop sending them out. This is the origin of the term feedback. The pathways by which these messages return function more quickly than others.

Feedback has been expanded to cover getting information back in all kinds of situations. Groups give feedback; it surfaces in social work. It clearly helps to provide such information so that we know how we are doing. *See* Biofeedback.

Female sexuality. *See* Sexual behaviour.

Feminist psychology. Before Simone de Beauvoir wrote her seminal book *The Second Sex*, there had been studies of sexual differences, but no attempt had been made to develop a specifically feminist psychology. Differences between the sexes seemed crucial and, somehow, justified the social status quo which feminists have come to denounce as the result of patriarchal attitudes: men had to be aggressive and leave home; women had to be nurturing and stay put. The first >insight of feminism was to claim that these were not biological givens but the product of social >conditioning – men and women weren't born like that but made like that by patriarchal society. The task of feminist psychology became the analysis of the origins of these differences to suggest how they might be changed.

Psychologists were not the first in the field. The feminist position was initially sketched out by literary critics and social commentators. De Beauvoir, Germaine Greer, Gloria Steinem and Betty Friedan were not empirical scientists, but their insights inspired a great deal of useful work in a number of key areas – >sexual behaviour, the ways in which men and women interact in conversation, the >self-esteem of women, >psychological androgyny, and the way >psychoanalysis viewed women. Much basic work exposed taboo areas and revealed that >incest, domestic violence and other abuses of women by men were far more prevalent than imagined.

Gill Meezy, in a pioneering study of unreported rapes in the Brixton area of London, suggested that far more took place than the literature recorded. Dale Spender showed that, in conversation, women were apt to listen and to nurture male tongues and >ego: ungrateful males, in return, interrupted them. Many authors showed that the self-esteem of women tended to be lower than that of men. This finding was allied to mental health work such as that of George Brown and Tirrill Harris, who showed that certain factors tended to trigger >depression in women, and that women were more likely to be committed to mental hospital for longer. Feminist psychology also pursued the reality of >sex differences and found that they were exaggerated.

The other impact was on developmental psychology (see Child development). Evidently, it was important to analyse how girls learned to play girlish roles as they grew up. Studies of >play, for example, led to a certain consensus as to the nature of the oppression of women. They identified key issues such as the kind of toys children of each sex were given, parental expectations and what kinds of actions won praise. Little boys got praise for being adventurous, little girls for being demure. Women's courses in psychology were set up, as were a number of journals such as the *Journal of Women's Psychology*. Feminist psychologists argued that identifying, and naming, these problems was only a first step. Real changes would involve major alterations to patriarchal society as a whole – a project as much political as psychological.

By the mid 1980s, however, many feminists wondered whether it was enough to attack patriarchal attitudes. Sandra Bem had, in her work on psychological androgyny, suggested a quite different way which took the best of the feminine and the best of the masculine and fused them into a new perfect human. The difficulty is that this, too, requires more than psychological insights. Feminist approaches to psychology have stimulated interesting thought and experimentation in the 1980s, but aim at more than mere psychology can deliver. *See* Horney, Karen.

- Simone de Beauvoir, *The Second Sex* (1949); S. Bem, *The Lenses of Gender* (1993); L. Eichenbaum and S. Orbach, *Understanding Women* (1983); Ann Oakley, *Taking It Like a Woman* (1984); S. Rowbotham, *The Past Before Us* (1989).

F

F

Field studies, studies that are based on observation in the real world and are contrasted with laboratory studies or experiments. From the 1920s, field studies were extremely unpopular as psychologists tried hard to establish their scientific credentials. Mere observation couldn't be really accurate and, anyway, it didn't permit the testing of hypotheses. A study in 1968 revealed that only 8 per cent of papers reported in the psychological journals were based on data obtained from field studies. However, the influence of >ethology (which built on observations of animals in the wild), the recent drive to make psychology more practical and relevant and the development of video filming as an investigative tool have reversed this trend to some extent.

Figure/ground. >Gestalt psychology made much of our ability, when looking at a picture, to distinguish the figure in the foreground which stands out from the rest of the ground (background). This ability to switch focus is interesting, and Gestalt psychologists devised a number of famous images to illustrate the point – one is the picture which can look like either a vase or two faces close together, another is the >Necker cube. The >brain's ability to see the same visual >stimulus as two utterly different images demonstrates a great deal about how our visual >perception is constructed. The figure/ground distinction is an important phenomenon in our understanding of visual illusions. *See* Vision.

Fixation, a term from psychoanalytic theory. If a person hasn't progressed properly through the stages of >psychosexual development, they may well remain fixated on a particular pattern of behaviour or love object. They are then likely to engage in infantile behaviour. Psychic energy which ought to be more widely spread remains essentially stuck to that one >stimulus. >Freud used fixation as a way of explaining 'inappropriate' sexual attachments.

Fixed-interval schedule. *See* Reinforcement.

Fixed-ratio schedule. *See* Reinforcement.

Flooding, a technique in >behaviour therapy. Flooding exposes a patient with a >phobia to what he or she fears most. Theoretically, it allows the patient to learn in one emotionally charged and 'massive' experience that his or her reaction to the thing that is feared is inappropriate. So, if I have a phobic fear of dogs, the therapist will first get me relaxed; then, over a few sessions, s/he will work through a hierarchy of my fears. I might first be asked to imagine a dog far away, then a dog closer, then patting a dog. Then I will be taken to see dogs in the street, asked to stroke them and eventually flooded by being put in a room with dogs or taken to a dog show.

There are different preambles used. Some therapists will work carefully up to an episode of flooding. Others believe that one massive dose will reverse the inappropriate learning that led to the phobia. Studies as to the effectiveness of flooding suggest it is considerable.

Formal operations, the final stage in >Jean Piaget's theory of intellectual development in which the teenager can now handle abstract, logical puzzles and strategies of reasoning. There is some doubt as to whether everyone reaches this stage, especially since P. Wason and P. N. Johnson-Laird have shown how poor university students are at solving certain logical problems. *See* Piaget, Jean; Thinking.

Free association, a technique invented by >Jung and then much used by >Freud. Theories of the mind have claimed since the 18th century that we build up networks of >association through habit and experience: say 'Table' and the reaction is 'Chair'. But Jung claimed that the speed of the association allowed one to tap into the unconscious >mind. He timed reactions and argued that if reactions were slow, then something was being suppressed. It was to facilitate these free associations that patients were allowed to lie on a couch and not see the analyst. This can be a useful technique but it is a pity that there has been too little empirical work (*see* Empirical approach) on what reaction times – that is, fluency of association – reveal. Freud slowly came to see that association was a valuable tool in analysis but not the pivot that it was first claimed to be. It remains an interesting, if under-investigated, technique.

Frequency, literally how often a >stimulus appears. It's an important variable in >learning, though there is a fine balance between greater frequency (which helps learning) and >habituation.

Freud, Anna (1895–1982). Anna Freud was born in Vienna – the youngest of >Freud's six children – and died in London. Her birth and childhood were shared with those of >psychoanalysis. She was the only one of Freud's children to grow up into his profession.

Her work was always geared towards children and their development. She dealt with neurotic distortions of personality at a time in a child's life when the unconscious mechanisms beneath are closer to the surface. What she observed and conceptualized, therefore, has implications for adult behaviour.

She started working with destitute children in 1919 when the effects of deprivation and separation of the young first struck her. She published carefully documented accounts: *Infants without Families*, *Young Children in Wartime* and *An Experiment in Group Upbringing*. She analysed adults, too, and was particularly successful at treating male patients.

Anna Freud believed that words were a prerequisite of the practice of psychoanalysis – which is where she differed from Melanie >Klein – and she would not work with children under the age of three. She was the first psychoanalyst formally to work out the >psychosexual stages which are now taken more or less for granted: the >oral stage (birth to 1 years); the anal stage (1 to 3 or 4); the genital stage (3-4 to 5–6); the >latency period (5 to 12); pre-puberty; and adolescence. The nub of her work is the interaction of these stages with the three psychic governors of personality and behaviour; >id, >ego and >superego. She was responsible for making British analysts so interested in work (often practical, preventive work) with children.

● J. A. C. Brown, *Freud and the Neo-Freudians* (1968).

Freud, Sigmund (1856–1939), the founder of >psychoanalysis. No short entry

F

can do justice either to Freud's work or to the controversy that he created. He worked first as a neurologist, and then won a scholarship to Paris in 1885 to study under the neurologist Jean-Martin Charcot and became convinced of the presence of an >unconscious >mind, and of unacknowledged sexuality. It took 13 years for these insights to hammer themselves into a complete theory – for Freud, the 1890s were the crucial decade. Then he turned away from physiology, saw the limits of >hypnosis and began the self-analysis of his own >dreams. This led him to write *The Interpretation of Dreams* and to formulate the basic notions of psychoanalysis. Freud argued that dreams were wish-fulfilments and that we repress many desires in the unconscious.

Everyone tends to simplify Freud into, and judge him by, only a few of his main theories. The central theories relate to dreams, to the organization of the mind into >ego, >id and >superego, to the >pleasure principle and to the role of >repression in establishing civilization as we know it. However, Freud was always torn between his desire to be a real scientist dealing with psychological 'facts' and his recognition of the human complexities revealed on his couch. He had to confront thoughts, feelings, actions, desires and intentions, but there was no physiological >language in which he could begin to handle them. In an interesting book, M. Jahoda has argued that Freud did not ignore the experiences or shirk the dilemma – which was part of his greatness. Like many psychologists, he saw that he could not be what the reductionist tradition taught him that he should be. Freud did more than study what made his patients neurotic. He looked at strange human behaviours – our jokes; our capacity to make and appreciate art; anthropological 'myths' of totems and taboos – in a persistent attempt to understand the hidden forces that drive and create human beings.

One of the oldest criticisms of Freud's ideas is that psychoanalytic theories are so comprehensive that they cannot be falsified. Paul Kline has shown this was not wholly true, listing experiments based on Freud's ideas. Nevertheless opponents of Freud, while emphasizing the unfalsifiability of analysis, have gone on to say that most attempts to test his ideas have, in fact, proved them wrong. Psychoanalysis thus has a strange status: it cannot be falsified and it is often false. Jahoda rightly points out the contradictions in such a position, and says that it is no good always trying to test Freudian ideas as if they were scientific hypotheses. Even the 'best' verification of psychology is still very tentative. Psychologists will have to accept that what they do is partly science, partly humanities, even partly art, and they are going to have to learn to speak in three different languages.

In 1981, the philosopher Brian Farrell argued that the correct model to apply to Freud's ideas isn't the logical positivist one but plausibility: do the concepts make it easier for people to make sense of their experiences, to knot a plausible story together? This may not be science but it does have a point. Freud wanted to study men and women as whole beings. He did not believe that we should study >memory or >perception or attitude changes or >eye contact behaviour as isolated fragments. In the scramble to become more and more specialized, many psychologists are now studying such minute particles of behaviour that it is hard to see what research has to do with people. The notion of total psychology, as it were, owes much to Freud.

One of the problems of assessing Freud's contribution to psychology is its sheer size. The 'complete' works show many revisions and shifts of emphasis. We lack an adequate biography, especially since there are documents still not made public and considerable controversy about Freud's personal life.

- B. Farrell, *The Standing of Psychoanalysis* (1981); Peter Gay, *Freud* (1989); M. Jahoda, *Freud and the Dilemmas of Psychology* (1977); E. Jones, *Freud* (1956); P. Kline, *Fact and Fantasy in Freudian Theory* (1972); J. Masson, *The Assault on Truth: Freud's Suppression of the Seduction Theory* (1985); F. Sulloway, *Freud, Biologist of the Mind* (1979).

Friendship, psychology of. Research shows that we tend to become friends with people from similar backgrounds and that a crucial element is >self-disclosure. *See* Bowlby, John.

- W. Willard and Z. Rubin, *Relationship and Development* (1986).

Frontal lobes, all the >cortex of the >brain that lies in front of the central sulcus (a deep groove in the folds of the cortex). From the time of Galileo in the 17th century, the frontal lobes were thought to be the seat of >intelligence. However, in 1939, Donald Hebb found that patients whose frontal lobes had been removed to help with >epilepsy didn't suffer in terms of >IQ. Theories of frontal lobe function depend most on brain research on what is missing if there are >lesions. Some damage to this part of the brain seems to affect movement programming. Other symptoms of frontal lobe damage are poor voluntary eye gaze, poor response inhibition, >aphasia, less spontaneity in behaviour, impaired associative learning, muddle in temporal ordering, spatial orientation problems. A few tests – notably the Wisconsin card-sorting test, the Semmes body-placing test and the Thurstone word-fluency test – are good for discovering the extent of frontal lobe damage. Many authorities argue that the main impact is often on personality: frontal lobe damage can lead to a more rigid, inflexible sort of behaviour. *See* Lobotomy.

Frustration. In everyday language, frustration is defined as the feelings evoked by not being able to succeed in one's aim – most commonly, sexual frustration. The word has two quite separate uses in psychology. 'Frustration' in >psychoanalysis and >psychodynamic theory means much what it does in ordinary language, but in >learning theory, there has been an attempt to qualify frustration, to turn it into a mathematical concept. The extent of frustration is the product of the force of the >drive multiplied by the number of times the animal tries to reach its goal and is prevented from doing so.

Fugue, literally a flight. A psychiatric state in which someone gives up their usual life and (usually) wanders far from home to set up a new identity. A brilliant example of the fugue state can be seen in Wim Wenders' film *Paris, Texas*, which starts with the hero wandering in the desert having lost everything

F

and forgotten everything. He only slowly begins to fight his way back to the reality he once knew. Such amnesiac fugue states are relatively rare.

G

G. factor. In >intelligence quotient (IQ), the g factor is the 'general factor' of intellectual ability. It is a statistical construct. Analysis of IQ test results makes it possible to extract a general factor responsible for most of the variance of scores. First identified by the British psychologist Charles Spearman, the g factor can be distinguished from scores for special abilities, such as verbal, mathematical, and musical performance. The g factor remained for a long time the most accurate predictor of educational achievement, though it was far from perfect. Given controversies about how fair IQ tests are to non-white cultures (*see* Jensen controversy), it has been suggested by C. Brand that speed of response is a much more accurate measure of general intelligence than anything else. Common sense, it seems, is true: to have a 'quick mind' is really to be more clever than average.

● R. Sternberg and R. Wagner (eds), *Practical Intelligence* (1987).

Galton, Sir Francis (1822–1911), eminent scientist who did some early work on 'hereditary genius' which is often quoted in >IQ controversies (*see* Eysenck; Jensen controversy). Galton argued that heredity accounted for much of the variance in intelligence and achievement, and supported the eugenics movement that advocated 'scientific' breeding and which now seems both bizarre and cruel. Galton was also a fanatical quantifier and his interest in that probably helped create a climate in which measurement rather than >insight was seen as the goal of psychology.

Galvanic skin response (GSR). Our skin has electrical resistance and GSR is measured by using electrodes placed on the skin. A high level of galvanic skin response generally indicates arousal. *See* Biofeedback.

Gambling addiction. Gamblers, just like alcoholics and drug addicts, cannot stop themselves carrying out the act they are addicted to. There are no sound figures for the numbers of compulsive gamblers, but the problem is acute enough

G

for there to be a large organization – Gamblers Anonymous – devoted to curing them. Normal gambling, like normal drinking, is perfectly socially acceptable so it is relatively easy for driven gamblers to hide their >addiction. No one is sure of the reasons for compulsive gambling, but addicts say that they feel compelled to continue because of the excitement and their self-delusion that luck is on their side. Despite the suffering of their families, gamblers believe that the next throw of the dice will make them millionaires.

Game theory. Psychologists use experimental games to study how people compete and co-operate. By offering players different options in games, researchers hope to understand complex social processes. Henri Tajfel found that even in trivial games, people develop strong team loyalties. This suggests that the game model has some basis in reality. Technically, the theory of games is a branch of mathematics applied to how people make decisions. In psychology it applies to social situations in which there are two or more decision makers or players; the outcome of the game depends on the choices players make and for each player there is an obvious preferred choice. The most interesting game is the two person Prisoners' Dilemma. In it, subjects are asked to think of informing on each other. If neither informs – ie. if they trust one another – both will get light sentences. If one informs, he may get a light sentence. If both inform, both are likely to face harsh sentences. It is interesting because, while each player can adopt an aggressive strategy that gives the best pay off against their opponents, each player in fact obtains the best result if both choose co-operative strategies. The psychological reason for interest in this is that it mirrors many real life debates such as the arms race, industrial negotiations and conflicts about pollution.

- Andrew Colman, *Game Theory and Experimental Games* (1982); Henri Tajfel and Jacob Israel (eds), *The Context of Social Psychology* (1973).

Gate theory, a theory in pain research. It is also known as the 'gate control theory'. The gate is a hypothetical mechanism in the spinal cord which influences the experience of pain. The gate can be open wide or almost closed, depending on a variety of factors which include the intensity of the actual pain >stimulus, the motivational state of the person and their expectations. The gate modulates signals from the skin before they are sent to the >brain for central processing. The theory has been devised to help explain the many different reactions to pain stimulus. *See* Pain.

- R. Melzack, *The Puzzle of Pain* (1973).

Gay psychology. The very word 'gay' as opposed to 'homosexual' illustrates profound shifts in attitudes, shifts that are partially reverting to their previous position under the shadow of AIDS. Until the late 1970s, >homosexuality was seen as a psychological disease. Then the American Psychiatric Association removed it from the >*Diagnostic and Statistical Manual* and acknowledged that being gay was just a different sexual orientation.

Somewhat evangelically, gay psychologists started to devise very positive theories of gayness. To be gay was to be authentic. It allowed men to explore their feelings and, more controversially, their promiscuous sexuality. It allowed women – lesbians – to cut themselves off from oppressive men. The advent of AIDS changed that aggressiveness, particularly for male gays. The Association of Gay Psychologists in the US, which was set up in the enthusiasm of the 1970s, now had to dwell less on Eros and more on Thanatos. They had to specialize in >loss and grief and, indeed, on how to prepare for death. Fortunately, there is no sign that the AIDS panic has led psychologists to consider homosexuality a disease again.

● J. Weekes, *Sexuality and its Discontents* (1986).

Gender differences. *See* Sex differences.

Genetic factors. Since the beginning of the century, psychologists have debated whether particular attributes are due to Nature (or heredity) or nurture (or the environment). (*See* Nature/nurture controversy). Advances in genetics and molecular biology have allowed biologically inclined psychologists to be far more specific than before in identifying which particular genes affect particular kinds of behaviour. For some problems, genetic factors are absolute. It's possible to predict from a genetic test whether a baby will be born with >Down's syndrome. However, for other conditions such as >schizophrenia, the evidence has to be assessed more delicately. The presence of a genetic market (itself still a point of debate) for schizophrenia doesn't prove that the disease is bound to erupt. Environmental causes do play a part so the geneticists now suggest that certain genetically disposed people will be more vulnerable to particular environmental stresses. There is fear that, as our understanding of genetic factors improves, all kinds of genetic engineering, both good and bad, will be possible.

Genital stage. A stage of psychosexual development postulated by >Sigmund Freud and >Anna Freud; also known as the phallic stage. The child goes through >oral, >anal and genital phases, during which s/he gets most libidinal pleasure from each of those erogenous zones. The genital stage leads into the >latency period. A person whose genital phase is properly resolved – without, for example, being made anxious by parents because they 'touched' themselves – should then evolve into a normal adult with normal desires who can obtain sexual satisfaction from genital contact with a person of the opposite sex.

Freud's theory was modified on the basis of observation of actual children by >Erikson, who suggests that the genital phase is marked by intrusiveness – especially in boys. Such a need to intrude makes genital-phase children talk aggressively, and there is also 'the intrusion into the unknown by consuming curiosity'. To the genital child, sex remains largely an apparently aggressive act between adults. Experimental research has shown, however, that children do not tend to progress quite so literally from seeking pleasure in one body area to seeking pleasure in another.

By putting so much emphasis on stages, Freud (like >Piaget with the development of the intellect) worked very much within the tradition of Victorian science. *See* Child sexuality; Oedipus complex.

● Paul Kline, *Fact and Fantasy in Freudian Theory* (1972).

Gestalt, a concept used in perceptual psychology. *Gestalt* is the German word for 'pattern'. The Gestalt school, which included Kurt Koffka and Max Wertheimer, was one of the few examples of a successful school of experimental psychology originating outside the United States or Britain. They claimed that the whole is greater than the sum of the parts. The >brain integrates phenomena so we tend to make patterns out of any stimuli (*see* Stimulus), even random collections of dots. The constellations in the sky are the original Gestalt, for human beings created patterns – Orion the Hunter, the Great Bear and so on – out of the stars. The Gestalt school also stressed the continually shifting nature of the >figure/ground, as in the famous diagram of the jug that could be also seen as two lovers. Depending on how the person sees it, the pattern could be perceived either way and would shift from moment to moment.

● K. Koffka, *Principles of Gestalt Psychology* (1935).

Gestalt therapy. Despite the use of the word *Gestalt*, there isn't very much similarity between the Gestalt school of psychology and Gestalt >therapy. The latter was largely developed by Laura and Fritz Perls. Its aim is to make someone responsible for their behaviour by getting people to focus on what they are doing now. Paying attention to the 'here and now' allows people to discover, and express, the rules and assumptions that guide their lives. The Perls also stressed the need for behavioural integration. If I shout that 'I love you' while thumping the table angrily, my behaviour isn't wholly consistent. Many recent Gestalt therapists get clients to act out how they feel and how they believe others feel about them. I might be asked to act out how I feel about my mother and then how I imagine my mother felt. But the Perls did not demand any particular techniques; theirs was more of a philosophy. At the heart of Gestalt therapy is the faith that the client knows everything s/he needs to know for change but doesn't know how s/he knows it or how to make change happen. More than most techniques, Gestalt stresses that the person isn't just responsible but capable. Hence Gestalt therapists use of the word 'client' rather than 'patient'. During the 1960s, this therapy acquired a radical tinge, helped because one of its gurus, Fritz Perls, enunciated what came to be seen as the ultimate hippy motto when he claimed that it was 'OK for me to do my thing' and 'OK for you to do your thing' and if the two coincided it was beautiful and OK to be beautiful. Perls actually denied having said this, but it captured nicely the free 'hippy' spirit of Gestalt.

● Fritz Perls, T. Hefferline and P. Goodman, *Gestalt Therapy* (1972).

G

Gifted children. In >IQ test terms, a child is generally considered gifted if he or she scores 3 >standard deviations above average, but this method isn't really useful for musically or artistically gifted children. The issue of how to cope with gifted children has been discussed since the time of >Sir Francis Galton. He never doubted the need to encourage them and even recommended 'breeding' through the marriages of intelligent parents. In 1892, the French psychologist >Alfred Binet published probably the first paper on gifted children.

Four main issues arise. First, how do you detect gifted children? It is probable that there are far more very able children in society than we normally believe. Julian Stanley set up in 1968 a programme at Johns Hopkins University in Maryland to identify mathematically gifted children and found that the ones he tested were far more capable of mathematics of a higher level than had previously been suspected. He devised another programme to teach them, coached them in summer schools and often gave them emotional counselling. As a result, many of his children sailed early into university and have since done well. However, this required a specific programme; without such programmes, the gifted children who emerge tend to do so because they have highly ambitious parents.

Second, are their gifts highly specific? The four-year-old Mozart could compose superbly but was he in other respects just like any other little boy? Stanley doesn't believe that many children are gifted in more than one area, although gifted children do tend to have a high general IQ. Giftedness is somewhat specific, and perhaps the more pronounced the gift, the more specific it is.

Third, how is society to handle such children? Should they be encouraged or should their gifts be ignored? Social attitudes to such children vary enormously. In Communist societies, they are identified young and given special training; they are favoured. In many Western societies, however, experts are anxious about pushing children too far, worried that this might damage them emotionally and socially. It also seems vaguely indecent that they should be so good so young. Joan Freeman suggests, however, that not giving a gifted child the chance to develop is in itself damaging.

Fourth, what happens to such children in later life? There are case histories which suggest that gifted children are emotionally deprived and often don't fulfil their early promise. The follow-up of highly intelligent children in Terman's sample (*see* Longitudinal studies) suggests that most succeeded but there's less good long-term information on gifted children. Critics point to the history of mathematical prodigies such as the American child Sidis who ended up burned out and doing vaudeville turns. Experts such as Joan Freeman say that such traumas occur perhaps because we don't know how to handle such children.

- Joan Freeman, *The Gifted Child* (1986); R. Sternberg and J. E. Davidson, *Conceptions of Giftedness* (1986).

Giles de la Tourette's syndrome, a neurological disease in which subjects swear, spit and develop other nervous tics. No one was much interested in what seemed a bizarre little malady until the neurologist Oliver Sacks began to study

G

it. He showed that sufferers of various neurological conditions often felt that, if they were cured of their disease and became normal members of society, they lost much of their personality. The Tourette patient develops a whole new character: from being a lively, extravert, dirty-joke cracking self, they become dull. Sacks wondered how patients can lose the handicaps but hang on to the gifts of the disease. *See* Mania.

● Oliver Sacks, *The Man who Mistook His Wife for a Hat* (1985).

Goals, simply objectives. Clinical psychologists started to use this term to give clients specific aims either in >therapy or in >counselling.

Goffman, Erving (1922–82), Canadian sociologist who developed >role theory. Goffman initially studied behaviour in hospitals. He claimed that concepts such as >personality were less important than the social and professional roles people had to enact. The doctor in his white coat acted the part of the doctor and that enveloped his own personality. Goffman expanded ideas first developed by >Jacob Moreno. Both saw life very much as a performance on a shifting set of stages, an >insight first offered by Shakespeare in *Macbeth* and *As You Like It* so perhaps it was less than blindingly original. But Goffman had a scientific problem that Shakespeare didn't have to grapple with; the famous soliloquy in *As You Like It* contains a powerful poetic image but it is a little vague to use as the basis of hypotheses.

Goffman argued that people took on the characteristics of their roles but never explained properly why certain doctors, for example, were gruff and secretive to patients while others had a sensitive bedside manner. Situations do determine behaviour – but not totally. Furthermore, as people become more aware of 'role theory' and 'role models', could they choose to act differently? Goffman was at his most persuasive in analysing powerless roles – that of the sick person or the facially disfigured. Since they have far less choice, their roles are forced on them. But what of those who love power and status? If human beings are nothing but the sum of their roles, where do people get their sense of their identity? Although Goffman never resolved this and other problems satisfactorily, he remains an important thinker, bridging psychology and sociology.

● Erving Goffman, *The Presentation of Self in Everyday Life* (1956).

Grasping reflex. One of the first things a baby can do is to grasp. Studies show that the grasping >reflex is important in helping the infant find the nipple and in developing eye/hand coordination. The grip of the newborn is surprisingly strong.

Grid. *See* Repertory grid.

Grief. *See* Loss.

Group cohesiveness, the tendency of groups to bond together and exclude strangers or members of outgroups. It's a phenomenon much studied by social psychologists. Traditionally, the family is the original group. It provides its members with shelter, food, affection, and a sense of belonging. Much psychology has studied the tension between the human need to belong to a group and the need to assert our own individuality. Many groups, especially religious ones, insist that members lay down their individuality for the greater good. Many people accept this with surprising meekness in groups as diverse as religious cults, Soviet society, Japanese criminal gangs and, according to some critics, the British Conservative Party. Some social psychologists complain that we are living in a period when the strength of traditional groups is waning. Thus people seek to belong to 'dangerous' groups such as those centred round cults or new religions in which the weak are easily exploited. The human need to be part of a group is strong. Henri Tajfel, for example, found that even when the only thing that knitted a group together was preferring one style of modern art to another, they soon develop group loyalty and tended to attribute many negative characteristics to those of the other group. In real political life, the importance of groups is great, but they tend to be drawn together by solid mutual interests.

* Henri Tajfel and Jacob Israel (eds), *The Context of Social Psychology* (1973).

Group dynamics, the processes that occur within groups. Theories of group dynamics differ wildly. Some psychologists stress that the >personality of the leader affects the way the group works, others claim that what is essential is the task at hand. Wilfred Bion, the psychoanalyst who first defined >group therapy, argued that the group reacts to its leader much as to a parent. Group dynamics can be very dramatic. The British House of Commons occasionally puts on a splendid display of group dynamics. The last time was in 1982 when the House was so incensed by Argentine actions that it demanded the Navy be sent to protect the Falklands Islands. Pacifists such as Michael Foot were affected by the mood and were as belligerent as Tory members. More sinister, group dynamics may lead people to accept actions which as individuals they would question. Ethics disappear if the happiness of the group is at risk. The most obvious recent examples of that are in cults and some extreme therapy groups.

Group homes. In the 1960s, it became clear that discharging long-stay psychiatric patients straight into the community was fraught with problems. Patients who had lived inside hospital for two to, in some cases, 30 years were terrified of the outside world (*see* Institutionalization). Some hospitals set up group homes in which eight to ten patients were trained to live together, taught how to shop, cook and clean house and encouraged to make more decisions for themselves. In a group home, they weren't isolated; they had the support of other patients and could call on the local hospital for help in a crisis. Group homes are, for some patients, a halfway house to independent living; for others, they remain all that they can cope with. Group homes have been an important part of the move to care for the mentally ill in the community, but in both the UK and the US, many communities do not have nearly enough group homes for the number of patients leaving hospitals.

Group hysteria, a situation in which the irrational beliefs of a group become totally unchallenged. The most obvious examples are Hitler's Nazi rallies and Beatlemania; in both cases, crowds totally lost control. Group hysteria was first identified by Gustave Le Bon in his seminal work on crowds, which, he said, do not behave like a collection of individuals but are swept by unfathomable surges of >emotion.

● Gustave Le Bon, *The Psychology of Crowds* (1890).

Group therapy. >Freud realized, after some years in practice, that one of the problems of >psychoanalysis was that it would always be accessible to only a few people. It is not surprising, then, that more radical analysts should try to use the principles of analysis to cure more people. The first-known course of group therapy was carried out by Wilfred Bion in 1941.

Group therapy has always used the basic principles of psychoanalysis, but it has become clear that treating a group involves dynamics very different from those involved in treating individuals – Freud spoke of the 'copper' of group analysis as opposed to the 'gold' of individual analysis. The group develops its own identity and members develop loyalty to it; in one-to-one therapy, the expert is all-powerful. Groups can be more democratic, and certain problems may be better handled in a group. One of the more obvious lessons that has been learned is that it helps to listen to people who have similar problems.

Pure analytic group therapy is rare. It is time-consuming, expensive and, in fact, the area in which its principles are most closely used is >family therapy. But a family is a very special group. In most areas there has been a proliferation of different kinds of groups, from >encounter groups on. The rise of >self-help groups is perhaps the most useful legacy of group therapy.

● W. Bion, *Experiences in Groups* (1961).

Guilt, a curious >emotion which is not very well explained by behaviourism or social >learning. Both explain shame perfectly well, for a child can be conditioned to feel ashamed about having done something wrong (*see* Conditioning). Shame, however, is linked to social >embarrassment, while guilt is more private, more intense. The most convincing explanation is >psychoanalytic (*see* Psychoanalysis). According to >Freud, guilt is the result of wishes arising from the >Oedipus complex: the simple expression by a son that he will marry his mother leads to vague fantasies bordering on rape and murder; the result is that the child is left with a deep sense of guilt. For Freud and his disciples, this secret guilt motivates the individual towards socially desirable >goals.

● Lucy Freeman and Herbert Streen, *Guilt – Letting Go* (1986).

H

Habit strength. This is a hypothetical construct. It is based on the idea that a habit is consistent and can be reliably evoked by certain stimuli. Its strength has to be inferred from observed behaviour. The probability of a stimulus evoking the same response, the strength of the response, its latency and the difficulty of extinguishing it all reflect habit strength. According to Clark Hull, the following equation holds. $_SE_R = f(_SH_R) \times f(D)$ where $_SE_R$ is the reaction potential to a stimulus; $f(_SH_R)$ is the habit strength and $f(D)$ is the drive at that moment. The greater the habit strength of a particular reaction, the harder it is to extinguish that particular reaction.

Habituation. As a >stimulus becomes habitual, we tend to respond less to it. A loud or sudden noise is generally a shock, but we get used to it. The longer the the pneumatic drill outside shrieks, the less we are startled by it. Habituation exists in all animals: snails, fish, insects, birds and humans all have a startle reaction to a new stimulus but then learn slowly to ignore it through habituation. The evolutionary value seems clear: habituation narrows down the stimuli that evoke flight or escape reactions.

Hallucinations, imaginary perceptions which seem very real to the person experiencing them. Hallucinations have an honourable history: the biblical prophet Samuel heard the voice of God; Joan of Arc heard the saints tell her that the Dauphin had to be crowned. In >psychiatry, however, hallucinations are seen as a sign of illness rather than of prophesy. For example, hallucinations are considered by some the first-rank symptoms of >schizophrenia.

Any of the senses – sight, hearing, smell, touch – can be involved, but probably the most common are auditory hallucinations – often described as hearing 'voices in the head'. The hallucinations that schizophrenics experience are often frightening and unpleasant to them: their voices accuse them of having committed terrible acts or command them to undertake acts of violence. The hallucinations can be odd. In 1951, M. Sechehaye described feeling as though

H

his mouth were full of birds, and later he saw 'people whom I had entombed in milk bottles'. Work with >LSD often produced hallucinations in subjects.

There are radically different theories to account for hallucinations. Biologically minded psychiatrists claim that the content of hallucinations is not very relevant, as they are a product of the malfunctioning >brain of the schizophrenic. Hence drugs such as >chlorpromazine control the hallucinations by suppressing the biochemistry of schizophrenia. More radical psychiatrists argue that the hallucinations may seem mad to us but they have a very real meaning for the schizophrenic. Not only do they protect the person from the hurts of the world but they have a skewed logic of their own.

● Mary Barnes, *Two Accounts of a Journey through Madness* (1971).

Halo effect, the tendency to assume that individuals with one positive characteristic must have others as well. For example, physically attractive people are thought to be of higher social status and morally superior and, as a result, they are more likely to get job offers. With the development of >attribution theory as an important model in personality theory, halo effects are being studied with new vigour. Why do people lump together positive attributes? This is not just an academic point for this tendency clearly influences a good deal of advertising and the marketing of anything from detergent to political candidates.

Handedness. Most human beings write with the right hand and use it exclusively for skilful manipulation of objects. Cave drawings show hunters using their right hands. The right side of the body is largely controlled by the left hemisphere of the >brain. Right handers usually have dominant right eyes, right ears and feet. They also tend to use the right hand to make gestures. Left handers are far less consistent.

To be left handed is generally considered a sign of disfavour. In some cultures the left hand is used for dirty acts like wiping one's bottom. The word 'sinister' actually comes from the Latin for left handed. As a result, there has always been pressure to get children to change if they show signs of left hand preference. About 2 per cent find this impossible; others find it difficult. With increasing tolerance the proportion of left-handed children has risen from 2 to 10 per cent. Arguments for the causes of handedness include both genetic and cultural ones. One genetic model suggests that all human beings are right handed and that left handedness is due to some defect, perhaps a lack of oxygen at birth. Twins are more likely to be left handed and are also more likely to suffer such damage. No simple genetic model, however, seems to fit all the facts.

The issue of handedness is especially important in trying to understand >language. In language, right-handed people have their language in the left hemisphere of the brain. Fifteen per cent of left handers have speech represented in both sides of the brain. It has been argued that stuttering occurs when left-handed children are forced to become right handed because the change creates a battle for control between the two hemispheres of the brain. The stutterer is caught between the two. Handedness also occurs in other mammals such as monkeys. *See also* Language; Lateralization.

Hawthorne effect. This was first noticed during a study of the workers at the Hawthorne industrial plant in 1926. The psychologists discovered that, during the study, the performance of workers improved for no apparent reason. After many attempts to find out why, it became clear that by studying the workers, by simply giving them extra attention, their industrial performance improved. The effect should be taken into account in any study.

Headaches. Increasingly, research has suggested that many headaches are >psychosomatic, caused by >stress and tension. It has also been suggested that a variety of techniques can be employed to reduce or eliminate them, including relaxation.

Head Start, an American programme of the 1960s which was designed to give under-privileged children compensatory education before entering school with the aim of remedying social injustices. The Westinghouse study, published in 1969, showed that, during those two pre-school years, Head Starters gained as many as 12 >IQ points but much of that had been lost by the time they went to school. However, the children did gain in self-confidence and in >motivation. Furthermore, local Head Start programmes varied greatly in quality. The Westinghouse study took little account of this when its generally negative findings were published.

Hearing. Human beings have a much less effective hearing sense than many animals. Our hearing is closely connected with our ability to understand >language.

The physiology of hearing is complex. Sound waves travel down the outer ear canal to the eardrum. This not only protects the interior structures of the ear but, by reverberating, it also conducts sound to the middle and inner ears, which is crucial for our hearing. Behind the eardrum are the three bones of the middle ear and, in the inner ear, the canals that govern our sense of balance and turn sound waves into signals to the >brain. The bones of the middle ear are set in an air-filled cavity, which is connected by the Eustachian tube to the mouth cavity so that its interior pressure can be adjusted. The sound waves that hit the eardrum are conducted across the three bones to the oval window, the boundary between the middle and inner ears.

The cochlea is the vital organ within the inner ear. *Cochlea* means 'snail' in Latin, and this bony cavity is coiled like that animal's shell. It consists of three separate canals filled with fluid and divided from each other by two membranes: Reissner's membrane and the basilar membrane. Resting on the latter through the entire length of the cochlea is the organ of Corti which contains hair cells; distributed around these cells are acoustic nerve fibres leading to the auditory part of the brain.

Sound comes into the cochlea in the form of pressure. One can imagine it as a travelling bulge. This bulge moves through the fluid in the cochlea, taking a different form depending on the frequency of the sound wave that has originated it. Different hair cells inside the cochlea respond to different frequencies.

As it travels up the cochlea, the bulge of pressure reaches a maximum, at which point specific hair cells react most and then the energy of the sound is converted into electrical and chemical impulses. These travel up the acoustic nerve into the auditory >cortex of the brain, where the sound is 'heard'.

As with >vision, the way we hear depends on many psychological factors, too including: how important material is, how much it fits in with what we expect and how emotionally-laden it is. *See* Dichotic listening; Pure word deafness; Selective attention; Signal detection theory.

● S. Handel, *Listening* (1989).

Hedonism, the ancient philosophy that puts sensual pleasure before anything else. It has been an important underlying concept in psychology since the task of psychologists is to explain what motivates people. Pleasure seemed a good candidate. >Freud argued that it is the reduction of tension that creates pleasure but, increasingly, experimental results such as those of J. Olds and P. Milner have shown that animals take pleasure in the *increase* of tension too.

● J. Olds and P. Milner, 'Positive reinforcement produced by electrical stimulation of the septal area and other regions of the rat brain' in *Journal of Comparitive and Physiological Psychology*, 47, 419-27 (1954).

Helping professions, a new term that covers psychiatrists, psychologists, social workers, psychiatric nurses. There seems to be no difference between the helping professions and the >caring professions.

Helplessness, learned, a concept developed by M. E. Seligman. He found that animals who were unable to escape from noxious stimuli soon stopped trying to do so. They lapsed into a miserable, whiny, powerless posture, and even when given the chance to escape, they didn't take it. Seligman then applied this idea to >social psychology, claiming that groups of powerless people can lose the will to improve their lot, becoming demoralized and thus totally inactive. The animal experiment research is sound; the social extrapolation is seductive and has been used increasingly to help explain the apathy of certain groups. *See also* Depression.

● M. E. Seligman, *Helplessness* (1975).

Hermeneutics, the study of meanings in social behaviour and experience. Hermeneutics is concerned with interpreting social experience rather than with general trends of behaviour. The meanings that it studies can be personal, conscious or unconscious.

Heroin, the most powerful narcotic drug, a derivative of morphine grown from the opium poppy. Since Thomas de Quincey's *Confessions of an English Opium-eater* (1821), students of human behaviour have been interested in why people become addicted to it and how they might be cured (*see* Addiction). It had romantic associations: not only De Quincey, but great poets such as Samuel

Taylor Coleridge, Charles Baudelaire and, later, writers such as William Burroughs were hooked. However, until the late 1970s, heroin was seen as the ultimate destructive drug: once a person was addicted, they could never get off. The withdrawal symptoms from heroin were believed to be terrifying; the craving would drive the addict back to the needle. This image of heroin as lethal kept down the number of addicts. In 1970, the British Home Office noted there were under 5000 registered addicts in all the UK – and it was assumed that those who were addicted were addicted for life. They were allowed to be prescribed methadone, which was itself addictive, on the NHS. With few addicts, that seemed a way of preventing addicts turning to crime. It didn't work. However, although there are still fewer than 5000 registered addicts in the UK, the Home Office accepts that there are many more, all unregistered. For many, methadone gives a kick itself. There has been growing evidence of the recreational use of heroin as well as more signs of addicts learning to live without the drug through groups like Narcotics Anonymous (NA). Controlled studies such as those by G. Stimpson suggest that the patterns of heroin addiction are changing considerably.

In the USA there has been a move away from heroin and towards crack, a derivative of cocaine. Ever since Thomas de Quincey became hooked in the early nineteenth century, those concerned for 'junkies' have tried to find a 'cure' for heroin addiction. It seems clear now that most of the techniques on offer can only work if the addict actually wants to stop. The two most frequently used techniques at present are (i) intensive therapeutic communes such as Phoenix House in South London where addicts live for nine months or more under strict rules and (ii) >self-help groups of ex-addicts such as Narcotics Anonymous, where people are befriended and counselled. It has been claimed that both approaches can work better than had been previously expected. Over a ten-year period, for example, some 48 per cent of addicts were found to be clean. However, the statistics in this field are dangerously unreliable.

● Tom Stewart, *The Heroin Users* (1987).

Heterosexuality. *See* Sexual behaviour.

Hierarchy of needs. >Abraham Maslow, the founder of >humanistic psychology, argued that humans had basically five sets of needs, which could be seen in the form of a pyramid. At the top is the need for >self-actualization, and, in descending order, the others are esteem, belongingness, safety and physiological needs (eg water, food, sleep, shelter). Only when one set of needs is met can one hope to meet higher-order needs. When an individual has enough rest, food and warmth, when he is safe and established in a human community which recognizes his worth, then and only then is he ready to try for self-actualization. Maslow found that most of the people who achieved this level were over the age of 60. Motivated by values that went beyond their own personal needs, they were also creative, self-sufficient and spontaneous, although they also needed privacy and solitude. The hierarchy of needs has remained an intriguing concept and has influenced the development of the personal growth movement.

- Abraham Maslow, *The Psychology of Self-actualization* (1968).

Hippocampus, a part of the >limbic system of the >brain, which looks like a sea horse (hence its name, the Latin word for sea horse) and is crucial in emotional behaviour. It lies in the anterior medial region of the temporal lobe – that is, deep within the interior of the brain. Patients with unilateral (one-sided) >lesions of the hippocampus have many defects. If lesions occur in the hippocampus in the right hemisphere, there are problems with tactile and visual image learning, face recognition, spatial >memory and spatial association. If they occur in the left, there will be difficulties with the recall of word lists, digit span and self-ordered word recall. The left hippocampus is clearly important for verbal memory, the right for spatial and visual memory.

Holistic psychology. This is less a specific school than a kind of approach, stressing the whole person and his/her spiritual needs. *See* Humanistic psychology.

Homoeostasis, equilibrium, a state of balance. It is an important concept in psychology because many theorists (eg >Freud) believe that human beings aspire to psychological equilibrium, a state in which they experience no tension. Perfect balance is just such a state. There is, however, growing evidence that some kinds of >personality crave imbalance, excitement, the >adrenalin of change and risk.

- M. Apter, *Reversal Theory* (1988).

Homosexuality, sexual attraction towards others of the same sex. Homosexuality in women is called lesbianism. Until the recent AIDS panic, the status of homosexuality had changed from being considered a sick perversion to an expression of authenticity.

Cultural attitudes to homosexuality have differed widely through the ages: the Bible condemned it; the Greeks thought the love between a young boy and an older man fairly proper; Victorian Europe not only damned male homosexuality but legislated against it in 1892 (lesbianism was politely ignored). Yet paradoxically, the English upper middle classes thought that boys will be boys. For example, the poet W. H. Auden carried around a diary in which he listed 'Boys Had' and wrote a very tender poem, *Lullaby*, celebrating the transience of one-night homosexual stands. All this perhaps shows the confusion that surrounds homosexuality, a confusion reflected in the theories of its cause. Initially, when homosexuality was seen as a sin, the task of psychology was trying to explain the sickness. No one could choose to be homosexual so what obliged these people to be like that?

>Freud argued that a homosexual phase was normal but that the child would emerge at puberty eager for genital gratification with the opposite sex. If not, a failure to resolve the >Oedipus complex was blamed. The growing boy never managed to identify with the father in order to give up his mother; instead, he identified with the mother who was probably strong. In 1981, M. D. Storms

suggested that the timing of the maturation of the sex drive is critical. If most of your social group are of the same sex, when your hormones switch on sexually, you will become homosexual. The theory predicts that early-maturing males with same-sex siblings will be more likely to be homosexual, and this is so. Storms' theory also explains British homosexuality nicely. In Britain, the high incidence of homosexuality among the middle classes has been attributed to the fact that young boys were packed off to boarding school. Oedipus had nothing to do with it: in a purely male environment, boys had to dote on other boys. >Behaviourist theories of sexual development stressed that too much affection on the part of the father could lead to male homosexuality. According to his son, the American psychologist >J. B. Watson had a pathological fear of homosexuality and never kissed his sons after they reached the age of two in order to make sure that they grew up 'healthy'.

All these early theories assumed that, although homosexuality was perverse, it was, thank heavens, rare. The first blow came with the publication of the >Kinsey reports on the sexual behaviour of males (1948) and females (1953). Kinsey stated that up to 38% of men and 14% of women had taken part in some homosexual behaviour and that perhaps 20 per cent of men had had a homosexual experience leading to orgasm and that 11 per cent of women had done so. In the late 1960s, the 'sexual revolution' radically changed the self-image of homosexual men and women. They 'came out', fought discrimination and stopped seeing themselves as a sick minority, instead arguing that they had made a positive choice to be gay or lesbian – ie homosexuality equals authenticity. Homosexual men claimed that, as gays, they could express their feelings; most heterosexual men were too insecure and stuck in macho stereotypes to do that. Yet gay men could also indulge in the kind of promiscuous sex that most heterosexuals dreamed of but could never get away with with women. Gays attacked theories of homosexuality as a sickness, and demanded to know why heterosexuality was considered the norm when, increasingly, research showed how many men had dabbled in homosexuality. Recent American research research published in 1990 contradicts Kinsey's findings. It claims that in the past year 98.3% of sexually active people were exclusively heterosexual. It is unclear if this is a reaction to AIDS, which may have pushed some bisexuals into total heterosexuality, or if Kinsey over-estimated the extent of homosexual behaviour. Accuracy is not easy to achieve in such surveys.

The advent of the AIDS panic dampened gay evangelical ardour but the effect on psychology and >psychiatry remains. It seems unlikely that we shall ever revert to the days when homosexuality was seen as a sickness.

There is little argument about whether female homosexuality has the same causes as male homosexuality. Kinsey found that there were far fewer women homosexuals than men. The lesbian stereotype pre-1970 and the feminist movement was not a flattering one. 'Dykes' were usually ugly large women who couldn't possibly get a man or, sometimes, fantastic fem vamps. The rise of feminism critically changed our view of lesbianism. Some feminists such as Dale Spender and Germaine Greer have argued that in a patriarchal society women did not often get that much out of sex. Men were brutal sexual partners interested only in their own sexual gratification. In *The Female Eunuch* Greer argued that male writers described orgasms as a form of murder. The bitch screamed with delight or pain. It didn't matter. Greer accused writers like Norman Mailer of fantasies of lust and violence where the two gave equal kicks. So, feminists argued, women might choose only to have other women as sexual partners as a conscious political choice because men are so violent. It isn't because they are deficient or unattractive that they avoid men but because women have more to offer both physically and emotionally. *See* Gay psychology.

- S. Cline and D. Spender, *Reflecting Men* (1987); Mary Daly, *Gyn/ Ecology* (1986); G. Greer, *The Female Eunuch* (1971); Baron Richard von Krafft-Ebbing, *Psychopathia Sexualis* (1886); M. Roper and J. Tosh, *Manful Assertions* (1991); J. Weeks, *Sexuality and Its Discontents* (1986).

Hormones, substances secreted by the >endocrine glands which are lodged in different parts of the body – especially the >pituitary, the pancreas, the thyroid, the parathyroid, the testes, the ovaries and the adrenal glands. Oestrogen (produced mainly by the ovaries) and testosterone (testes) are the major sex hormones. Hormones act as biochemical messengers to regulate the function of various organs. They also play a crucial role in determining mood and also in >stress. In stress, the release of >adrenalin by the adrenal glands affects our reactions.

- P. J. B. Slater, *Sex, Hormones and Behaviour* (1978).

Horney, Karen (1885–1952), a psychoanalyst who was the first major feminist critic of >Freud and remains an important figure in psychology. Penis envy didn't exist for her; instead, she believed that social and cultural forces made women unconfident and drove them to seek total fulfilment in personal relationships. She replaced the >ego, >id and >superego with the ideas of the true and false self. Insecurity made most of us adopt false selves. Horney also posited a number of neurotic needs that people have, including needs for power and intimacy. She claimed that people either move towards, against or away from people giving few of us any hope of normal happiness. The division of the >personality into the true and false self anticipated the ideas of >R. D. Laing. *See* Neo-Freudians.

- Karen Horney, *New Ways in Psychoanalysis* (1939).

Humanistic psychology, an approach to psychology which emphasizes the wholeness of people. It originated as a reaction against experimental psychology. Humanistic psychologists stress the need for psychology to respect people, their feelings, their creativity and their potential for growth. At the root of much humanistic psychology is the belief that the organization of society and the constraints we are conditioned to accept mean that the lives of most of us are much less than they could be. It's easy to see humanistic psychology as a revamp, with a touch of >Freud, of old romantic ideas of the 19th century. Probably the most influential psychologist of the movement was >Abraham Maslow who developed the notions of >peak experiences and >self-actualization. He argued that few people had enough peak experiences, and that it was equally rare to find individuals who had achieved their true potential and grown fully into what they might be (ie achieved self-actualization).

In various kinds of groups, therapists offered individuals the chance to explore and find themselves. These concepts were noble and reflected a very American attitude to psychology: people should get the best out of their lives. However, the concepts were always a little vague, and there never was any proper methodology that showed independently how to achieve more peak experiences or true self-actualization. Yet some of the ideas of humanistic psychology are valuable, for the scientific approach can all too easily become arid. *See* Encounter groups; Group therapy; Hierarchy of needs; Holistic psychology; Nature/nurture controversy.

- John Rowson, *Ordinary Ecstacy* (1988)

Human nature. The debate as to whether there is some essential thing as 'human nature' is covered in the entry on the >nature/nurture controversy. Cultural variations are very widespread, but there are some aspects of human life common to all societies. All human beings talk; most bring up children and protect them; in most societies, marriage exists and usually the marriage of one man to one woman; there are sexual taboos against >incest and marriage of members of one's family who are too closely related by blood. People from one culture can recognize the emotional expressions of people from another culture to a surprising extent. These various cross-cultural similarities all suggest that all human beings are somewhat the same irrespective of their cultures. That's not surprising, given our basic biology. It's also ethically useful to remember our basic, common humanity as it highlights the need to treat people humanely. Human nature has given rise to human rights.

- A. Chapman and D. Jones, *Models of Man* (1980).

Hunger. 'We eat to live, not live to eat,' says Harpagon in Molière's play *L'Avare* (*The Miser*). Hunger is seen in psychology as one of the chief motivating >drives. It was measured by Clark Hull in terms of the period of time an animal can go without food. However, as much work has shown, hunger is not a model for all drives because not every drive is as regular or easy to satisfy.

Hyperactivity, excessive activity in children, combined with inability to concentrate and difficulty in >learning. This is a modern notion – no children were thought to be hyperactive 40 years ago. Hyperactive children are more physically demanding and inattentive than average. A common estimate in the UK and US is that 5 per cent of the elementary school population is hyperactive, with more boys than girls being identified. There's much controversy as to the cause. Minimal brain damage, food allergies, lead poisoning, mothers who drink or smoke during pregnancy – all have been put forward. Medication – usually Dexedrine – is claimed to make children more attentive and cooperative, but little is known about the long-term effects. That is worrying as there are quite specific short-term effects – for example, increased heart rate and raised blood pressure.

● R. Kneedler, *Special Education for Today* (1984).

H

Hypnosis. There are some who claim that hypnosis is not much more than relaxation, while others say it is an altered form of >consciousness. People feel as if they are not in conscious control. Someone who has been hypnotized may seem to be asleep, but they can reply to questions and carry out orders. Hypnosis has been used to get people to remember things that they have apparently forgotten or to do things when awake such as stop smoking. Police forces round the world have experimented with hypnosis in the hope that it will make witnesses remember details their conscious >memory has blanked out. The Israeli police have been leaders in this esoteric field and claim it has helped to solve a number of murders. What is curious about hypnosis is that subjects who are easily hypnotized are not necessarily weak or stupid. Hypnotic suggestibility seems positively linked to >intelligence. Hypnosis has been used both honourably and dishonourably. >Freud, for example, used it to gain some of his early insights. Some National Health clinicians use it to treat >psychosomatic disorders, especially to try to clear up eczema. There have also been many cases of hypnotists using their skills either to gain power over people or to make them look ridiculous in front of an audience. *See* Posthypnotic suggestibility.

● A. Gauld, *A History of Hypnosis* (1991).

Hypothalamus, a structure in the midbrain which is involved in a diverse number of functions including appetite and some aspects of emotional behaviour.

Hypothesis testing. In theory, the testing of theories to work out their truth depends on (1) formulating specific hypotheses and the consequences that follow them, and (2) designing experiments which will eliminate some of these hypotheses by proving them wrong in particular circumstances. In practice, as K. Simonton has shown, scientists do not behave in this rational manner, but tend to try to prove their hunches are right, rather than examining the flaws in their theories.

● K. Simonton *Scientific Genius* (1989).

Hysteria, one of the first psychiatric disturbances to be recognized. The hysteric is exaggeratedly emotional, becomes frantically attached to certain ideas and is highly manipulative. Hippocrates knew of it, and because doctors in the 18th century thought it was due to a disorder of the uterus (and thus exclusively a condition of women), they called it 'hysteria' from the Greek word *hustera* (uterus). The book that represented the start of >psychoanalysis was Josef

Breuer and >Sigmund Freud's studies in hysteria. One of their hysterical patients, Anna O, terrified Josef Breuer by saying she was pregnant by him, and her hysteria forced Freud to confront the emotions and >fantasies that could well up in patients. This mythical view was influenced by two facts: (1) it appeared more in women than in men (and as a result there was a certain sexist view of it); and (2) there seemed to be a confused clinical picture. Here there is confusion. Neurologists use it to refer to non-organic disorders where there isn't a clear >brain malfunction. Psychoanalytic psychiatrists use it to refer to particular conflicts and to see the condition in apparently non-sexual patients who act seductively. The American Psychiatric Association >*Diagnostic and Statistical Manual* no longer uses the term.

- Ilse Verth, *Hysteria; the History of a Disease* (1965).

Iconic memory, >memory for visual images (from the Greek *eikon*, 'image'). It stores just sensory items and not information about items.

Id, one third of the great trinity of the >mind that >Freud described: >ego, id and >superego. Freud was not the first to conceive of the id; he drew on the work of George Groddeck to posit a structure in the >unconscious. The id is the name he gave for the depths of the mind, very primitive, wild and unrestrained. The id is an unorganized reservoir of psychic energy whose only aim is to maximize pleasure, and here the >pleasure principle rules unfettered. The id is also sexual and aggressive. Freud argued that, when children are very young, the id controls all behaviour. He described the child's first thought processes as >primary process thinking, the purpose of which is the immediate satisfaction of all the id's needs and desires. This remains the id's goal for the rest of life but, as the child grows older, the rampant id has to contend with the guilt-tripping superego and the realistic ego, which spoil all its fun. In a striking image, the British psychologist Don Bannister described Freud's theory as depicting a perpetual battle between a sex-crazed monkey, a puritanical spinster aunt (the superego) with a bank clerk in between (the pragmatic ego).

* Sigmund Freud, *The Ego and the Id* (1923).

Identical twins, twins who emerge out of the splitting of one egg. For their scientific importance, *see* Twin studies.

Identification, a concept in >psychoanalysis. Literally, the process by which someone is not really themself. He or she extends their identity into someone else, borrows from someone else or confuses their identity with someone else. As a result their ego boundaries are weak. In infancy, it is perfectly normal. In adolescence, identifying with a hero and seeking to emulate him or her may actually be a spur to achievement, but it can lead to difficulties if it is not outgrown.

Identity, a topic that is beginning to surface again in psychology with the renewed interest in >consciousness. William James asked how we knew in the morning that we were the same people who had gone to bed the night before. He claimed that the stream of consciousness cemented our identity. It was taken for granted until recently that sane individuals had one coherent identity. >Role theory then suggested that this might not be so. Psychologists have drawn on the work of Roger Sperry with split-brain patients to suggest that we may be a bundle of different identities. Robert Ornstein offers the theory that we have a variety of brains (*see* Brain) such as the >cortex and the >limbic system.

Although there is much evidence to back this view, most of us feel we stay the same person day in, day out. We thread a consistent story out of our lives. Is that illusion? Habit? Is our way of thinking about our identity going to change radically? It seems unlikely that our everyday notion of identity will change, but psychologists are likely to continue to wonder at our potential for many selves. *See* Self; Self-concept.

● Jonathan Glover, *Personal Identity* (1989); Robert Ornstein, *Multimind* (1988).

Ideology in psychology. This is not really recognized as a topic but, in fact, different schools of psychology have very different ideologies. The world as the >behaviourist sees it is different from the world seen by the psychoanalyst (*see* Psychoanalysis). However, few practitioners are willing to admit that these ideological conflicts deeply affect their attitudes towards psychology. Rather they see their work as a quest for truth, and believe that their opponents are sadly deluded. In this, psychology is unlike other sciences. When physicists made discoveries that superseded those of Einstein, no one condemned him as a charlatan who would have been better advised to have remained a clerk in the Swiss patent office. Yet in the great controversies between psychoanalysts and behaviourists, experimentalists (*see* Experimental method) and humanists (*see* Humanistic psychology), all sides pour polemic on each other with great relish.

● H. Kendler, *Psychology: A Science in Conflict* (1982).

Idiographic. The approach that concentrates on the individual case as against the 'nomothetic' approach which seeks to establish general laws in psychology. The difference between these approaches has been a central area of debate. Some theorists claim that human beings are too variable to establish laws of psychology – only basic processes of sensation and >perception can be described in such scientific terms. Others, like B. F. Skinner, claim that psychology has to seek general laws. Dissatisfaction with experimental psychology's insights has inspired new nomothetic techniques. For example, Harré *et al* have devised ways of critically using autobiographies. They are not the only relevant data in understanding a person's life but they are essential. Careful questioning of the subject, reference to some objective tests, can make the case history more reliable. The idiographic approach offers depth and the revived interest in it shows that its advocates believe psychology must conform to some scientific principles.

● David Clarke, N. de Carlo and Rom Harré, *Motives and Mechanisms* (1985); Liam Hudson, *Human Beings* (1975); William Runyan, *Life Histories and Psychobiology* (1984).

Idiots savants, mentally handicapped children or adults who have one remarkable skill such as a photographic >memory or numerical ability. The character 'Raymond' in the 1988 film *Rain Man* verged on being an idiot savant.

Imagery. Mental images have been an area of interest in psychology since 1879 when the first psychology lab was set up in Leipzig. >Introspection as a technique for studying them was abandoned when it was realized that results were contradictory. With the rise of >cognitive psychology, however, new studies have focused on imagery. Cognitive psychologists such as Ulric Neisser accepted that mental images were private but they claimed that subjects could answer questions about details on a part of an image that they described as being near more rapidly than they could about those that they described as far. This would be the same in ordinary >vision if they were looking at a landscape.

● U. Neisser, *Cognitive Psychology* (1976).

Imagination, a faculty of thinking that psychologists have tried to study under the guise of >'creativity' or by trying to see what makes artists tick. Imagination appears linked to >intelligence and yet it is often very specific. It seems that one can identify at an early stage children who are good at inventing >fantasies and who like doing so. It may be possible to develop such creative skills. Various theories claim that certain kinds of upbringing facilitate the development of the imagination, but none is wholly convincing.

Imitation. This is crucial in psychology in two senses. Originally, social psychologists were interested in seeing whether people imitated the actions of others more powerful than they were. For example, if they saw a violent TV programme were they more likely to act violently?

A. Bandura found some evidence for that, although it has proved hard to show that all viewers of a violent programme will be more inclined to act violently. Rather, some will, and therefore the question is: what makes that small group imitate?

Secondly, from the work of T. Bower and others, it became clear that infants only a few days old can mimic such actions as sticking out their tongue, a capacity that seemed to disappear for a few months, before returning in a more conscious form (*see* Child development). This ability to imitate has been taken as proof that, from very early on, the baby is a social creature, reaching out to the world and able to respond rather well to its signals. *See* Ethology.

● A. Bandura, *Social Foundations of Thought and Action: A Social Cognitive Theory* (1986); T. Bower, *Development in Infancy* (1972).

Impotence, a sexual dysfunction – the inability to achieve an erection – which affects approximately 10 per cent of men. Slag (1983) in a study of 59-year-old veterans found that 34% had erection problems. Masters and Johnson (*see* Sex therapy) argue that its causes are often psychological: the man feels anxious and guilty about sex. Psychoanalysts believe the causes to be deeper: the impotent man hates women and denies them. An additional factor may be that men (especially American men) feel under pressure to perform – particularly in these post-feminist times.

To overcome impotence, Masters and Johnson recommended a variant of >behaviour modification: couples were told that they could touch each other but on no account could they have full intercourse. They had to relearn their erotic skills. The two sex therapists claimed a high success rate. The ethics and efficacy of their treatment have both been questioned.

- Z. Luria, S. Friedman and M. D. Rose, *Human Sexuality* (1987); H. Masters and Virginia Johnson, *Human Sexuality* (1988); J. Slag, 'Impotence in Medical Clinic Outpatients', *Journal of the American Medical Association* (1983); T. Szasz, *Sex by Prescription* (1980).

Imprinting, literally a process by which a behaviour is stamped (or imprinted) into the organism. When successful, it leaves the animal 'knowing' what species it belongs to and should mate with. The phenomenon was discovered by >Konrad Lorenz, the ethologist. He found that greylag geese were imprinted, or developed an awareness of the image of their mother and their species, during a critical period in the first few days after birth. If animals were not in a normal environment, they would tend to have something else imprinted. As a result, many of the geest brought up by Lorenz thought that he was their mother and that they belonged to the same species as him.

This concept has been applied to human psychology. It stimulated the work of such psychologists as >John Bowlby and C. Trevarthen, who showed that mothers and babies are very delicately programmed to respond to each other. However, there is also evidence that the higher up the phylogenetic scale you go, the less important imprinting is. Higher animals are less totally fixed by their biology.

- John Bowlby, *Attachment and Loss* (1972); *A Secure Base* (1988); Konrad Lorenz, *King Solomon's Ring* (1952).

Incest, sexual intercourse between individuals regarded as too closely related to marry each other. This is psychologically a very important concept. According to >Freud, all normal children unconsciously desire incest – Oedipus stands for all of us. Freud suggested that the resolution of the >Oedipus complex, with its acceptance of the >incest taboo, is wholly crucial to the child's development. This theoretical emphasis on incest did not mean, however, that there were studies of actual incest. For one thing, it was assumed that children who grew up together would be sexually safe with each other – an idea that can be found in Jane Austen's *Mansfield Park*.

Despite the theoretical interest in incest, it was something of a shock when researchers discovered that there was much real incest. Incest is usually forced upon a child – through sheer force, fear or >guilt – and the psychological damage caused by it is intense. People have described, years after the events, how ashamed, angry and/or guilty they feel, and >self-help groups now exist for the victims of incest. In psychological terms, incest is restricted to blood relatives; it is not the same as sexual abuse within families (*see* Child abuse) because that often occurs between a stepfather and children by a previous marriage. However, as sexual abuse has become an issue, it's become clear that even 'pure' incest is fairly frequent. Statistics are hard to establish, but in 1988 in the UK there were 516 prosecutions for incest and the National Society for the Prevention of Cruelty to Children (NSPCC) claims that this is just the tip of the iceberg.

● Sigmund Freud, *Totem and Taboo* (1917); J. Renvoize, *Web of Violence* (1980).

Incest taboo, a concept borrowed from anthropology. In most societies, there are prohibitions on marriage between close kin. >Freud seized upon this evidence when elaborating the >Oedipus complex. A Czech study suggests, however, that in-breeding may not be as disastrous as imagined.

Individual psychology, a form of >psychoanalysis devised by >Alfred Adler in rivalry to >Freud. Adler stressed that the infant is born feeling powerless and, as a result, human beings are driven much more by a need for power than by sexual energy. Adler also argued that the infant has 'social interest', ie a need to respond to and succeed among others. His conviction of the importance of power led him to suggest three key concepts of individual psychology: the >inferiority complex, the >superiority complex and >masculine protest.

Individual >therapy aims to encourage a more socially useful way of life and to improve personal relationships so that the person can do without either an inferiority or a superiority complex. Follow-up studies have been few, especially as Adler's ideas never attracted the numbers that those of Freud and >Jung did. Still, his concepts did influence >family therapy and encouraged the development of child guidance services in Vienna, the first such services in the world. The *Journal for Individual Psychology* still exists.

● Alfred Adler, *The Psychology of the Individual* (1924).

Industrial psychology, the area of psychology which studies behaviour at work. Soon after the turn of the century, American psychologists began to develop relationships with companies in a desire to use the new knowledge of human behaviour to improve the efficiency of workers. Many psychologists were impressed by the work of Charles Taylor who devised ways of making industrial processes more efficient, although Taylor's >time-and-motion approach had critics from the start. Many psychologists also wanted to improve conditions in industry, realizing that people would not work at their best if they were under too much >stress. Industrial psychology developed concepts such as >job satisfaction and job stress.

Infant development. *See* Child development.

Information processing, an approach to psychology which argues that the way to conceptualize the >brain is as a channel for processing information. As a metaphor this has been enormously influential since the late 1960s in >perceptual psychology, in >cognitive psychology and in some aspects of >child development. *See* Artificial intelligence.

● S. Papert, *Mindstorms: Children, Computers and Powerful Ideas* (1980).

Innate ideas, ideas or capacities that a child is born with. *See* Nature/nurture controversy.

Insight. There are two senses of insight. R. W. Lawler describes how, over a period of ten weeks, his six-year-old daughter Miriam gained insight into how to add up – in other words, she mastered an intellectual skill. Studies of >creativity identify a similar experience that has been called 'the Eureka experience'. Newton, when the apple fell, enjoyed a Eureka experience – he suddenly solved an intellectual problem and gained insight into the process of gravity.

However, the term 'insight' also has a >psychodynamic use. It's a quality which those who are being assessed by psychiatrists and social workers are said either to possess or to lack. Even here it has different senses – intellectual insight, emotional insight and, more specifically in >psychoanalysis, becoming aware of the link between one's childhood experiences and one's adult behaviour. According to some theories, the task of analysis is to restore the insight that a patient had before becoming neurotic; others (including >Anna Freud) claim that it is only by going through analysis that one can develop true insight.

Given the central role of insight in many psychotherapies, it's been surprisingly little researched. A. Bandura has quipped that insight tends to be spotted by a therapist when his patient starts to explain things in terms of the theory that the therapist holds dear. However, this isn't insight so much as conformity. In general, to deny that you have the problems that the professionals say you have is to lack insight.

● A. Bandura, *Principles of Behavior Modification* (1969); Anna Freud, 'Insight: Its Presence and Absence in Normal Development', *Psychoanalytic Study of the Child*, 36, pp. 241–19 (1981); R. W. Lawler, *Computer Experience and Cognitive Development* (1985).

Instinct. At first, psychologists argued that people did things because their instincts led them to. A British ethologist, W. Thorpe, argued that there are six instincts: eating, drinking, sleeping, having sex, eliminating waste products and taking care of the body. An instinct is biologically determined. It is not learned, although it may not manifest itself unless the organism goes through certain experiences. The British psychologist William MacDougall was the first to formulate a theory of human >motivation in terms of instinct. For example, why do we seek the company of others? Because we have an instinct to be gregarious.

In other words, we are gregarious because we are gregarious. MacDougall later changed his terms, replacing 'instincts' with 'propensities' – which didn't add much really!

>Freud believed that the psyche had a fixed store of energy which it always sought to discharge, and that energy came from instincts. Men and women sought sex, not because it gave them pleasure, but because it relieved them of tension. Freud ignored the fact that human beings indulge in sexual foreplay which heightens tension; the object of having sex was, for him, to get rid of, to discharge, sexual tension.

The views of MacDougall and Freud have this in common: humans react; they do not act. They do not do things out of choice; they are driven to do certain things by biological needs. When they have fulfilled these needs, they are happy. Therefore, inertia, a state like death, is the ultimate in human delight. When Freud propounded the >death instinct, he was elaborating on this view.

Instinct fell somewhat out of fashion as a concept during the >behaviourist years but was reintroduced by the >ethologists. Both >Lorenz and Tinbergen claimed that many patterns of animal behaviour could only be explained as instinctual. They cited a variety of patterns of innate response as proof of the existence of instincts. More recently, stress on genetic factors has confirmed the importance of instincts.

- N. Tinbergen, *The Social Behaviour of Animals* (1962); E. O. Wilson, *Sociobiology* (1975).

Institutionalization. The damaging effects of being kept in a hospital were hinted at by Henry Maudsley in a lecture in 1870. Since then, it's been repeatedly shown that people who stay long term in institutions such as hospitals, >asylums and prisons become increasingly helpless, do not like making decisions for themselves and find it hard to re-enter the outside world. Various techniques to cope with this include teaching them activities of daily living such as shopping, cooking and budgeting. Some new forms of institutions such as >group homes have been created to provide halfway houses for the highly institutionalized so that they have time to develop the skills they'll need for life outside.

- P. Brown, *The Transfer of Care* (1985); T. Szasz, *Cruel Compassion* (1994).

Intelligence. Much debate has centred on whether intelligence is a product of heredity or of the person's environment. The issues are similar to those in the >nature/nurture controversy with the additional >trauma that those who claim that intelligence is largely inherited have been accused of racism. *See* Eysenck, Hans Jurgen; G factor; Jensen controversy.

Intelligence quotient (IQ), a statistical construct derived from scores on intelligence tests. People tend to think that IQ is the same as >intelligence but it isn't. It's the score given to indirect measures of intelligence. *See* Intelligence testing.

Intelligence testing. There has been more energy devoted to validating >intelligence quotient (IQ) tests than to any other psychological tests. The IQ test is actually based on a number of tests including the >Stanford Binet test and the >Wechsler scale, both with a history of more than 50 years. They include separate sections covering verbal ability, mathematical ability, performance IQ and spatial ability. Research has shown that one factor – the >g factor – accounts for most of the variance on IQ test scores, but there are also clear differences in specific abilities.

There are many reasons for being critical of IQ tests. First, the form that the questions take assumes that there is one correct answer, and they favour convergent over divergent thinking (*see* Cognitive styles). Second, the answers are not >culture-free – some general knowledge of the prevailing culture is required. The relatively poor scores of blacks and Hispanics may be partially due to such cultural factors, although there is also the oddity that Chinese and Japanese people tend to score higher than Europeans on tests based on European cultures! Third, the tests presume that >intelligence remains constant. It may sound odd to say that a person was more intelligent in 1983 than in 1984 unless there is some reason for the change. But in fact detailed research has revealed that intelligence isn't constant; individuals' IQs do alter. Richard Lynn found that the IQ of Japanese children has been rising steadily since 1910. As far back as 1948, Alice Heim and J. A. Wallace discovered that when undergraduates took IQ tests every week for eight weeks, their results got better and better even though they got no feedback about how they had previously done. Petty and Field found that the IQs of children over the age of four were rather unstable.

These technical criticisms apart, there's been much political argument about how honest some of the raw data used in studies have been and about the uses to which IQ tests have been put. Much of the best early evidence for the value of IQ testing came from the British psychologist >Sir Cyril Burt, who was later found to have invented much of his data. The political issues around intelligence testing were highlighted in the >Jensen controversy. *See* Head Start.

- H. J. Eysenck and L. Kamin, *The Intelligence Controversy* (1981); R. Fancher, *The Intelligence Men* (1985); R. Lynn, 'IQ in Japan and the United States Shows a Growing Disparity', *Nature* (1982); J. Khalfa (ed), *What is Intelligence* (1994); P. Kline, *Intelligence* (1992).

Interaction, literally acting together. We speak now of how people interact together – that is, how they talk together, how they coordinate (or fail to coordinate) >body language, >eye contact and all the delicate cues that go to make up social interaction.

Internalization, to make part of one's mental furniture something that was previously outside. Good Jews internalize many prohibitions such as not travelling on the Sabbath and accept this as the Law of God. Some middle-class girls used to internalize the taboo on going 'too far' before marriage. The film *Billy*

Liar has as a running gag how Billy tries to bed his very resistant fiancée who has internalized 'decency' splendidly.

Interviews. Tests of how good interviews are at predicting how well people will do in jobs have shown that they are not very effective. Psychological tests and observing how well trainees do on the job are superior. Interviewers often have poor technique, asking inappropriate questions and spending much time impressing candidates. Useless qualities such as good looks are given too much weight (*see* Halo effect). Some psychologists offer training on how interviewees can handle interviews, but the value of such training is itself debatable.

These criticisms aren't revolutionary; they have been publicized over the last 20 years. However, despite this, interviews remain the favourite way of hiring people – a sign that it's hard to change ingrained social habits. *See* Personality tests.

- C. F. Connell, L. Okensberg and J. M. Converse, *Experiments in Interviewing Techniques* (1979). J.T. Dillon, *The Practice of Questioning* (1989).

Introjection, a concept from psychoanalytic theory. It describes the process by which the functions of an external object are taken over by its internal representation. It's what happens when we internalize something. I may 'hear' my father giving me advice in my head long after he has died.

Introspection. The technical meaning of introspection is slightly different from the everyday one. Ordinarily, we say someone is introspective when they think a lot about themselves and their motives. In psychology, however, introspection is an experimental method, the aim of which is to analyse one's own >consciousness rather than feelings. The German psychologists of the Wurzburg school who used this method at the turn of the century hoped thereby to find out the basic constituents of consciousness; they were not interested in feelings. Instead, like physicists had found the atoms of matter, they hoped to find the atoms of the mind. Unfortunately there was disagreement between observers as to what subjects experienced when they introspected. The minute thoughts and feelings that were evoked when one subject saw a simple >stimulus like a feather were radically different from those of another subject, and the confusion that resulted caused the technique to fall into disrepute. The rise of >behaviourism also encouraged its demise, when psychologists such as >Watson and >Skinner argued that psychology didn't have to study consciousness.

It became clear, however, that vetoing introspection denied psychologists useful data – after all, human beings do think and even think about thinking. From the 1960s onwards, some investigators began to use self-report techniques. In these, a subject would say what he thought or felt about a subject or anything else. There have even been studies of mental >imagery using such principles. Rom Harré, among others, has argued that researchers should use various forms of introspection but not imagine it to be privileged. It is simply one technique among others. We aren't perfect witnesses to our own thoughts and feelings, but we do have something to say about them. Psychology cannot rule evidence gathered by such methods as inadmissible. Introspection is back. *See also* Self-report techniques.

- D. Dennett, *Consciousness Explained* (1992); G. Humphreys, *Thinking* (1951); B. Lyons, *The Death of Introspection* (1989).

Introversion. *See* Extraversion/introversion.

Intuition, the ability to grasp the solution to a problem without any very clear sense of the steps that lead there. Psychologists have seen intuition as a key element in >creativity. There's very little explanation of what makes a person intuitive, but possibly one of the important aspects is the ability to see connections between very different stimuli (*see* Stimulus). *See* Insight.

IQ. *See* Intelligence quotient.

J

Jealousy, the feeling of not wanting someone else to possess the beloved. Surveys show that many people describe themselves as somewhat jealous. >Freud argued that the roots of jealousy are found in the parent-child relationship. Each child is doomed to be jealous of the parent of the opposite sex who is a rival for the affection, and attention, of the mother or father. Psychologists have little to say about jealousy beyond this that isn't common sense. Jealous types are often obsessed with their beloved and insecure. Hopka, an anthropologist, has claimed that jealousy is rare in societies that do not emphasize private property and do not base social recognition on marriage and heading a household.

- P. Hauch, *Jealousy* (1981); R. B. Hopka, 'Cultural Determinants of Jealousy', *Alternative Lifestyles*, 4, 310–56 (1981).

Jensen controversy, a controversy relating to >intelligence testing. In 1969, Professor A. R. Jensen wrote a scholarly article for the *Harvard Educational Review* (*HER*) in which he argued against the orthodox view that blacks do less well in >IQ and other tests because they have been environmentally deprived. Jensen claimed that it was the blacks' genes, not their poor childhood environments, that made them less intelligent. This was seen as a racist argument, despite the fact that Jensen stressed that he was simply pointing out the basic statistical trend for the race. His enemies then tried to muzzle him, he claimed in his preface for *Genetics and Education*, a book of reprints on genetics, race and >intelligence. The *HER* board denied that it had commissioned the article as it stood in its final form; members of the 'notorious Students for a Democratic Society', as Jensen described them, tried to attack him; the popular press hounded him, publishing lurid versions of his findings that Hitler himself could have penned. Such is the stuff of scientific martyrdom.

However, a detailed reading of Jensen's work reveals that he drew unwarranted conclusions from his evidence. Jensen argued that programmes aimed at helping black people such as >Head Start had failed. But a small proportion (less than 10 per cent) of the children in the programmes did have a rise in IQ scores (often by 10 to 15 points) or an increase in scholastic performance. Surely we should try to understand what made such programmes unsuccessful for the majority? It is not an argument to say the problem is insoluble. Because 1000 wrong formulae don't solve a quadratic equation, it does not mean that quadratic equations cannot be solved. Given Jensen's logic, mathematicians would have given up years ago. IQ is only one measure. You cannot evaluate the educability of a child totally in terms of it. All the remedial education programmes did not have the aim of boosting IQ, yet because they failed to do so in most cases, Jensen dismissed the value of compensation for a poor environment.

Jensen accepts that IQ is not intelligence *per se* but only a measure. He estimates its heritability at 0.80, whereas the heritability of scholastic perform-ance is far lower – around 0.62 (1.0 would be perfect heritability). He cites studies where black children have improved scholastically but failed to register much IQ gain. He admits that, during testing, nervous children, many of them black, often scored 8 to 10 points under their true level. Jensen retested them, putting them at ease, and their scores went up, but how many other testers don't do that? Specifically, how many testers, whose published results Jensen used, didn't bother to retest?

There is a logical confusion at the heart of Jensen's argument. If IQ is not everything, why be so bothered if you cannot raise it? Even more, why not try to understand why a few programmes did succeed? Jensen's conclusion, how-ever, is that black children are not suitable for an academic education. It would be much better if we didn't torture them with book-learning; they're bound to fail. But if you ensured that their aspirations were more realistic – Oh! to be a cotton picker! – they'd be happier.

Jensen's work influenced the sociobiologists, and he was supported by >Ey-senck. The controversy led to many articles on the nature of intelligence and the validity of IQ tests.

- H. J. Eysenck and Leo Kamin, *The Intelligence Controversy* (1981); A. R. Jensen, *Bias in Mental Testing* (1983); Leo Kamin, *The Science and Politics of IQ* (1974).

Job satisfaction. Industrial psychologists (*see* Industrial psychology) have ar-gued that whether people are satisfied in their jobs depends on the following factors: pay; status; interest in the job. Interestingly, in post-industrial societies, there is increasing pressure on companies to ensure workers do get job satisfac-tion, as it seems to make them more productive and less likely to leave their employment.

Jokes. According to >Freud, the pleasure that we derive from jokes and plays on words are due to two factors. First, they allow forbidden material to slip out from the >unconscious to the conscious >mind because they appear harmless. For example, Freud shared one joke in which a man, instead of saying that he was going to meet a friend '*à tête à tête*', used the phrase '*à tête à bête*'. (*Bête* is the French word for 'stupid'.) It would not be acceptable to call the man stupid outright but the play on words made it more acceptable. Second, the compression in jokes – the 'psychic economy' – made them pleasurable; we enjoy their cleverness. Freud's ideas now seem incomplete, but few psychologists have followed them up.

● Sigmund Freud, *Jokes and Their Relation to the Unconscious* (1905).

J

Jung, Carl Gustav (1875–1961), a Swiss psychoanalyst who was >Freud's greatest disciple and, after a famous row, his greatest rival. Jung was the son of a Protestant pastor and studied medicine at the University of Basle. In 1900, he joined Emile Bleuler, the famous Zurich psychiatrist who did much pioneering work on >schizophrenia. Jung started to work on word >associations and, in 1906, contacted Freud. He became a regular member of the Psychoanalytic Centre in Vienna, but there were always differences between the two men. Jung could never accept Freud's stress on sexuality; he was much more interested in spirituality. Jung quarrelled with Freud both because Freud made a dogma of the theory of sexuality and because Freud would not let Jung analyse his >dreams as this would mean losing his authority. The break caused both men much pain. Jung went on to develop >analytical psychology. He aimed to understand the mystical and spiritual aspects of life Freud rather derided. He elaborated some very interesting concepts such as the >collective unconscious and the >anima and animus. His followers were exceptionally loyal to him, even when he became fascinated by the occult. He devoted much energy to the study of alchemy, saying that it held fundamental clues to human >personality, a claim dismissed as absurd not just by 'scientific' psychologists but by Freudians, too.

Jung's reputation has been dented by the fact that he did so little to defend Jewish psychoanalysts against the Nazis and seems to have accepted their triumph without any protest. He continued to edit the leading German psychoanalytic journal which never breathed criticisms of Hitler or how Jewish analysts were being treated. *See* Psychoanalysis.

● F. Fordham, *An Introduction to Jungian Psychology* (1969); C. G. Jung, *Archetypes of the Collective Unconscious* (1934), *Analytical Psychology* (1934); A. Samuels, *Jung and The Post Jungians* (1988); A. Stevens, *On Jung* (1990).

K

Kinsey reports, the first serious survey of sexual behaviour. In 1938, Alfred Kinsey (1894–1956), a zoologist, was asked to give lectures at Indiana University on the biology of sex and marriage. He found there were almost no statistical surveys of sexual behaviour, and he had no information to give students when they asked questions such as 'Is >homosexuality abnormal?' As a result, Kinsey himself set about creating a survey. He believed human sexuality could be studied objectively and told his assistants to ask intimate questions frankly – for example, they were to ask subjects if they masturbated, not if they 'touched themselves'. The publication of the first report (on male sexual behaviour) in 1948 and the second (on female sexual behaviour) in 1953 was important for two reasons. First, they provided an enormous amount of data on normal sexual behaviour. (Krafft-Ebbing and other sexologists had previously focused on the bizarre and abnormal.) Second, Kinsey assumed that sex was a perfectly proper area of scientific enquiry.

The results of the surveys shocked the United States by unveiling that many of its citizens had had sex before marriage and outside marriage and even dabbled in homosexuality. Kinsey helped persuade the public that sexual practices which were considered repulsive and abnormal were fairly widely practised. For instance, he found that by the age of 20, 82 per cent of males and 33 per cent of females had masturbated to orgasm; that 48 per cent of women had had intercourse before marriage; that 50 per cent of married men had had at least one extramarital affair; that 37 per cent of men and 13 per cent of women had had at least one homosexual relationship to orgasm. His statistics became the foundation on which subsequent work such as that of Masters and Johnson was built.

Kinsey neglected to report, however, that nearly all his subjects had been working at the local university. When this was revealed, some argued that what he had really shown was that intellectuals were oversexed – 'decent' Americans didn't go in for those kinds of perversions. However, the Kinsey reports, like Freud's work, were a major step in dismantling the taboo on sexuality which was a relic of Victorian morality.

- Alfred Kinsey, *Sexual Behavior in the Human Male* (1948) and *Sexual Behavior in the Human Female* (1953).

Kinship, degrees of blood relationship, crucial in >incest taboo.

Klein, Melanie (1882–1960), an important psychoanalyst who had a tremendous influence on the way we now think about the emotional development of children. Her influence has been both direct and indirect and has been especially powerful in the area of very early childhood. She believed, from observation (of children from the age of 18 months) and deduction, that children had an >unconscious and a >death instinct more or less from birth. This led to an ideological upheaval and split in the psychoanalytic world in the 1920s (especially in Britain where the two rivals, Klein and >Anna Freud, lived and worked). Klein parted company with Anna Freud and the Freudians in general, and had great influence on analysts such as D. W. Winnicott, >Wilfred Bion and the work of the Tavistock Clinic in London. She was an important pioneer of >play therapy.

One of Klein's major books – *Narrative of a Child Analysis* – tells of a short wartime analysis with a boy called Richard. Lots of his drawings are analysed, and there are detailed descriptions of every session – exactly what Richard did and what Klein did and her interpretations, how Richard resisted them and expressed his deepest feelings in actions and drawing. It is generally regarded as one of the best accounts of the complex benefits of analysis with children.

As a person, Klein aroused strong feelings due to what she described as her 'passionate nature'. Opponents found her overbearing, inflexible and 'grossly overrated'. Friends found her warm, lively and fun to be with, though her daughter broke off relations with her. *See* Object relations.

- H. Segal, *Klein* (1980).

Kleptomania, an >obsessional neurosis revolving around stealing, particularly shoplifting. Curiously, a number of kleptomaniacs are well-to-do, hitherto respectable middle-aged women. It's been argued that kleptomania in them is a >cry for help. Kleptomaniacs often also feel depressed. There were a number of cases in the 1970s and '80s in Britain in which wealthy women were caught stealing from department stores when there was no financial need for them to steal. It has been claimed that they actually wanted to get caught as they were starved of attention. There is no doubt that this kind of unnecessary theft is a symptom of psychological unease but many policemen are cynical about this view. It is true that it isn't always easy to tell who steals out of distress and who steals 'professionally'.

Labelling, the process of diminishing an individual by totally defining him of her in terms of some handicap or illness. A typical 'label' is 'schizophrenic' or even simply 'handicapped' or 'disabled'. Labelling theory suggests that affixing labels to people creates stigma since it suggests that all who wear that label are the same and cannot look after themselves.

Lacan, Jacques (1901–81), French psychoanalyst who argued that >psychoanalysis needed to return to >Freud. Lacan dismissed the changes that the >Neo-Freudians brought about. The return to Freud meant, in effect, a detailed analysis of Freud's work and its >language. Lacan was deeply influenced by >semiotics. His actual writings remain rather obscure and he has been accused of deliberate obscurity. His fame grew so great that by the end of his life he tended to see patients only for a few minutes. To those sceptical of psychoanalysis, his fame and the fact that it remains extremely hard to understand his ideas because he refused to express them clearly is proof of its tendency to glory in its own mystifications.

- Jacques Lacan, *The Four Fundamental Concepts of Psychoanalysis* (1977); Alan Sheridan, *Jacques Lacan* (1985).

Laing, (R)onald (D)avid (1927–89), Scottish psychiatrist who became a radical guru in the 1960s. He drew on >existentialism and was seen as an 'anti-psychiatrist' because he was so critical of the profession and its theories and practices. He said that >schizophrenia was the result of >labelling in the family, arguing that schizophrenia was not a disease but a reasonable response to >stress and that often the mad are really the most sane people in a crazed world. Laing's insights helped change psychiatric practice: psychiatrists now talk to the families of the mentally ill more; and it has become more accepted that family stress triggers episodes of schizophrenia. The enthusiasm for anti-psychiatry faded, especially as better research contradicted Laing's claims. It showed that showed that most psychiatrists did classify similar symptoms as schizophrenia. He lost his driving force as a theorist, and later focused on childbirth.

- A. Collier, *Laing* (1982); R. D. Laing, *The Divided Self* (1960) and *The Politics of Experience* (1968).

Language, a system of communication usually involving words. Language is important since it has long been taken as the distinctively human capacity, together with reason. Different schools of psychology approach language very differently. A number of intrepid psychologists, eager to bridge the species gap, brought up chimpanzees with much affection, and expertise, as if they were their own children. Despite being so privileged, the infant chimpanzees stubbornly refused to talk. They could out-leap, out-handle and out-manipulate human babies but could not master language. At best, some chimpanzees managed to learn a few sounds and to link them to objects.

Human babies are not born with the full-blown ability to talk. Language develops through the early years of life until, by the age of five or six, children should have the ability to speak normally. A study of speech development in children of all classes in Newcastle in the north-east of England showed that there are no fixed age points at which the first word, the first phrase or the first sentence should appear. Most children start to use words with meaning between the ages of 8 and 30 months. If, by the age of five years, children have not developed intelligible speech so that they can use proper phrases and sentences, then they need help. However, nothing is worse for the development of language in a child than for parents to panic about it. The child can become nervous and self-conscious about speaking, and this can retard him or her.

At first, babies learn to use their voices. They cry and shout, gurgle, make sounds such as 'oo' and 'aah' which will form part of their first words. Between the ages of 10 and 14 months, most children say their first word. This is usually associated either with a person – 'Ma' – or with pointing at things. Between the ages of 18 and 24 months, most children will start to put together phrases of two to three words. Good examples are 'No bath', 'Too hot', 'All gone' and other virtuoso performances that make parents feel they have given birth to a future Shakespeare. The use of correct sentences begins at about 18 to 20 months. Children now constantly imitate and repeat what is said to them, echoing adult language and so learning to speak. Yet they can also produce phrases or sentences they have never heard. By the age of 3¾, 63 per cent of children can use sentences properly; a year later, this rises to 88 per cent. Gordon Wells, a psychologist at Bristol, has shown how the learning of language depends on parents repeating words, inviting their children to take their turn at speaking, and correcting mistakes. The remarkable extent of this 'teaching' (both social and verbal) escaped most psychologists until Wells' painstaking work. This work has provided facts where previously controversy about language learning had reigned.

American psychologist >B. F. Skinner offered what turned out to be an inadequate theory. Skinner claimed that children learn to speak through

>reinforcement. The child imitates his parents talking and is rewarded by them when he does so correctly – he echoes their words, they smile at him and say he's good. Skinner did not see verbal behaviour as being much different from any other kind of conditioned behaviour (*see* Conditioning).

>Noam Chomsky has argued that this view is totally inadequate. Chomsky initially refuted Skinner on the grounds that all children learn to speak whether their parents are reinforcing or not. Language is a universal, and because of this, Chomsky suggested that there had to be 'hard wired' into the >brain a language-acquisition device. His ideas on the nature of the linguistic wiring of the brain stem from his highly influential linguistic analysis. In 1957, he said that the surface grammar of a language is not the best way of representing it. The surface structure of a sentence 'A wise man is honest' could be analysed into the subject 'man' and the predicate 'is honest', but the >deep structure of the sentence is different. Chomsky offers the following as a picture of the deep structure much more in terms of meaning: there will be 'an underlying proposition' with the subject 'man' and the predicate 'be wise' which can be transformed into the usual grammar of speech. So

(A man)	(Is wise)	(Is honest)
|	|	|
subject, noun	verb	verb
phrase	phrase	phrase

yields the utterance 'A man who is honest', which yields 'A wise man is honest'. The deep structure is a system of two propositions which interrelate so as to express the meaning 'A wise man is honest.'

Ambiguous sentences can also reveal how the same surface structure can conceal two different deep meanings. For instance, consider the sentence 'I disapprove of John's drinking.' It could mean that I disapprove either of John's drinking or of its character – he drinks so clumsily. This ambiguity is possible because there are two different deep structures, but these differences have been obliterated by the transformations into surface structure and the words obscure the meaning. In deep structure, the meaning is clear. Chomsky argues that this scheme allows us to understand why we can understand sentences we have never heard before. The deep structure meaning is always available and one can attach new words to it.

Chomsky has not been content only to describe a linguistic theory; he also claims that the deep structure is neurologically 'wired in'. Language is learned but the ability to learn it depends on certain innate systems in the brain. Studies of children show that they understand sentences they have never heard before and that they produce utterances they have never been told. In other words, since they produce sounds, words and sentences that have not been reinforced, any theory of verbal behaviour that depends on reward is inadequate. Chomsky's ideas initially caused a great deal of controversy as psychologists had tended to deny the existence of >innate ideas and to maintain that complex behaviours were largely learned. Today language learning is seen as learning a skill that is partly intellectual, partly social. The painstaking accumulation of evidence from conversations between children and parents emphasizes how such things as turn-taking are taught.

- Noam Chomsky, *Syntactic Structures* (1957); J. Greene, *Language Understanding* (1986); G. Wells, *Learning through Interaction* (1981).

Language areas. Most of our knowledge of the brain areas involved in language come from studies of disease (*see* Aphasia). If a person does not talk and has a >lesion of the >cortex of the >brain at point A, anywhere in Broca's area, it is held that point A is crucial for >language. Physiologists have become cautious of arguing that point A 'contains' language for it may either receive, code, decode, retain, integrate or do something else to language, but they have isolated a number of crucial areas: X is the posterior speech cortex known as Wernicke's area; Y is the anterior speech cortex known as Broca's area; Z is the motor cortex that controls the musculature involved in speech. Areas Y and Z are found only in one hemisphere of the brain. In most right-handed persons, the language areas are in the left hemisphere (*see* Lateralization); left-handed people have their language behaviour and ability stored but in both the left and the right hemispheres.

The destruction of part of Z will not lead to anything worse than a thickening of the voice and other muscle difficulties that can fade away. Destruction of part of X or Y, however, usually leads to aphasia, a very wide-ranging condition in which a person cannot speak or understand speech normally. Aphasia can clear up quickly, but this hardly ever happens if the posterior speech cortex (X) is destroyed. Nevertheless, it would be wrong to imagine that this is the only or main speech centre; rather, it seems to be one of a number of crucial structures.

Latency of response, the length of time it takes for a >stimulus to arouse a response.

Latency period, the period when a child does not show any overt sexuality. >Freud reckoned that this begins at the end of the >Oedipus complex, at about the age of seven, and it lasts until the start of puberty. During it, the child reverts to a more intellectual mode of functioning, keeping repressed and latent the emotions that will soon erupt in adolescence.

Latent content, the hidden meanings in what patients in analysis say – hidden, that is, from themselves. >Dreams, >daydreams, >jokes are usually crammed with latent content. One task of analysis is to bring the latent content to the surface.

Latent learning, not immediately observable >learning. In 1923, E. Tolman showed that even laboratory rats could make internal 'mental' maps of a maze, but they would only use that learning when there was some advantage to be gained from it. If the >behaviourists are right, why doesn't learning immediately show up as a change in behaviour?

Lateralization, the specialization of the two different cerebral hemispheres of

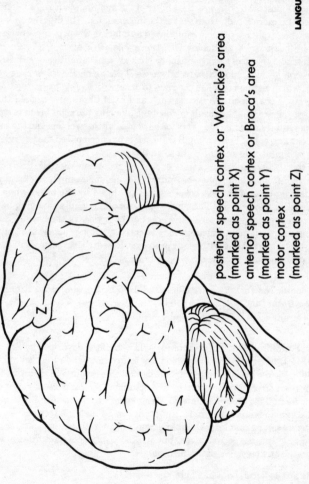

posterior speech cortex or Wernicke's area
(marked as point X)
anterior speech cortex or Broca's area
(marked as point Y)
motor cortex
(marked as point Z)

LANGUAGE AREAS

the >brain. Each hemisphere is responsible for different functions. Ever since Sperry's research in 1968 (*see* Consciousness), it has been supposed that the left hemisphere is responsible for language, logic and mathematical thinking while the right is responsible for creative, emotional and artistic thinking. In 1979, Johnson found that, with age, the ability of the non-linguistic right hemisphere declined far more rapidly than that of the linguistic left. The differences between the two hemispheres became established as a fact in the popular >imagination through books such as Robert Ornstein's *The Psychology of Consciousness*, which stated that the right hemisphere has mystical qualities (*see* Brain, for a discussion of this), and Barbara Edward's *Drawing on the Right Side of Your Brain*, which claimed to teach the rigid to draw with feeling by letting the right brain guide the pencil. Physicists such as Fritjof Capra also argued that the greatest science was the result of doodling, allowing the right brain to come up with potential solutions – don't try too hard to solve the problem and the solution will float into being! Some computer theorists have compared the left side of the brain to digital code and the right to analog.

In the 1980s, some doubts were expressed about how rigid the distinction is into two different hemispheres. Andrew Gevins, for example, claimed that a detailed analysis of the electrical signals produced by the brain when doing simple tasks showed that there were very complex, rapidly changing patterns of electrical activity between many areas on both sides of the brain. The basic dimensions of left-right functions may be correct, but in practice, the brain taps both sides when dealing with many problems. Research increasingly shows that the pattern is more complex. *See* Split-brain studies; Handedness.

- F. Capra, *The Turning Point* (1982); B. Edwards, *Drawing on the Right Side of Your Brain* (1983); Robert Ornstein, *The Psychology of Consciousness* (1976); H. Gardner, *Multiple Intelligences* (1993).

Lateral thinking, a kind of unfocused, 'wild' >thinking developed by Edward de Bono. In this, you deliberately don't try to arrive at the direct solution to a problem. Rather you go around it, hoping that this detour will throw up lateral rather than direct creative options and solutions. De Bono offers various techniques for making oneself go lateral, recommending >brainstorming in particular. De Bono claims that lateral thinking can be highly effective, but critics counter by saying that lateral thinking may be generally amusing and occasionally throw up unexpected ideas, but it's more of a gimmick than a serious conceptual strategy. *See* Lateralization.

- Edward de Bono, *Lateral Thinking* (1984).

Laughter. Darwin observed that some animals laughed and claimed babies did so when tickled as long as it was not by a strange man! It is, however, notoriously difficult to study because it can't be easily set up in the laboratory. Laughter is an important behaviour. It is found in some apes as well as in humans.

In 1908, >Henri Bergson argued that we laugh when 'something mechanical is encrusted on the human', or, more simply, when human beings act like mechanisms. That's why we roar when lovers fall out of cupboards in farces or the Keystone cops collide into each other. However, because it is now clear that children begin to laugh in a variety of situations, Bergson's theory may be too narrow. Psychologists have tended not to study it in isolation, concentrating instead on the study of humour, rating >jokes as to how funny, aggressive, etc they are. This is a pity since laughter remains powerful and intriguing. The journal *Humor* reports often on the use of laughter and humour in therapy. The case histories are intriguing, but, empirically claims that laughter is therapeutic remain unproven.

● H. Bergson, *Le Rire* (1908); David Cohen, *The Development of Play* (1993); *Humor*, an inter-disciplinary quarterly, is published by Mouton, the Hague.

Law of effect. *See* Effect, law of.

Lead and its effects on IQ. Recent studies show that children brought up in an environment where there is a higher than average amount of lead (either in the form of lead paint or in air pollution) have a lower >IQ. It is not wholly certain that this is directly attributable to the ingestion of lead rather than social class. The results have also focused attention on the role of aluminium as well as lead in brain disease. *See* Brain.

● M. Smith, *Lead and Human Performance* (1989).

Leadership. What interests psychologists are the different styles that leadership can take and how these affect the ability of groups to carry out tasks. In 1939, Kurt Lewin and colleagues identified three basic styles – authoritarian, democratic and *laissez-faire*. The autocratic style is where the leader tells a group what his orders are. The co-operative one is where the leader accepts suggestions and then decides on the right action and in the democratic style the leader is simply the person who expresses what the group decides. The democratic style was best in enabling the group to do its work while maintaining emotional well-being. Research showed that authoritarian leaders provoked hostility, while the democratically led group was more cooperative and its members praised each other more. The research on styles of leadership has been mainly of interest to psychotherapists and, to some extent, to >industrial psychology as companies want to know which leadership style will produce the best results.

● K. Lewin, *A Dynamic Theory of Personality* (1936).

Learned helplessness. *See* Helplessness, learned.

Learning, a crucial concept in psychology. We learn a huge variety of complex skills in life – from speech, to how to make friends, to driving. Despite this, the psychology of learning has tended to focus on fairly artificial experimental situations. John Watson argued that psychology should study how people learn to type, to shoot and many other ordinary activities. In reality, studies have honed in on how people learn lists of adjectives or how rats learn to find their way around a maze. This experimental tradition has made it possible to isolate some crucial factors that affect learning such as >recency (how recently did we perceive the >stimulus we are meant to learn), frequency (how often have we seen that stimulus), >contiguity (was that stimulus next to another stimulus we had already learned), the >law of effect and the motivating power of different kinds of >reinforcement. It has also been established that we tend to learn new skills in the way that we learned old skills (*see* Learning sets; Reinforcement).

The experimental tradition has, however, meant that there was for a long time less work undertaken in how we learn a variety of more sophisticated behaviours like the complex social roles that become second nature to us. For example, when I go on a first date with someone, I have a reasonable idea of how to behave. Unless I am socially deficient, I will try to be interesting and charming. I will not keep talking about my ex-girlfriend. How do we learn that? Psychology is much vaguer in such areas. It has also been argued that some capacities, especially language, are not learned in the ways predicted by classical experimental psychology (*see* Chomsky, Noam).

A third important area of the study of learning is its neurophysiology. To learn something is essentially to remember it so as to have it available when it is needed. There has been much recent progress in psychology. Rats reared in a rich environment, in a cage full of gadgets, develop a larger cerebral >cortex than average. McCormick has recently found that a wide variety of classically conditioned learned responses may be stored in the >cerebellum. Rats whose eyeblink was conditioned to puffs of air lost that response when a tiny slice of their cerebellum was removed. The unconditioned eyeblink remained normal however. In humans, the >hippocampus seems to play an important part in learning as patients who have lost both the left and right hippocampus show serious learning difficulties.

● W. Hill, *Theories of Learning* (1988).

Learning curve, the graph which shows how competent people are when plotted against the number of learning trials they have had on a particular task. This can also be applied to animals. Typically, the more exposure the quicker the solution. The discovery was first made by >E. J. Thorndike who found that cats coped faster and faster with getting out of his 'puzzle box'. We speak now of a learning curve for certain jobs which means that with time people get more adept at coping with routine problems.

Learning set is a state of preparedness in which certain problems are solved in certain ways. If an individual has a learning set, he or she will tend to look for solutions of a particular type. For example, if I usually do the *Daily Blather* crossword, I will have learned that the setters of that puzzle tend to use the plays of Shakespeare. I will not find it hard to solve the clue 'room for a pig' as a result – 'Hamlet' will occur to me quite quickly. But if I have no such learning set because I usually do the *Daily Trumpet* crossword which is more literal, I may well be mystified. 'Sty' is too short. Where problems are similar, a learning set may be a help. However, it tends to create problems and rigidity in the face of new problems.

Lesbianism. *See* Homosexuality.

Lesions, brain, damage or injury to the >brain, caused by disease or trauma (eg from a car accident). Much brain research depends on matching the site of a particular lesion with a specific loss of function. However, even if you find that a person with a lesion in area A can no longer perform a particular function, there isn't an instant logical answer. You can't be sure if area A encoded, stored or effected that particular function. *See* Language areas.

Levels of processing, a theory about how >memory works. It claims that information may be processed at a number of levels. The strength of these levels depends on how the information is organized, the emotions it is associated with and its links with other memories. Superficially processed information will be forgotten fairly quickly, while information which has roots in many different levels will be remembered for longer and be harder to extinguish.

Libido, sexual energy or force, a concept developed by >Freud. The libido is the force that drives a person to satisfy his or her desires. Initially, Freud saw libido as pure sexual energy, but later, he decided that the term covered both sexual and other life-enhancing >instincts. It is a mistake to equate libido with sex. Freud meant it as a generalized life-giving force in opposition to the >death instinct, Eros against Thanatos. In 1923, Freud altered his views when he suggested that it wasn't the >id, but the >ego that is the great reservoir of the energy of the libido.

Lie detector, technically known as a polygraph. For psychologists, the critical issue is whether there are clear signs of lying. Lie detector enthusiasts claim that there are physiological changes which register untruth such as >galvanic skin response. Scepticism about both this and the so-called 'truth drug' remains. *See* Biofeedback.

Life events, significant events in life. This concept arose in the 1960s through the research of George Brown into the onset of >depression. Brown found that major and traumatic events such as divorce, bereavement, losing a job (*see* Loss) were likely to trigger >stress and depression in people who had been just managing to cope. It didn't matter whether it was their heredity or their experiences that made them vulnerable; the life event was the trauma that pushed them into a breakdown. The surprise was that happy events such as marriage or getting a promotion can also trigger such breakdowns.

In 1967, two psychiatrists, Holmes and Rake, drew up a list of life events that can cause stress and depression; they also assigned points to each one.

Life event	Points
Death of husband/wife	100
Divorce	73
Separation Imprisonment Death of close relative	60–69
Personal injury Illness	50–59
Getting married	50
Loss of job Retirement Pregnancy Change in health of family member	40–49
Sex difficulties New family member Business readjustment Change in financial condition Death of close friend Change to different kind of work Change in number of arguments with spouse/partner Large mortgage	30–39
Moving house Trouble with in-laws Change in living conditions Trouble with employer Son/daughter leaving home Wife/partner beginning or stopping work Change in working hours/conditions	20–29
Holidays Christmas Minor violation of the law Change in eating/sleeping habits Change in number of family get-togethers Changes in recreation	10–19

According to Holmes and Rake, a score of 60 points within six months or 150 points within a year can lead to both mental and physical trouble. For example, people with serious heart disease frequently have scores of 400–600 points for two or three years. What remains odd is why happy events, some not unlike >Maslow's >peak experiences, should have such damaging results. Humankind cannot bear too much ecstacy, perhaps? If so, why not? No psychological theory has grappled with this paradox properly.

● G. Brown and T. Harris, *The Social Origins of Depression* (1975); T. Holmes and R. Rake, 'The Social Readjustment Rating Scale', *Journal of Psychosomatic Research*, 2, 213–18 (1967).

Lifespan development, an idea developed by the psychoanalyst >Erik Erikson. He has claimed that >Freud was wrong to argue that after adolescence there were no more stages of development. Erikson has argued that throughout life people develop and change. They are deeply affected by their past but they can, either through >therapy, accident or sheer determination, change. For Erikson, the key choice at any critical point is whether to turn towards life, >creativity and the chance of fulfilment or to take refuge from those challenges. Erikson's ideas have become more influential as people live longer and – especially in the US – as psychology has become part of popular culture. Even the over 60s expect to grow and develop now. Lifespan development lasts from womb to tomb.

● E. Erikson, *The Lifecycle Completed* (1986).

Limbic system, a name coined by Broca in 1878, from the Latin *limbus*, 'border', or 'hem'; the term for an area of the midbrain. It contains the following structures: the >hippocampus, the septum, singulate gyrus. It was first thought that these controlled smell, but in 1937 J. W. Papez suggested that the real link was >emotion. However, now that is seen as being too simply a description of what the limbic system's role might be.

Linguistics, the study of >language, how it is produced and the social interactions that surround it. It has become an important area for psychology largely because of >Chomsky's pioneering work.

Lithium (carbonate salts or citrate), a drug used in manic-depressive illness (*see* Mania). It has some side effects, including drinking and passing a great deal of water, trembling and weakness, confusion, slurred speech, diarrhoea and drowsiness. Psychiatrists have become wary of patients becoming psychologically dependent on it.

Lobotomy, also called prefrontal lobotomy; cutting the connections between the frontal lobe and the rest of the >cortex of the >brain. When it was believed that the frontal lobe was not responsible for any specific functions, lobotomy became a favourite operation for the relief of >epilepsy. The technique became controversial when it became clear that it had damaging side-effects. Lobotomized patients did not simply resume their old >personality free of epilepsy but changed. They showed profound symptoms of apathy, often becoming inflexible and uninterested in anything; they seemed to have lost a human spark. The operation was widely performed in Britain, the United States and Italy, and there were allegations that neurosurgeons were keen to carry it out since such patients were an interesting group to research. As public awareness of the adverse effects of lobotomy developed in the late 1950s and early 1960s, this helped kindle interest in the issue of psychiatric patients' rights. Patients' rights groups fought hard to get the operation banned, seeing it as one of the worst abuses of psychiatric power. It is done rarely now.

Locus of control, a theory which argues that people can be seen as significantly different by whether they see their destiny as being in their charge (inner locus of control) or at the mercy of external events (outer locus of control). This theory has become influential with the growth of >attribution theory.

Loneliness. The effects of loneliness tend to include >depression and low >self-esteem. Lonely people are more vulnerable to physical illnesses, too.

Psychiatrists have yet to find a cure. In industrial societies, many people feel lonely, and the growth of groups to help socially inadequate people learn communication skills was a feature of psychology in the 1970s. American studies suggest that 20 per cent of adults feel 'moderately' lonely each week.

● A. Peplov and D. Perlman (eds), *Loneliness: A Sourcebook of Current Theory, Research and Therapy* (1982) R. Weiss, *Loneliness* (1973).

Longitudinal studies, research carried out on the same >sample over a long period of time. The most famous of these is Terman's study of the very intelligent which has lasted since 1925 and is based at Stanford University. Longitudinal studies do not have to be as long as that. Their advantage is that they make it possible to follow up how a particular life developed and the way in which early influences work over decades, and to achieve a richness of data that more conventional tests lack. Their problem is that they are expensive and complicated to administer.

Lorenz, Konrad (1903–89), ethologist involved in devising a number of important concepts such as >imprinting and >bonding. Lorenz helped revive interest in the study of animal behaviour, and he hoped to use his animal work to further human morality. He argued that one reason for human >aggression was that, unlike other species, we tend to kill at a distance and so do not see the death throes we inflict. Humankind, therefore, doesn't kill to survive. He shared the Nobel Prize with N. Tinbergen and Karl von Frisch in recognition of their work in founding >ethology. As with >Jung, questions have been raised about Lorenz' dealings with the Nazis. His books include *King Solomon's Ring* (1952) and *On Aggression* (1966).

Loss. This refers to bereavement and divorce and has even been extended to cover losing a job, experiencing a separation or losing a limb. The psychological consequences of all these traumas have similarities – mainly that the person who loses either someone or something grieves for what has gone. >Freud was the first to argue that the pain of loss is not as simple as it seems; there are darker, less generous feelings involved with it.

It is normal to grieve when we experience loss. Many primitive cultures have elaborate rituals for dealing with grief, as did many in the West until the recent past, Irish wakes being perhaps the best known. By the 1950s, however, it had become less socially acceptable for people to grieve openly and emotionally at the death of a loved one, and some spoke of death as the new taboo. There has never been a very satisfactory explanation of why that should have occurred, although it may have something to do with the fact that people now rarely die at home. Instead, they die in hospitals, and where once the family would have laid out the body of their loved one, this role has been taken over by the funeral home. Death has become unfamiliar and worrying, and grief has become an embarrassing reminder of its realities.

Starting in the 1960s, however, a number of groups of bereaved people began to argue with the help of psychiatrists such as Colin Murray Parkes and Elisabeth Kubler Ross that accepting death took time and required grieving. Kubler Ross identified a number of stages that people go through in grief. First, they tend to deny that they have lost someone (*see* Denial). They fantasize that the person isn't really dead, which is much easier to do if they haven't actually seen the body. Then they begin to get angry: why did the person die and leave them? Kubler Ross claims that one reason for the anger is that, when people die (or marriages end) there are often many things left unsaid and many issues unresolved, but now there is no hope of resolving them. Finally, grieving people move towards acceptance.

A feeling of loss is only possible if we have first become attached. Given the transience of life, to be involved is to court certain loss, and for some, childhood experiences leave too much pain and make them unwilling to risk further attachments and further loss – no love, no loss, an equation that would seem to guarantee contentment but doesn't work for most people. *See* Attachment theory; Bowlby, John; Defence mechanisms; Life events.

● Elisabeth Kubler Ross, *On Death and Dying* (1969); C. Murray Parkes, *Bereavement* (1972).

Love. >Freud said that the great task for psychology was to enable people to love and to work – *Leiben und Arbeiten*. A 1966 survey in the United States showed that 75 per cent of couples named love as the primary reason for marrying; 24 per cent identified a desire for children; while sex, at 8 per cent, came a poor third. Our first loves are our parents, and it has been said that we tend to seek partners who echo the style of that love. The son who has a domineering but fussy mother looks for a similar wife, or one that is the complete opposite (to escape mama). This hypothesis is exceptionally difficult to prove, but some apparently prosaic social psychological research confirms it in a general sort of way. We tend to fall in love with people from our own social, economic and cultural group. Most people will marry someone who was born within a few miles of their own birthplace and who is of their own educational level.

Love, the 17th-century French writer La Rouchefoucauld noted, is 'self-love *à deux*'. He anticipated the Freudian view that love always includes a healthy (or perhaps unhealthy) amount of >narcissism. Some writers speak of love as fulfilling deficit needs, so that the partners complement each other; the humanistic psychologist Abraham contrasted 'deficit love' and 'giving love'. Theorists about why we fall in love argue among themselves: it may be to fulfil social expectations (Greenfield, 1965); because we happen to be intensely physiologically aroused (Walston, 1971); because love seems to be the correct label for the emotions we are feeling; or as a response to a hope signal (Miller and Siegel, 1972). A telling point from an Economic and Social Research Council survey is that it was only at the last minute that social scientists included 'love' as one of the possible reasons for living together, yet 78 per cent of the sample gave that as their reason for doing it. The Harlows, two animal behaviour researchers, suggest that being unloved as a child tends to make it hard to become a loving parent, but this cycle of deprivation is better proven in monkeys than in humans.

This notion that there is a social psychology of love clashes with romantic notions of the chemistry of love. The only evidence for that comes from the discovery of pheromones, scent released by sexual excitement which produces love or at least sexual attraction. However, detailed research shows no evidence that the modern love potions containing pheromones actually work – except as a way of making money.

● R. Sternberg and M. Barnes, *The Psychology of Love* (1988).

LSD, lysergic acid diethylamide, 'acid'. A drug used in the 1960s in various experiments and 'recreationally'. Subjects reported frightening >hallucinations. It has also been used by some therapists, notably the Dutch psychiatrist Jan Bastiaans, as a way of bursting through repressed traumatic memories.

Luminance, the amount of light emitted by an object in a given situation. Used in >perceptual psychology.

Lunacy, an old term for >madness. The word derives from the Latin word *luna*, 'moon': the moon was thought to affect the >mind, intermittent forms of insanity reflecting the moon's phases.

Lunatic asylums. *See* Asylums.

M

Madness. The term is rarely used now. It is considered demeaning to say a patient is 'mad'. *See* Depression; Lunacy; Mental health; Schizophrenia.

Malnutrition. Infants and children who suffer a prolonged period of malnutrition seem to suffer a reduction in >IQ (*see* Intelligence testing) and may later also have eating difficulties. Few references in psychology deal with this important topic, reflecting the >Anglo-American bias of much psychology. It's basically a Third World problem and too few psychologists in these parts of the world have so far attended to it and any possible remedies.

Mania, a form of psychiatric illness in which the person is especially active and energetic. A manic person can be engaging but is generally unrealistic. It is not unusual for manic patients to buy expensive goods and plan to 'conquer the world'. Some successful individuals have many manic traits but manage to keep enough grip on reality not to confuse their >fantasies with things as they really are. Pure mania is rare. Estimates say it is likely to occur in 6 out of 1000 lives once. The more common form is manic-depressive illness in which a person's mood swings from the positive and hyperactive to the profoundly depressed.

The treatment for manic-depressive illness assumes that it is a chemical disorder, blaming an imbalance of >brain control mechanism. However, this does not take into consideration whether patients enjoy the bouts of mania. The neurologist Oliver Sacks, in his studies of >Giles de la Tourette syndrome patients, touched on that difficult issue. Patients who are cured of the manic tics often mourn the loud, energetic personality that goes with them and which is lost with the cure.

The most common treatment for mania is >lithium, which can't begin to tackle the psychological complexities.

● Oliver Sacks, *The Man who Mistook His Wife for a Hat* (1985).

Manic-depressive illness. *See* Mania.

M

Marital counselling, >counselling whose aim is to mend marriages and other significant relationships. Such counselling can use a variety of models, but except in >family therapy, they tend to be loosely based on common sense and being honest about feelings. Some counsellors like to show partners specifically how they are either failing to communicate or to meet each other's needs. For example, the woman may constantly interrupt the man; the interruptions make him feel threatened; he lashes out in revenge or drinks too much. Or the man may not listen to what the woman says; she becomes apathetic and depressed; he feels she doesn't care for him; she feels he doesn't care for her. Either way, a spiral of misery starts. Marriage counselling may also involve >sex therapy, although it doesn't have to.

Research into why marriages are unhappy point to (1) sexual unhappiness, (2) emotional conflicts and (3) financial conflicts, but there are some bad marriages which have good sex and perfectly good marriages which have bad sex. Initially, it was always the aim of marriage counsellors to persuade partners to stick together, but slowly it has come to be recognized that the best >therapy may be to help the partners end amicably what is an unhappy union.

In Britain, most marriage guidance counselling is done by the Marriage Guidance Council which, because many of its clients were not married, relaunched itself in 1988 as Relate.

Marxist psychology, an approach rather than a school of psychology. It was fashionable during the late 1960s and 70s, especially because Marcuse analyzed it in his *Eros and Civilisation*. Marxist psychology highlights the concepts of class and alienation. Much research shows that class has important consequences – especially for the way children grow up, the opportunities they get and the problems they are exposed to. Working-class children are significantly more likely to do badly in school, to have lower than average >IQ, to get in trouble with the law, to marry early and even, remarkably, to be exposed to damaging amounts of >lead which will probably harm their intellectual development. Working-class adults are more likely to suffer a variety of both physical and mental illnesses – especially >schizophrenia. Many non-Marxist psychologists recognize the importance of class. The more distinctively Marxist concept is >alienation. Marx argued that in capitalist societies the conditions of production divorced the workers from their work. They didn't own what they produced, either economically or psychologically. They were merely cogs in a great industrial machine. Novels such as Dickens' *Hard Times* and H. G. Wells' *Kipps* describe better than anything else the feelings of alienation. Alienation, modern Marxist psychologists argue, creates misery. The concept has been used by radical thinkers such as >R. D. Laing to explain the inability of certain individuals to feel comfortable and get on with the world.

● R. D. Laing, *The Politics of Experience* (1968).

Masculine protest, a concept from the Adlerian (*see* Adler, Alfred) school of >individual psychology. When women realize that they are discriminated against, they sometimes begin to imitate the actions of men. They protest by adopting some male characteristics such as aggressiveness. Although Adler wrote about this, the evidence is slight. Certainly some feminist writers and theorists have been as aggressive as men. They would, however, balk at the idea that this was masculine protest. The concept is dated and sexist.

Masking, a phenomenon in visual >perception when one >stimulus is 'masked' and thus not seen because another one takes precedence. Masking plays a role in some visual illusions.

Maslow, Abraham (1908–1970), American psychologist who is one of the fathers of >humanistic psychology. He introduced some important concepts such as >peak experiences and >self-actualization, in which a person achieves his or her full potential. *See* Hierarchy of needs.

● A. A. Maslow, *Farther Reaches of Human Nature* (1968).

Masochism, the enjoyment of pain. This is a controversial subject, both in >psychoanalysis and in >feminist psychology. It was the Marquis de Sade (1749–1814) who probably first wrote about masochism and its ambivalent delights. Masochism can't really be understood without understanding >sadism. It is unclear too whether people are pure masochists – only into receiving pain – or whether they vary, sometimes also playing the sadist. Reliable statistics on how many masochists there are in the population don't exist. In the USA, one interesting finding is that 35 per cent of transvestites and fetishists were also excited by sado-masochistic practices.

The 19th-century sexologists Krafft-Ebbing and Havelock Ellis both recognized masochism as an important sexual deviation. >Freud made it more central. The extent of masochism is unclear partly because enjoying anything from sexual teasing to sheer brutality could be evidence of masochistic tendencies. The psychologist Weinberg has argued on the basis of interviews with prostitutes that usually the masochist sets the limits in a sado-masochistic relationship. But sometimes, that doesn't happen. It has been estimated, in the USA, that 250 to 500 deaths a year may be due to sado-masochistic practices which 'go too far'. Many myths surround masochism such as, in the UK, that public school boys brought up by fierce nannies who spanked them love, as adults, to be spanked. Another one is that many women are secret masochists and enjoy being treated roughly during sex. The evidence for both these propositions is at best anecdotal, at worst very dubious. Even though phone boxes and contact papers are full of personal ads for 'Strict Mistresses' who will provide bondage and other forms of sweet torture, there is no sound survey evidence to suggest that many men dream of being spanked. Secondly, feminist psychologists argue that the idea that women love pain is patriarchal rubbish which suits males – and male psychologists – and has done so for centuries. Yet there are clearly some women who accept relationships with men that are more about pain than about pleasure. Robin Norwood has argued that this is due to their own disturbed relationships with their fathers.

- Robin Norwood, *Women Who Love Men Too Much* (1988); R. Stoller, *Perversion, the erotic form of hatred* (1975).

Masters, W. H. (1915–) and Johnson, Virginia (1925–), pioneering students of sex and developers of >sex therapy. Masters and Johnson argued that the physiology of sex deserved detailed study, and they carried out these studies in a very dispassionate way. They dissected how both men and women arrive at >orgasm and found that women reach a series of plateaus marked typically by high states of arousal. The levels of arousal shift progressively higher and are measured through pulse rate, breathing, heart rate and other classical physiological indicators. They probably should be credited with the discovery that women find it easier to reach orgasm when they are on top because it allows them to control the rhythm of friction. Their sex therapy seemed at one time highly successful but there has been controversy about it as some have claimed that it doesn't work as well as claimed while others maintain its ethics are dubious.

Masturbation, once believed to cause >madness, blindness and other ills. It is now seen as a relatively ordinary form of sexual activity. Morals have changed with the fashions in scientific explanation.

Maternal deprivation, the notion that children who are not looked after by their mothers suffer a variety of psychological problems because they are 'deprived' of their mothers' affection. The idea owed a great deal to the work of the animal psychologists, the Harlows, who found that infant monkeys clung even to 'mothers' made of wire mesh. In his work following 44 juvenile thieves, >John Bowlby argued that most of them had 'gone wrong' because they had lacked the stability and affection of a mother. Feminists have attacked the concept because it makes women feel guilty if they don't take on full-time mothering. They would feel they were harming their children if they went out to work. Bowlby in the 1980s finally accepted that a father could provide the >love and care needed and so avoid maternal deprivation. The concept is also linked to >separation anxiety.

Maze. An important device in psychology since much early >experimental work involved rats running down mazes to find their rewards. Some mazes were veritable labyrinths; other ones (eg T-mazes) were much more simple.

Mechanistic models, models of psychological function which claim that human beings are physical/chemical machines, that the >brain is simply a physical organ and that its actions wholly explain the >mind. Mechanistic models of the brain tend to reflect current technology. Originally the brain was viewed as a supercomplex telephone exchange, now the favoured analogy is the computer. Mechanistic models deny the existence of the mind/body problem by claiming that the mind is all brain. This solution, however, doesn't explain why we feel that our intentions cause our behaviour or why many people believe that they can control their actions through their wills. Increasingly, the thought experiments of philosophers such as Daniel Dennett (*see* Consciousness) suggest that these simple analogies don't encompass the peculiar properties of human >consciousness. The view that consciousness is fragmented may also affect the status of these models.

- A. Chapman and D. Jones (eds), *Models of Man* (1980); Daniel Dennett, *Brainstorms* (1985).

Medication. *See* Antidepressants; Benzodiazepines; Chlorpromazine; Lithium; Monoamine oxidase inhibitors; Neurotransmitters; Psychopharmacology; Psychotropic drugs.

Meditation, a process by which one attempts to lose conscious attention; an old religious practice of monks in the Western and Eastern worlds well before the chic of Zen and the Indian gurus. In the 14th century, Thomas à Kempis set out rules for meditating on Christ, as did St Teresa of Avila. Psychologists became interested in the late 1960s when meditation seemed to offer a way of exploring alternative states of >mind and of getting high without drugs. Experiments showed that, during meditation, some adepts could achieve remarkable feats: one Indian managed to reduce his need for oxygen to the point where he could live for 3 days in a covered space; his accomplishment was reported in the science journal *Nature*. More prosaically, it has been argued that learning to meditate is useful in combating >stress and high blood pressure and in calming the heart. David Shapiro has also suggested that it can help with a variety of psychological disorders.

The most popular form of meditation is probably transcendental meditation (TM), although both Zen and Zazen have had their adherents. Some of those practising TM have claimed that if sufficient people meditate, they could influence worldwide events, including the price of shares on the stock market. There's no proof of this, but the value of meditation to the individual seems relatively well established even among sceptical psychologists. Meditation is now used as part of a number of techniques of >psychotherapy.

- D. Shapiro, *Meditation: Self Regulation Strategy and Altered States of Consciousness* (1980).

Memory, an important topic since >Ebbinghaus. Studies initially discovered that we had two different memory systems – short-term memory which can hold no more than seven items for a period; and long-term memory. It was then suggested that there is also a pre-short term memory in which you rehearse items before you can pass them into memory. Psychologists have established a number of laws on how we remember. These include that we remember most recently given information best, also the items at the start and end of a list – and not those in the middle – and material that has emotional meaning for us.

Long-term memory is the greater part of our memory, which retains events, ideas, etc for days, months and years. Experimentally it is easy to divide long-term from short-term memory but the precise biochemical manner in which it works is still controversial. Long-term memory must be involved not just with remembering events but, crucially, with our sense of identity: when I wake up each morning I remember who I am.

Neuropsychologists have long hoped to find the biochemical 'memory trace' that will reveal just how memories are stored in the >brain. But they have had to use information from chicks, sea slugs and brain tissue recently to investigate the biochemistry. Wilder Penfield, the great neurologist, found in the late 1930s that electrical stimulation of the human >cortex did evoke the most remarkable long suppressed memories. Patients who were operated on under local anaesthetic came out with strings of ancient memories when their cortex was stimulated by electric currents. The memory traces were clearly there, dormant. Penfield's work fascinated those interested in memory but was hard to progress, though it did confirm that memory was largely encoded in stories, scenarios, the film script in the >mind. Memories are stored in chunks. Chunks may be held together because they all deal with one topic or they have subjective significance.

Long before psychology was a science, orators knew a great deal about how to use mnemonic cues (*see* Mnemonics) to remember huge tracts of speeches. Frances Yates (1966) in her *Art of Memory* has shown the retrieval cues classical and Renaissance orators used. But the biochemistry of memory remained highly speculative – and still is. There have been some interesting advances that show how >learning changes the >synapse. Work on day-old chicks shows that as they learn to recognize their mother both the number of synaptic vesicles and the length of the synapse increases. The rate of firing of neurons (*see* Neuron) also increases dramatically in the hours after learning. This looks as if a memory trace is being laid down. If these changes in the structure of the synapse don't take place the chick can't learn. Work on sea slugs suggests that two substances play a key part in consolidating memories – the hormone serotonin and cyclic AMP. Both these substances affect the electrical properties of individual synapses. Memory is curious because, while the psychological research on it has a long and sophisticated theory, psychologists are only now beginning to see how important it is for our sense of ourselves. My >identity is crucially dependent on what I remember, and how I remember what I have done. What has been less investigated is the role of emotions in creating and dissipating long-term memories. We tend to remember Marlow's >peak experiences – the night a child was born, for example – and 'peak' pains. Do we do so accurately? In some circumstances we edit experiences, or blot them out entirely. Each of our life stories is made up of how we string together our long-term memories. Psychology has yet to accept fully the remarkable mix of cognition and emotion involved in long-term memory, as experimental psychologists have focussed on the strategies by which we recall and retrieve. *See* Amnesia.

Short-term memory, the first and immediate stage of memory. William James first described it. It has severe limits. Most theories suggest that one can hold no more than 7 ±2 items in short-term memory. These items are very vulnerable. They can be forgotten quickly especially if new material comes along. Some theories of memory suggest that short-term memory is quite distinct from long-term memory. Recent work in levels of processing theory claims that the reason for the rapid decay of short-term memory items is that they are processed in a very superficial manner. *See also* Amnesia; Identity.

- Alan Baddeley, *Working Memory* (1993); Gillian Cohen, *Memory* (1986); G. Horn, *Memory Imprinting and the Brain* (1985); A. R. Luria, *The Mind of Mnemonist* (1969); Frances Yates, *The Art of Memory* (1966).

Menopause, the 'change of life' when women stop ovulating. Hormonal changes accompany it as women secret less oestrogen. The psychological consequences can be severe and can include >depression, >embarrassment because of hot flushes and a very fluctuating >libido. Hormone replacement therapy (HRT) has been considered something of a boon because it helps even out the hormonal imbalances which cause some of the problems associated with the menopause.

- A. Kahn and L. Hugney Holt, *Menopause – The Best Years of Your Life?* (1987).

Mental handicap, an arbitrary term. Children with an >IQ of under 80 are usually considered mentally handicapped though they can often be taught to manage a wide range of skills. Mental handicap does seem to be largely genetic and irreversible. However, improved training programmes and a higher expectation of what the mentally handicapped can achieve has led to many of them leading better lives.

Mental health. >Madness has long been seen as a calamity or a terrible illness, and researchers have devoted most of their work to studying the negative aspects of mental health. However, a new and interesting idea has emerged – that of positive mental health. Especially in the United States, there are endless schemes and brands of >therapy aimed at keeping you mentally healthy so that you can maximize your potential and make the most of your >mind and soul. Many of these notions are absurd, but some have a decent pedigree (*see* Maslow, Abraham) and appear partially to achieve their aims.

Factors that promote mental health include avoiding >loneliness, having a confiding relationship, being able to speak frankly about problems, having interesting work and not being under undue financial or emotional >stress. Sharing problems with people who suffer similar ones seems to be an important key to preventive >psychiatry; >self-help groups such as Alcoholics Anonymous do prevent stress, at least for some people to some extent.

The early psychologists such as >Freud and >Watson hoped that the new science would not just cure people of their psychological ills but would also give those who were not actually ill the insights they needed to best use their capacities (*see* Insight) It's an old hope that started during the Enlightenment of the 18th century with the ideal of the perfectibility of man. Watson suggested that psychology students drew up a 'balance sheet of the self' to see where they could improve themselves. This practical, optimistic idea lay dormant from the 1920s to the late 1950s, when >humanistic psychology began to argue that psychology ought to help us maximize our potential to reach >'self-actualization' in >work, >love and >play. Much of this was therapeutic hype of the sort that

143

the humorist James Thurber poked fun at in 1936 (*see* Introduction), but psychology ought, in principle, to be able to help people make the most of their capabilities and overcome their handicaps. In an increasingly self-conscious world, the interest in positive mental health is likely to grow.

● J. Newton, *Preventing Mental Illness* (1988).

Midlife crisis, when people in their 40s question where they have gone so far with their lives and feel that they are running out of time. This is often a time of psychological disturbance. It is, however, one of those concepts that create 'symptoms': now that experts have identified the mid-life crisis as a legitimate, 'real' crisis, more people suffer from it. *See also* Menopause.

Mind. One of the most problematic terms in psychology and philosophy. Is the mind non-material, akin to the soul, or is it the brain itself? From Descartes to the early 20th century scientists could not abandon the idea that humans had souls. There are some like the Nobel prize-winner Sir John Eccles, who still believe you cannot equate mind and brain, but most psychologists accept that the mind is 'in' the brain. *See* Consciousness; Dualism.

Minnesota Multiple Personality Inventory. The MMPI is a standard questionnaire testing >extraversion and introversion.

Mnemonics, mental devices which allow people to remember long sequences of information by flagging particular things. Usually, these are the initial letters of the things needed to be remembered – for example, the names of the Great Lakes of North America can be remembered via the word 'HOMES' (Huron, Ontario, Michigan, Erie, Superior). However, Frances Yates has shown how Renaissance scholars discovered that the Romans had used visual images very effectively. A Roman orator, having to remember a long speech, would identify each section of his oration with a niche in the amphitheatre in which he would be appearing; as he spoke, he would 'collect' the section from the series of niches.

Monoamine oxidase inhibitors (MAOIs), drugs that inhibit the action of MAO which itself reduces the levels of >adrenalin and >noradrenalin.

Mood swings, sharp swings from excitement to >depression, from high to low; a symptom of manic-depressive illness (*see* Mania).

Moreno, Jacob (1889–1974). Romanian psychoanalyst who founded >psychodrama and devised the technique known as >sociometry. Moreno emigrated to the United States where he set up a school of psychodrama. After his death, his third wife continued to teach psychodrama, giving devotees a real feel of historical continuity. *See* Dramatherapy.

Mother/child interaction. In all schools of psychology, what the mother gives the child is crucial. Neither the psychoanalysts nor the behaviourists realized that babies are well-programmed, 'wired' by Nature, to receive what their mothers or other care-givers have to offer. >John Bowlby argued that good, warm mother-child interaction was essential to the social, physical and emotional development of the child (*see* Bonding); those deprived of a bond with their mothers tend to have behavioural problems in their teens and later life. Psychologists in the 1970s, using video equipment to film how babies and mothers interacted, were able to plot an intricate web of behaviour. Gordon Wells (1981) charted the way that >language developed, with the mother repeating things. The Harvard psychologist Jerome Bruner showed that, when mothers taught children to play games such as >peekaboo, they also taught social values and how to take the initiative in starting them. Corwyn Trevarthen found that mothers respond to the pattern of their babies' cries. These discoveries all suggested that babies are born with capacities for social >learning and that mothers are their first teachers. Feminists argue that fathers and other loving care-givers could do this just as well, something Bowlby resisted initially very forcefully. He now concedes that he was wrong.

A very detailed study was carried out by Klaus and his colleagues on the effects of the first few days, even hours, of the mother-child relationship. Klaus and his team divided 28 women about to give birth into two groups. The first group of mothers were given a brief glimpse of their babies after they were born, identified them again 6–12 hours after the birth and then visited them for 20–30 minutes every four hours for feeds. The other 14 mothers were given much more extended contact with their babies: they were allowed to hold their newly born children and spend one of the first three hours after birth with them; during the remainder of their stay in hospital, they had an extra five hours' contact with their children every day.

The effects of this extended contact were found to be considerable when Klaus and his team saw the mothers again 28–32 days after the births. The women were asked if they let their babies cry for food and if they could leave them without feeling any pangs of >guilt on doing so or, at least, thinking about them while they were gone. The mothers who had had less contact with their babies after birth were significantly more willing to let their babies cry for food and they were more apt to go away from them without thinking of the babies' needs. Klaus's study shows how early postnatal behaviour does affect the bonding of the mother to the child.

In the late 1970s and early 1980s, much developmental psychology devoted itself to mapping out the ways in which the child becomes socially skilled through interaction with its mother and/or father. *See* Child development; Imprinting; Postnatal depression.

- John Bowlby, *A Secure Base* (1987); K. Kaye, *The Mental and Social Life of Babies* (1982).

Motivation. What drives people to do things has been a crucial area for psychology since its beginnings. Early psychologists tried to find a general law that would cover all motivation. They highlighted some basic biological >drives – hunger, thirst, sex and sleep. What motivated people and animals were simple needs to replenish deficits of these. Such theories are known as 'drive reduction theories' because the organism is motivated to reduce the level of the drives.

Clark Hull provided the most comprehensive of such theories. However, while this model made sense for food, drink and sleep, it did not easily fit sex. What is a sex deficit? Some perfectly well adjusted people have no sex lives. Then, in the late 1940s, psychologists found that rats and babies are driven by curiosity. They will seek to explore new territory as long as it doesn't appear unsafe. However, it doesn't follow that you are motivated to replenish a lack of curiosity. Drive-reduction theories also don't explain what makes a particular individual act in a particular way. Some argue that the best psychology can do is to frame general laws of motivation. Others claim this misses the point. Understanding what makes an individual do something is crucial for motivational studies. It is an ambition psychology should not forget. Theories of motivation have failed to deal with this issue adequately. That failure suggests that for more complex motives the only ways forward are either through self reports or through psychoanalytic techniques which will expose the real motivation underlying actions.

● D. McClelland, *Human Motivation* (1988).

Motor skills, skills which depend on movement and often on the coordination of >perception and movement. Walking and reaching for an object are both motor skills.

Multiple personality, a very rare condition, given the Hollywood treatment in *The Three Faces of Eve*, in which a person does have different and separate personalities. Not to be confused with >schizophrenia.

● John Rowan, *Subpersonalities* (1989).

nAch, the 'need to achieve'. *See* Achievement motivation.

Narcissism, concept named after the Greek, Narcissus, who fell in love with his own reflection in a pond. It was originally used by >Freud to describe two kinds of self-love: first, the infant's >love for him/herself before he or she can form >object relations; and second, the love that turns back to the self after withdrawing in a crisis of rejection from the real world. Narcissism can be defensive and prevent the development of ordinary relationships with others, but it can also be healthy, boosting a person's sense of >self-esteem.

● Sigmund Freud, *On Narcissism* (1914); S. Pulver, 'Narcissism: The Term and the Concept,' *Journal of the American Psychoanalysis Association*, 18, 319–41.

Nature/nurture controversy, a perennial debate going back to John Locke. Is a baby born with any >innate ideas or capacities or is everything learned? This dispute is now debated in scientific rather than philosophical terms. Are abilities or even personality traits the result of genetic inheritance or the environment?

Locke argued that, when a baby is born, its >mind is a *tabula rasa* (literally 'scraped table') and everything is learned from experience – nurture triumphs over Nature. But Locke's ideas were even controversial when he developed them in the 1680s. Other philosophers, such as Spinoza, Leibniz and (later) Kant, claimed that experience could not account for all >learning. There had to be a structure, an organization of the mind that was capable of assimilating the experiences the infant was exposed to. In the late 19th century, the philosophical debate became a scientific one. Those who favoured Nature argued that heredity (*see* Genetic factors) determine abilities and >personality; those who favoured nurture claimed that learning and >conditioning alone shaped human beings.

At first, nurture had it largely its own way, at least in >Anglo-American psychology. The behaviourists, for example, played down heredity. >J. B. Watson said that if he were given the care of children until they were seven, he could totally shape their futures. The ideology of psychology, especially in America, favoured the importance of experience and learning. Psychological techniques could change people for the better. Initially, this was not seen as a left-wing position. The pre-eminence of nurture was challenged in the 1970s by some psychologists such as >Hans Eysenck and the sociobiologists who have claimed that heredity is crucial, with the result that they have been identified with right-wing politics (*see* Jensen controversy; Sociobiology). More controversial is the position of the left-wing psycholinguist >Noam Chomsky, who says that Locke was so wrong that his arguments can be ignored. Chomsky suggests that the capacity to learn >language comes from 'Nature' and is 'wired' into all human beings, and this may be true of other aspects of our ability to communicate.

It has become clear that neither the extreme Nature nor the extreme nurture position is generally true. Some >longitudinal studies such as the Colorado Adoption Project are trying to unravel in more detail than ever before the contribution of both and how they interact. The complexity of the interaction between genetic factors and environment has often been ignored. For example, much intelligence is heritable but it is also affected by nutrition, background and simple teaching. It is also true that no amount of special skills will turn someone with a low >IQ into a nuclear physicist. Attempts to isolate genes that are responsible for particular abilities or personality traits continue, but the genes themselves can only unfold in an environment that permits it.

- Robert Plomin, John De Fries and David Fuller, *Nature and Nuture in Infancy and Early Childhood* (1988); E. O. Wilson, *Sociobiology* (1975).

Neckar cube, a cube which is so drawn that, when observed, it appears to reverse itself – first one edge, then another, seems to be the leading one. The >brain has no apparent control over these alternations. Our alternating >perception of the cube is cited as an illustration of how, in perception, the brain tests hypotheses.

- R. Gregory, *Eye and Brain* (1980).

Needs. *See* Hierarchy of needs.

Negative reinforcement. This is not the same as punishment, although it is often confused with it. Negative reinforcement is, in fact, the avoidance of aversive or unpleasant stimuli such as electric shocks or anxiety attacks. Negative reinforcement is biologically sensible: it rewards the animal whose response to the appearance of danger is to hide efficiently. However, the responses that negative reinforcement rewards can also be inappropriate and defensive. A good example is someone who has a >phobia about dogs – the sight of a dog produces (given previous classical >conditioning) unpleasant physiological stimuli and the person then avoids the dog. There is reinforcement because the unpleasant physiological responses disappear, and as a result, the behaviour (avoiding dogs) is strengthened. The person has 'learned' to have a phobia about dogs.

Responses which are negatively reinforced are very hard to extinguish. Popular culture acknowledges their force in >jokes – for example, 'I wear a red rose to keep elephants away.' 'But there aren't any elephants here.' 'It works then, doesn't it?' *See* Aversion therapy; Reinforcement.

Neo-behaviourism, an approach which developed out of >behaviourism. The neo-behaviourists were willing to allow the study of some non-observable behaviours such as >thinking as long as there were external indications of what thinking achieved. Neo-behaviourism, in its turn, developed into >cognitive psychology.

Neo-Freudians, a school of American psychoanalysts including Harry Stack Sullivan and Erich Fromm, who replaced both the biological and individualistic emphasis of >Freud with a concern for interpersonal relationships. They also stressed the link between the individual and his culture.

Sullivan stated that 'the environment flows through the living cell' – that is, a person can't be seen as distinct from his or her social environment. This led Sullivan to an interest in communication. >Karen Horney, another leading neo-Freudian, argued that people could only realize their potential through good personal relationships. She said that individuals tend either to move away from or towards other people, and when extreme, either tendency is destructive. Erich Fromm, influenced by Marxism, claimed that, while everyone has common biological drives – to eat, sleep, drink, etc – it is through interaction with society that people define themselves.

The neo-Freudians were diverse and did not form a school with a neat set of theories. Rather, they offered a set of alternatives to Freud while recognizing the value of his work.

● J. A. C. Brown, *Freud and the neo-Freudians* (1966); E. Fromm, *Man For Himself* (1949); H. S. Sullivan, *The Interpersonal Theory of Psychiatry* (1953).

Nervous system, the basic distribution of nerves in the body. There are two parts: the *central nervous system*, which consists of the >brain and spinal cord; and the *peripheral nervous system*, the nerves of which extend from the brain and spinal cord to the rest of the body. Included in the peripheral nervous system is the *autonomic nervous system*, which governs the organs of blood circulation, breathing, digestion, excretion and reproduction, and which is not normally under conscious control.

Networking, making contacts with other people and, through them, further contacts. The term is now applied to therapy groups as well as to business. Networking is seen as part of the 'New Age' sub-culture which offers a mix of >encounter groups and mysticism.

Neural networks. The existence of neural networks (ie networks of nerves) has been deduced both from connections in the brain anatomy and the ways in which neurons are linked in the >brain. Memories may be encased in specific neural networks, and >language may be based in overlapping sets of networks. This overlapping may be the reason why, if one network fails, it may be possible to employ other pathways to reinstate the 'lost' speech. The specific organization of neural networks is hard to establish. *See* Neuron.

Neuroleptics, drugs which depress the central >nervous system and are used in the treatment of psychotic conditions. Neuroleptics calm >schizophrenics, but have to be distinguished from tranquillizers. Well-known neuroleptics include chlorpromazine and other phenoziathines. There are anxieties about their side-effects, especially >tardive dyskinesia.

Neurology, the physiological study of the >brain and the medical speciality which treats brain diseases.

Neuron, the basic unit of the >nervous system; the nerve cell. The neuron is made up of the *soma* (cell body), several branched processes (projections) called *dendrites*, and the *axon*, a single long process. These processes either receive information and send it back to the >brain or spinal cord, or they convey signals from these to organs, muscles, etc. They connect with each other via synapses. *See* Neural networks; Sensory neurons; Synapse.

Neurosis. Arguments rage over whether this is a psychiatric illness or merely a part of the human condition. The term is commonly used in both senses. Thus, psychiatrists speak of neurotic patients while some very successful people, such as the American film maker Woody Allen, make a wonderful living out of examining their supposedly crippling neuroses. Allen is clearly not sick. >Freud saw neurosis as a defence against overwhelming >anxiety. Usually, neuroses are less disabling than >schizophrenia. The neurotic can function and usually has some insight into his, or her, problems. Freud believed that if neurotics achieved >insight into their problems, they would resolve them. It has not turned out to be so simple. Many neurotics come to cling to their symptoms which gain them sympathy, attention and an excuse for bad behaviour. Tranquillizers are often used as treatment, as are various talk therapies. What distinguishes neuroses from psychoses is that neuroses are believed to respond to psychotherapy. Those who claim that a measure of neuroticism is perfectly normal include >Hans Eysenck. His theory of >personality has >neuroticism as a key personality trait. People who score high on neuroticism are anxious and easily shamed. Neurosis would seem to be both part of the human condition and, taken to extreme, a psychiatric condition.

Neuroticism, a personality trait measured by >Eysenck. Neuroticism involves high >anxiety as well as a tendency to feel shame and >guilt.

Neurotic personality, a person who suffers from excess >anxiety. This is not really a scientific term.

Neurotransmitters, chemical substances which pass a nervous impulse either to the next >neuron along the line (across a >synapse) or to an organ (eg a muscle). To identify a chemical as a neurotransmitter, it should be present at the nerve end; it should be released when the neuron fires; a cell that can be activated should, when artificially exposed to the chemical, mimic what happens if the nerve is stimulated; there should be an uptake mechanism in the synaptic space to inactivate the chemical. There are at least eight substances that fit these criteria, including >dopamine, >acetylcholine, >serotonin, histamine, >noradrenalin and glutamate.

Much treatment for particular illnesses involves affecting neurotransmitters, either by boosting or suppressing their working. >Chlorpromazine, for example, reduces dopamine action and is used to combat >schizophrenia. Imipramine, on the other hand, increases serotonin and noradrenalin action by lengthening the time they can act on a receptor; it is used as an >antidepressant. The isolation of neurotransmitters has had a major impact on the development of drug treatments.

N

Noise. In psychology and information theory, noise is what conceals or distorts a signal. Studies of >hearing have tried to identify the levels of noise at which it becomes impossible to hear messages, or they become grossly distorted. Certain signals or stimuli (*see* Stimulus) such as one's name tend to get through even the thickest noise, suggesting that there is some kind of filter or device that is primed to receive really important signals. Some evidence also suggests that mothers respond acutely to the sound of their baby crying. Psychologists are also interested in the effects of noise. Prolonged, intense noise can cause >stress.

Non-directive therapy. In theory, this is a form of >therapy in which therapist and client are equals and the latter is not told what to do, or cajoled or persuaded. Carl Rogers first used the term but then switched to >client-centred therapy. One reason was that it became clear to him that it is virtually impossible for a therapist to be non-directive. Studies of how non-directive therapists behave show that they still tend to give advice and offer instructions. It seems difficult to exclude direction from the therapeutic relationship.

Non-rapid eye movement (NREM) sleep, periods of sleep when the eyes do not move behind the eyelids. Originally it was thought that no >dreaming took place during such sleep, but it was later found that those who were woken up from NREM sleep did sometimes report themselves in the middle of a >dream but less often than in >rapid eye movement (REM) sleep.

● Ian Oswald, *Sleep* (1980).

Non-verbal behaviour. *See* Body language.

Non-verbal communication, systems of communication that do not depend on words. This became a fashionable concept in the 1960s even though writers and philosophers had long known that gestures and posture expressed much. For instance, >Darwin studied non-verbal communication even though he didn't label it as such when, in 1872, he published *The Expression of the Emotions in Animals and Man*, for he looked at signals – especially of alarm – that different species make. Non-verbal communication is not a >language for it tends to convey specific signals in specific situations only, but, despite its inflexibility, it can be effective. Primate research has identified a vocabulary of signals that various species such as the baboons employ to warn of predators. In some species, there are fairly elaborate rituals which involve signals of threat and submission – eg the threat display of wolves.

Human beings also engage in non-verbal communication – usually to show off power or to express sexual attraction (*see* Body language). Different cultures have different ideas of personal space which means that sometimes non-verbal communication can go awry. For example, friendly Arabs will think it natural to stand very close to whomever they are talking to, whereas Europeans will find such proximity threatening.

Noradrenalin, a >neurotransmitter involved in the biochemistry of >depression. Recent theories suggest that it is broken down and rendered inactive by monoamine oxidase (*see* Monoamine oxidase inhibitors). The neurotransmitter becomes inert and contributes to the listlessness of the individual.

Normal. Psychologists agree that it is very hard to define what is 'normal' behaviour in any set of situations as these differ from culture to culture. In Western Europe, for example, children are reared in nuclear families, but elsewhere, they may be reared by extended families. At best, there is only normal behaviour within a particular class or culture and even that is debatable. Many psychologists are worried by the fact that the discipline is much more interested in studying abnormal than normal behaviour. Most people spend most of their time behaving normally, but few good studies have mapped out what that is. A recent useful technique has been self-monitoring. In this, a person wears a bleeper and, whenever it bleeps, jots in a diary what they are doing. As a result, they build up a detailed picture of how they spend their time. One engaging study by the psychologist E. J. Dearnley concluded that he spent too much time in the pub!

- E. J. Dearnley, 'Experimental Self Monitoring', paper presented to British Psychological Society Annual Conference, reported in *Psychology News*, 7 (1981).

Normal distribution, a statistical concept originally formulated by >Sir Francis Galton. When he plotted the measures of a variety of human characteristics, he found that they fitted a hump-shaped curve. Most people's scores were in the middle so the curve was highest there. Galton called this curve (with fewer individuals at either extreme) 'normal distribution'. It is important in psychology because many statistical tests depend on finding out how different from this normal distribution the scores of a particular >sample are. Once they differ from the norm, then you can begin to ask why. *See* Skewness.

Null hypothesis, the hypothesis that psychology experiments seek to disprove. It says that a particular independent variable has no effect or that the results of a study are due to chance. Experiments usually try to define how low the probability is that the null hypothesis is correct. This figure is called the 'significance level'. The acceptable level is usually p.05, ie that there is less than a .05 or less than $\frac{1}{20}$ chance of the null hypothesis being true. *See* Significant difference.

Nurturing, what parents ought to be for children. To nurture is to look after, to care for, to support the development of. Children who are deprived of nurturing suffer all the problems of >maternal deprivation. *See* Bowlby, John; Mother-child interaction; Nature/nurture controversy.

N

Obesity. The psychology of obesity has long interested psychologists. Two basic models have been offered, the first being physiological. We overeat because there is something askew in the appetite-regulating part of the >hypothalamus. Mice with >lesions in their hypothalamus never stop eating. The second model is a compensatory one. Obese people seek to compensate for lack of >love or success by stuffing themselves. Since 'stuffing' has sexual meanings, too, the explanation sounds plausible. >Freud argued that some people remain stuck at the >oral phase and they seek gratification through food. Susie Orbach has suggested that some women eat in order to make themselves unattractive, to avoid the stereotypes of a patriarchal society and take themselves off the sexual market. *See* Anorexia, Bulimia.

● Susie Orbach, *Fat Is a Feminist Issue* (1979).

Objective psychological test, a test where the format – and in some cases, the answers – is predetermined. There are clearly defined, explicit rules which give the individual little latitude for qualifying answers. Unlike >projective tests, the examiner is similarly constrained. An objective personality test might ask, 'Do you like going to parties?' with the option of answering 'Yes' or 'Sometimes' or 'No'. The respondent is not given the opportunity to qualify his or her answer – for example, 'I accept every invitation to parties but people rarely invite me,' 'I have lots of invitations to parties but I always refuse them,' 'I will always go to parties but only if I think there will be a lot of women/men/alcohol/loud music/soft music/no music/lively conversation/good food,' 'Either going to, or abstaining from, parties is of no interest to me. What I really like doing is . . .' Therefore, the 'objectiveness' of an objective test and the ease of comparing one individual's results with those of others may be gained at the expense of getting really relevant and specific information. Nevertheless, objective tests play an important part in psychology. The skill lies in knowing how to interpret them and realizing their merits and limits.

Object permanence, also sometimes known as 'object constancy'. The ability to know that an object stays the same even if it disappears from view. >Jean Piaget found that infants under the age of six months tended not to think that. As far as their >egocentric selves were concerned, if an object disappeared from view behind a pillow it ceased to be – to be was to be perceived. However, Tom Bower has suggested that Piaget was wrong, after a series of experiments which showed that babies' eyes follow the likely path of an object after it has disappeared from view.

Object relations, a development of >psychoanalysis which shifted emphasis from the instinctual >drives that >Freud made so much of. Its two most influential thinkers were >Melanie Klein and the British analyst R. Fairbairn. Object relations theory suggests that an >instinct doesn't just seek to satisfy an impulse in order to discharge tension; rather, it seeks appropriate objects. People, Fairbairn argued, are not just frantically pleasure-seeking. The term 'object relations' suggests, furthermore, some kind of relationship between subject and object. Although this is not the same as the theories of the >neo-Freudians, there are parallels between the two movements in the way that both seek to move away from classical psychoanalysis while retaining much of its core.

Oblique rotation. >Factor analysis is a method which extracts the underlying connections from data, teasing out which factors account for most of the variance. Oblique rotation is a technique which makes it possible to extract the corrolations between factors. The personality theorist R. B. Cattell favours an oblique rotation and has produced 16 personality factors ('16PF'). >Eysenck, on the other hand, claims that Cattell's factors are not independent, and the intercorrelations in turn 'require to be submitted to factor analytic studies'. Eysenck claims that Cattell's 16PF can be reduced to three personality dimensions. *See* Correlations in psychology; Orthogonal factors.

● R. B. Cattell, *The Structure of Personality and Environment* (1979); H. J. Eysenck, *The Structure of Human Personality* (1953).

Observational studies, research which does not tamper with 'natural life' but merely seeks to record as fully as possible what is going on. This sounds easy but it is, in fact, notoriously difficult to capture the various cues, stimuli (*see* Stimulus), responses and sequences that make up even a minute of 'ordinary' behaviour. In the last ten years, the advent of cheap, portable video cameras has made observational studies far easier since these can film what is happening and later on the psychologist can analyse the tapes. As a result, there has been a growth in the number of such studies.

Obsessional neurosis, one of the more distressing of the neuroses. Someone who suffers from it will feel compelled to carry out the same task time after time – for example, hand washing or making sure that all the doors in a house are locked or the gas is turned off. According to >Freud, obsessions are, like all neuroses, a defence. By engaging in this meaningless activity, the person wards off some underlying crippling >anxiety. Obsessional >neurosis is not easy to cure. Some behaviour modification techniques (*see* Behaviour therapy) work well, but psychoanalysts complain that such techniques deal just with the symptoms, not with the underlying causes of the behaviour.

Occupational psychology, the area of psychology that examines how people work, job satisfaction, the stresses they suffer, how to provide the best incentives and how to devise the most effective tests to find out if someone will be able to perform a job well. Its original aim was to maximize industrial efficiency but it has become more widely used recently, partly as people expect more from their working lives. Until recently, most men defined their identity in terms of the job they did: now, they are less one dimensional. Industrial psychologist, John Topliss, has argued traditional >personality tests don't offer a good way of testing how well people perform. The best way is to try and train them on the job. C. Cooper and M. Smith have recommended ways of dealing with >stress at work. The growth of occupational psychology reflects changing concerns about work.

● C. Cooper and M. Smith, *Job Stress and Blue Collar Work* (1985).

Occupational therapy, the use of work in therapy. If nothing else, it helps to pass the time in hospital. OT departments often offer some kind of craft work and very simple industrial tasks. In theory, the idea is to retrain patients to work in order to regain skills and confidence. In reality, however, most OT departments get patients to do menial jobs, such as packing, at low rates of pay. Consequently, the experience is far from positive.

Oedipus complex. >Freud claimed that Sophocles' tragedy *Oedipus Rex* encapsulated the human dilemma. The boy is in love with his mother; his father is his rival. Furious >jealousy rages in the boy who wants to kill the father and possess the mother. Freud got the idea of the Oedipus complex from his own self-analysis as well as from Sophocles. Given the secrecy surrounding sex, it was not too clear what possession of the mother actually meant. Incest or just the exclusion of the father? Oedipal boys resolved their problem by identifying with their fathers and thus, by proxy, 'love' their mothers. Experimental attempts to prove the Oedipus complex have never been very successful since it is hard to interview six-year-olds on such emotive topics. *See* Electra complex.

Olfaction. *See* Smell.

One- and two-tailed significance tests: different statistical techniques. One-tailed tests are used when the expected direction of a difference has been specified in advance because they take into account only one 'tail' of the probability distribution. Two-tailed tests are proper when there has been no prior prediction of the direction of a difference, whether, for example, the introduction of variable A (taking a vitamin) will improve or diminish performance on a particular test.

One/off law. A >neuron in the >brain is either on or off, firing (ie in a state of excitation) or not.

One-trial learning, >learning in which the subject masters the task in one go; the opposite of >trial-and-error learning. One-trial learning occurs in classical >conditioning usually when there is a very strong, unpleasant >stimulus such as a drink which causes vomiting (in the treatment of alcoholism). It has also been argued that, in human beings, magical or superstitious belief often occurs as a result of one-trial learning – eg 'I only have to see one >vision of a saint to become a truly religious man.'

Ontogeny, the development of the individual. This term is frequently used in the phrase 'ontogeny recapitulates phylogeny'. What this means is that the way an individual grows repeats the way the species did. The most quoted example of this is that human embryos have gills because our ancestors were once adapted to marine life.

Operant conditioning, a form of >conditioning identified and developed by >B. F. Skinner. Skinner noticed that in classical conditioning, autonomic responses, which are usually not under any kind of conscious control, are often strengthened. Skinner worked with naturally occurring behaviours and then strengthened them. Thus, while >Pavlov conditioned dogs to salivate at the ringing of a bell, Skinner conditioned pigeons to direct their natural pecking at a ping-pong ball so that eventually they were able to peck a ball to play ping-pong. For Pavlov, the point of the study was to show that dogs could learn to salivate to a non-food >stimulus. He didn't then *use* this canine ability. In operant conditioning, the idea is to produce useful sequences of behaviour – like birds playing ping-pong.

Skinner argued that, in real life, operant conditioning is much the more significant process. It underlies how we learn many behaviours such as driving a car or even reading poetry, both of which are under our conscious control. He also argued that our feeling of control was an illusion since our '>reinforcement history' actually determined our actions.

Operant conditioning is both impressive and a well-established concept, but to claim that it accounts for all >learning is extreme. Skinner even devised a utopia based on responsible operant conditioning.

● B. F. Skinner, *Science and Human Behaviour* (1953).

Opponent processing, a theory in colour >vision developed by E. Hering in the 19th century initially. According to this theory, there are six primary colour qualities – red, green, blue, yellow, black and white. In the >brain, there are independent >neural networks that correspond to each of these but these networks are not independent. Rather, they are organized into three pairs of 'opponent process' – red/green; blue/yellow; black/white. The colour perceived depends on the balance of the first two pairs which make up the hue system. Thus, if the light from an object tips the red/green balance towards the red and the blue/yellow balance towards blue, the object will be seen as violet. If both hue systems are in balance, no colour is perceived.

In the 19th century, there was no neurophysiological evidence for the theory, but recordings from single-cell electrodes now suggest that many cells do behave rather as the theory suggests. For instance, in some animals, if a yellow light is seen, not only do yellow responsive cells fire but the cells responding to blue are inhibited. *See* Young Helmholtz theory.

Oral stage, the first stage in >psychosexual development according to >Freud. During it, infants experience the mouth as the erogenous zone. They mouth, kiss, eat and suck with relish and these actions are their main ways of communicating with the outside world. >Erikson in his analysis of eight stages suggested that a successful transition from the oral stage was important if infants were to develop basic trust, the trust that would underpin a good mutual relationship between mother and child. There have been many critics of the oral stage who claim that it is wrong to see it as an exclusive stage. However, in his analysis of Freudian ideas, Paul Kline concluded that there was some evidence that infants do relish oral activities for a particular period.

- Erik Erikson, *Childhood and Society* (1963); P. Kline, *Fact and Fantasy in Freudian Theory* (1972).

Organic disorders, in medicine, a disease or condition in which structural changes in organs can be found, as opposed to 'functional' disorders, in which function is disturbed with no apparent changes in structures. In >brain disease, if a disorder is organic, it was traditionally seen as being *not* of psychological origin. Therefore, if a >lesion causes a person not to recall faces, there was no need to waste time trying to understand what deep psychological causes, such as >repression, might be at work. However, this is not particularly logical. Some imbalance in the brain could be caused by emotional factors. Recent work which shows that high expressed emotions can lead to outbreaks of >schizophrenia suggests this, and it might be that we will discover both emotional and organic changes in some states of schizophrenia.

Organizational behaviour, the study of how organizations behave and how people behave in organizations. It has become increasingly important and psychologists are now employed by many large corporations. Initially, many psychologists were critical of how people behaved in companies, and many analyses tried to compare life in the corporate jungle with life in the real jungle. The executive ape sought status and rewards much as his ancestors fought for nuts, berries and mates. More recent work in >occupational psychology, however, has shown a rather different trend. Executives have become much more self-critical. Many are beginning to realize that corporate life isn't good for their health. Feminists have been dismayed to find that when women progress in organizations they now pay the same health price as men used to. Some studies, not surprisingly, show that managers are reacting to this situation. They want different rewards. There is evidence in the USA that the initial tendency was to believe that managers were becoming less willing to manage. The subsequent trend towards self-employment, towards self-development within a career has helped to make this a crucial area for psychologists in industry. Much attention is now being paid to how to restructure work within organizations so that people don't leave. Some organizational experts argue that in the 1990s the typical organization will be less a pyramid (with its rigid hierarchies) and more a circle, with people 'networking' despite different levels of jobs. It's an intriguing possibility. Japan may remain, for now, the only country where the original corporate man and woman still thrive.

● F. Blackler and S. Shimmin, *Applying Psychology in Organizations* (1984).

Orgone, an entirely mythical substance that played a large part in the work of >Wilhelm Reich. Reich argued that one of the main reasons for the rigidities of >personality which caused unhappiness and which he called the 'character armour' was a lack of orgasms. After a period of trauma, Reich found the solution in the Milky Way in outer space: there was abundant orgone which prompted the flow of orgasms. Reich, still taken seriously, then invented a device called the 'orgone box', which resembled a wooden telephone box without a telephone and which was able to collect orgone. The person deficient in orgasms had only to step inside to have a wonderful experience. Reich was eventually arrested by the US Food and Drugs Administration for fraud in the selling of these orgone boxes. He seems, however, to have been sincere in his belief in the existence of orgone.

● D. Boadella, *Wilhelm Reich* (1985); C. Rycroft, *Reich* (1980).

Orienting reflex, the reflex that causes us to turn towards a sudden, unexpected >stimulus such as a sharp noise. Studies show that with this reflex there are sharp changes in heart rate, muscle tone and >brain waves. As a result, animals (including humans) are better prepared to cope with what may turn out to be danger. If such a noise recurs, however, we respond less and less to it because of >habituation.

Orthogonal factors. In >factor analysis, these are factors which are uncorrelated. In analyzing data, psychologists can use a procedure known as orthogonal rotation. This keeps the angles between factors at 90 degrees. If one imagines the factors as lines on a graph, they are rotated to keep the angle between the different factors at 90 degrees so that the factors can be studied independently of each other. It's a technique which has been used in the study of intelligence.

In his studies, L. L. Thurstone identified seven factors or 'primary mental abilities'. J. P. Guilford, on the other hand, favours orthogonal rotation and insists that there are at least 120 distinct intellectual abilities. Guilford and his students set themselves the task of determining how many of these 'logical factors', or distinct intellectual abilities, actually exist and constructing a measure or test of each. *See* Correlations in psychology; Oblique rotation.

Outgroup, a group outside the main or central group. It is often used as a scapegoat for society's problems and evils. Jews in Nazi Germany were the classic instance.

P

Pain, a feeling, usually physical, which is uncomfortable and serves as a warning signal. The pain of burning, for example, tells us to move our hand away from the flame. The pain felt in most conditions does warn that something is wrong and is, therefore, a shock. The physiology of pain is well established. Impulses received by pain receptors in the skin travel very rapidly to the >brain partly through the use of the >volley principle. However, the psychology of pain is more problematic. The same amount of pain >stimulus doesn't produce the same intensity of pain. A person's motivations and expectations will affect the way pain is felt. Pain research has established that subjects differentiate many sorts of pain, ranging from the sharp to the slow and thudding. Relaxation and mental attitude can help diminish the feelings of pain. Such complexities have led doctors to set up pain clinics which teach people how to handle pain – especially that associated with long chronic illnesses. *See also* Gate theory.

● R. Melzack, *The Puzzle of Pain* (1973).

Paradoxical intention, a therapeutic technique in which sufferers are asked to imagine or do that which they fear most. One of its originators, Viktor Frankl, explained how, if people were frightened of having a heart attack, he would get them to try having a heart attack. When they did, they, of course, found that they could not bring one on. Frankl argued that the experience often helped people to get a better perspective on their fears. This technique could also be interpreted as a >one-trial learning experience.

● Viktor Frankel, *Logotherapy* (1967).

Paradoxical sleep. *See* Dreams.

Parallel distributed processing. A new theory that attempts to understand how the >brain integrates sensory information. It used to be thought that visual information was broken down in the superior colliculus, a structure in the

>cortex literally half-way between the retina and area 17 of the cortex where visual information is integrated. As a result, information about what an object was and where it was would be processed separately. Recently, it's been found that the analysis of visual information isn't done in such a compartmentalized way. Information about different parts of the visual >stimulus keeps on being processed in parallel. The information is combined to achieve a complete sensory image. Other senses also appear to work in this way.

- James McCelland and David E. Rumelhart, *Parallel Distributed Processing* (1986).

Parameter, a descriptive summary of some characteristic of a population.

Parametric test, a test which involves estimating a population >parameter.

P

Paranoia, a state of >mind in which people feel persecuted (by real individuals or by 'voices in the head') and that people are conspiring against them. It is considered a major symptom of >schizophrenia: some schizophrenics are called 'paranoid schizophrenics'. The causes of paranoia are assumed to involve some form of >organic malfunction as well as contradictory experiences in childhood. Some see it as a personality disorder.

Biological psychiatrists believe that feelings of paranoia are caused by organic factors and do not have any particular meaning. However, some psychoanalysts try to explain paranoid fantasies. One of the more interesting attempts is the concept of the 'paranoid schizoid position' introduced by >Melanie Klein. She used it to describe normal development in the first few months of life. The infantile >ego is very fragile and easily gives way to fears of annihilation, and to get rid of these, they are projected outwards, and things and people are characterized as being wholly good or wholly bad. Klein argued that schizophrenic disorders are rooted in this process. In some patients, the >splitting of objects and self is so extreme as to lead to paranoia.

- Melanie Klein, *The Writings of Melanie Klein*, vol. 3 (1946).

Paranormal phenomena. Psychology has long been perplexed by paranormal phenomena such as >telekinesis, >telepathy, >extrasensory perception (ESP) and >clairvoyance. These would, if proved, show that >mind could affect matter in ways that defy physical and psychological laws. Scientists have demanded that those who believe in the existence of such phenomena should produce especially rigorous proofs, and experimental designs to test for them have to be tougher than designs in ordinary psychological studies. However, believers in the paranormal argue that telepathy and other phenomena are not easily replicable, as they tend to be spontaneous and often occur at emotionally charged moments.

Over 100 years after the creation of the Society for Psychical Research in Britain, there is still remarkably little agreement on the worth of the evidence for various paranormal claims. Since 1975, the position has become more complicated because a number of physicists – and psychology defers to physics as a proper, exact science – have put forward speculative models of how subatomic matter works which makes some paranormal claims slightly more plausible. The debate over the paranormal shows no sign of resolution, and it generates powerful emotions. On the 'pro' side, there are groups such as the Society for Psychical Research; on the 'anti' side, there is the Committee for the Study of Phenomena Deemed Paranormal and others.

● Brian Inglis, *The Paranormal* (1984); D. Rhine, *New Frontiers of the Mind* (1973).

Parapsychology, the study of areas of human behaviour in which >mind seems to triumph over matter. There has been a Society for Psychical Research since 1880. It has sponsored investigations in >clairvoyance, >telepathy, >extrasensory perception (ESP), psychokinesis. Those who believe in the paranormal claim that science is unfair to them. It demands far more rigorous standards of proof from them than from other branches of psychology. Conventional psychologists respond by saying that the claims of parapsychology are so incredible that they need to be tested with this degree of rigour. There is some evidence that paranormal skills do exist. *See* Paranormal phenomena; Psychokinesis.

Partial correlation, the correlation between two variables with the effects of a third variable held constant. A study of the aggressive behaviour of subjects who have drunk eight lagers in temperatures of 10É and 25É might well find a partial correlation between alcohol, heat and rowdiness. You would say heat partially correlates with rowdiness.

Partial reinforcement. In >operant conditioning a condition in which >reinforcement isn't given every time the required behaviour is shown. It is also known as intermittent reinforcement. >B. F. Skinner showed that it was very powerful in establishing behaviour because the animal, or person, persisted in behaviour even when it wasn't rewarded every time.

Pattern recognition. A crucial ability in visual >perception. We have to be able to recognize patterns and to judge how these match patterns we are used to seeing. If you weren't able to recognize patterns, you couldn't make sense of the visual world. The ability to do so seems to depend on the >temporal lobe.

Pavlov, Ivan (1849–1936), Soviet physiologist who discovered how animals could be conditioned. Pavlov's classic experiment was in dog >conditioning. The prospect of food prompts the automatic response of salivation in dogs. Pavlov rang a bell just before food was given to his dogs. The bell came to signal food, and the dogs eventually began to salivate whenever they heard the bell, even if food did not always arrive shortly after it rang. The bell became, therefore, the conditioned >stimulus, its sound sufficient to make the dog salivate. This conditioning provided the model for much >learning theory, and >J. B. Watson, the behaviourist, used Pavlov's ideas to explain how we form chains of behaviour.

Pavlov stayed on in the USSR after the 1917 revolution and his laboratory was protected by Lenin personally. He was to have a remarkable effect on the development of psychology and >psychiatry in the Soviet Union. Marx had argued that human beings are social animals and that our personalities are moulded by our social interaction – rather like Locke, he had assumed that human beings became what they were through experience. A Marxist psychology would, therefore, play down the influence of biological and organic factors. Pavlov's influence was such, however, that the post-revolution Soviet Union developed forms of psychiatry and psychology which Marx would have denounced: mental illness and the basic foundations of >personality were seen as organic. Psychologists such as Lev Vygotsky who opposed this idea were persecuted, and it has taken over 50 years for Pavlov's domination of Soviet psychology to be challenged.

- David Cohen, *Soviet Psychiatry* (1989); J. Gray, *Pavlov* (1981); J. Valsiner, *Developmental Psychology in the USSR* (1988).

P

Peak experience, part of the jargon of >encounter group culture. The term was coined by Fritz Perls, the founder of >Gestalt therapy, and >Abraham Maslow, one of the fathers of >humanistic psychology. A peak experience is a sublime 'high'. Making love and having the earth move, watching a magnificent sunset, winning a takeover battle – all were peak experiences. Maslow wanted to increase the number of peak experiences that people had because, he claimed, these were highly creative. Encounter groups were supposed to create opportunities for more peak experiences, but, unfortunately, these group experiences tended to be outside real life. With the decline of 'happy chic', peak experiences have become a shade *passé*.

Peekaboo. Psychological interest in the game of peekaboo was stimulated by Jerome Bruner, the Harvard psychologist. He showed that, as mothers taught their offspring to play peekaboo, they didn't just teach them the game but also a set of social rules that were crucial for learning how to interact with others. Bruner discovered that, at first, mothers took the initiatives in the game, but from nine months on, infants would begin to demand the game be played with them. He also showed that, by 15 months, most infants understood the rules of peekaboo, even though they could not, of course, articulate them. Bruner's description of how young children learn to master peekaboo is an important and elegant display of child psychology at its most revealing. *See* Child development; Mother/child interaction.

- J. S. Bruner, K. Sylva and H. Jolly, *Play* (1981).

Peer group, a group of people of the same age and class; a term usually used in child psychology.

Penfield, Wilder (1891–1976), Canadian neurosurgeon who, in order to treat >epilepsy, opened up the >brain while patients were conscious, using only a local anaesthetic. In order to find the location of the epileptic focus, he then applied a low electric current to parts of the >cortex of the brain. Patients responded with memories, sometimes sad, sometimes ecstatic. Penfield's research was important in revealing how much is stored in the brain and the complex layers of >consciousness, and in mapping the sensory and motor areas of the cortex.

Penis envy. According to >Freud, all girls envy the fact that boys have a penis. This is responsible for their castration anxiety and affects their >psychosexual development. However, even Freud's admiring biographer, Ernest Jones, has suggested that this phallocentric view was perhaps a shade extreme. Feminist psychoanalysts have argued that Freud was essentially sexist in believing that women regret that they aren't men. Some, such as the British psychoanalyst Juliet Mitchell, have claimed, however, that feminists have misunderstood Freud. *See* Feminist psychology; Horney, Karen.

● Juliet Mitchell, *Psychoanalysis and Feminism* (1985).

P

Perception. Because different theories account for how the eyes, ears, nose and skin take in information from the outside world, each of these is treated separately. *See* Hearing; Pain; Pitch, Perception of; Smell; Taste; Touch; Vision. In every case, the process of perception involves a complex interplay of >receptors and >central nervous system functions.

Perceptual defence, a phenomenon in which subjects take longer to recognize and read sexually suggestive words. Women take even longer than men. It's not entirely clear if this is due to some in-built filter or is an example of subjects not really wishing to shock the experimenter.

Perceptual psychology, the study of how we hear, feel, taste, see and smell. *See* Hearing; Pain; Pitch, perception of; Smell; Taste; Touch; Vision.

Perceptual set. *See* Set.

Peripheral nerves, the nerves that radiate from the >brain and spinal cord (ie the >central nervous system). *See* Nervous system.

Personal construct theory, a theory of the >mind which argues that everyone is a scientist, in the sense that we all seek to make sense of the world as we experience it. In reality we all construct our own universe. The task of the psychologist is to understand each individual method of construction – how the individual made their world. It was developed by George Kelly who invented the >repertory grid test to work out various ways of dealing with it.

● D. Bannister and F. Fransella, *Inquiring Man* (1986).

Personal growth, a concept fostered by the therapy movements of the 1960s and 1970s. To grow is to become freer, more aware of one's own needs and more >self-actualized. Believers apart, the concept has come to be viewed with increasing cynicism as a legacy of the narcissistic late 1960s. *See* Therapy.

Personal space. Every person feels that there is a small area that surrounds their body which is theirs. If others enter into it, unless they are lovers or sometimes parents, it is experienced as a threat. Different cultures have different measures of personal space. For example, an Arab will come much closer to you while talking than a Briton. The Briton, unless trained to expect this sort of proximity, will feel pressured. If the Briton stays his usual reserved distance away, the Arab will feel disliked.

Personality, in theory, the relatively stable and enduring characteristics of an individual. We expect a person who was amusing and warm on Saturday to be also amusing and warm on Sunday unless there are good reasons for some change. To have an unstable personality makes a person, at best, odd, at worst, sick. This belief in the stability of the personality predates scientific psychology. Greek drama and society are full of descriptions of heroes who have some constant personality attributes – for example, Heracles (Hercules) was brave and persevering which is why he managed to carry out his 12 labours. Psychologists took over this underlying concept without, until recently, much analysis of its roots. Most theories of personality, therefore, try to describe different personality types and to account for them. Well-known personality theories include those of >Freud, >Jung, R. B. Cattell (*see* Oblique rotation), >Eysenck, Henry Murray, and W. Mischel.

This last argues that personality doesn't really exist at all – it is simply an artifact created by psychologists! Freud, on the other hand, saw personality as linked to >psychosexual development; there are, he said, oral, anal and genital (phallic) personalities. Jung focused on >extraversion/introversion, a distinction later taken up by Cattell and Eysenck. Eysenck has argued that personality consists of a number of >traits, and the task of the personality theorist is to identify all these traits and devise proper ways of measuring them. Eysenck has so far done this with extraversion/introversion, >neuroticism and >psychoticism. He has said that the essential differences are biological, based on differences in the excitation of the >cortex. Many critics argue that the trait measures devised by Eysenck miss out what is unique about every person. Henry Murray has argued that all human beings are alike in some ways, similar in some ways and unique in some ways. His theory was first articulated in 1938 but still remains valuable. First, he argued that we all have a large variety of needs. Some are basic, such as food; others are complex, such as a need for intimacy. He did not think that it was possible to devise a neat formula for understanding personality. Rather, he claimed that different psychologists viewed personality in very different ways. If you thought of personality as the face, some were fascinated by the nose, others by the ears. He wanted to see psychology focus on the individual details of people's lives. He would have been disappointed by some developments. Mischel, for example, in his own influential theory has argued that behaviour is a product of particular situations. Put me in an office with a demanding boss and I will feel nervous and inadequate. Mischel's ideas are close to those of role theory. The study of personality has focused on similarity to others but many psychologists do now finally recognize that it needs to deal better with individual quirks and agendas.

- C. J. Carver and M. Scheier, *Perspectives on Personality* (1989); J. Eaves, H. J. Eysenck and N. G. Martin, *Genes, Culture and Personality* (1989); W. Mischel,

Personality and Assessment (1969); Henry Murray, *Explorations in Personality* (1938).

Personality disorder, a concept which is essentially used when referring to disorders which are neither psychiatric illnesses nor behaviour disorders. When a personality disorder is dealt with, the focus is on the person's enduring characteristics rather than on what he or she does in certain situations. The most common personality disorder is >psychopathy, and some would also include >paranoia.

Personality tests, tests that seek to quantify differences not in abilities but in characteristics. There hasn't been the same controversy over personality tests as over IQ tests (*see* Intelligence testing; Jenson controversy) despite the fact that, paradoxically, they are even less reliable. No personality test has the same depth of validation as the >Wechsler scale or >Stanford Binet intelligence test has.

There are well over 5000 personality tests – ranging from the Intercollegiate Basketball Instrument, which tests whether you have the >personality to be a good basketball team member, to tests of >extraversion/introversion (*see* Minnesota Multiple Personality Inventory. Personality tests use different techniques from intelligence tests: yes/no answers, multiple choice questions, selecting from a range of points from 0 to 7 to quantify feelings, and sometimes >projective techniques. Most tests are nomothetic – that is, they seek to establish general laws based on similarities between certain groups – but there have also been some attempts to develop individual idiographic tests to provide systematic in-depth information about one person. The quality of personality tests differs hugely, from the relatively well validated to the wholly spurious.

The first personality tests were created in the United States for personnel work. From 1921, the Psychological Corporation provided employers with an expert service which included tests for hiring people. There have been doubts as to the value of personality tests ever since. It is hard to construct a test which is technically accurate. Good tests need to have >face validity, >reliability, >test/retest reliability and some predictive value, but few manage all these at a high level of accuracy.

Furthermore, most tests consist of paper-and-pencil questionnaires with little latitude for expansion or explanation. The fact that I answer 'Yes' to the statement 'I like going to parties' may not mean that I actually go to parties very often, and there may be a number of reasons for my staying at home. I may not be invited to any parties. I may not like to admit that I am actually nervous of parties and so stay away, only pretending to love them in order to save face. I may live in a culture in which parties are not given – say, in a highly religious one where people only gather for worship or business. Extrapolating from answers to a questionnaire any real life behaviour remains fraught with problems.

Considerable evidence casts doubt on the ability of personality and ability tests together to predict how well people will do in certain jobs. John Toplis has argued, for example, that a much better predictor would be to put people on a short course that is very relevant to the job and then to find out how well they do (*see* Interviews). However, people like doing personality tests and, because of this, newspapers and magazines often run them. There is some evidence that people tend to believe that they can be used to get insights into their own behaviour.

- O. K. Buros, *The Eighth Mental Measurement Yearbook* (1978); H. J. Eysenck, *Psychology is About People* (1966); P. Kline, *Handbook of Psychological Testing* (1993); D. Shelley and David Cohen, *Testing Psychological Tests* (1986).

Personnel psychology deals principally with how to select prospective employees and, in competitive labour markets, how to keep them at their jobs. *See also* Training.

Person perception. Psychologists have applied many of the techniques used in the study of >perception in general to find out how we perceive people. Person perception is very complicated. How we perceive others depends greatly on our expectations and attitudes, and concepts such as >attribution theory are central to this; factors such as physical attractiveness also matter greatly. Robert Zajonc has argued that our perceptions of others are heavily influenced by 'hot cognitions' which seem to be processed much more quickly than ordinary impressions (*see* Primacy effect).

- Carol Izzard, Jerome Kagan and Robert Zajonc, *Emotions and Behaviour* (1984).

Phallic stage. *See* Genital phase.

Phobia, an irrational >fear focused on an object, animal, situation, etc. Almost anything can be the focus of a phobia. Common phobias are >claustrophobia, >agoraphobia, herpetophobia (fear of snakes), and arachnophobia (fear of spiders), but there are also exotic phobias such as thunderphobia.

Theories differ as to the cause of phobias. In one famous study, which has been re-analysed by historians of psychology, the behaviourist >J. B. Watson created a phobia in a little boy called Albert by banging a steel bar heavily when the child saw a white rat. Little Albert, who had previously been perfectly friendly to the beast, became terrified of the rat. Psychoanalysts say that, because phobias have deep causes, superficial attempts at >behaviour modification (ie the reverse of the Little Albert experiment), treating phobias as if they were due to inappropriate >learning, are doomed to failure. Rather, phobias are a defence against >anxiety, a means of avoiding the object that produces the anxiety. The apparent object of the phobia isn't really what the person is frightened of; the phobic object is only a symbol for part of the self. Thus, if I feel claustrophobic, it isn't because I'm really over-anxious about lifts but because I fear some part of my >personality.

Psychoanalysts have predicted that, as a result, behaviour modification

P

167

techniques would never really work with phobias – the immediate phobia might be cured, but the return of the repressed fear would ensure that a new phobia would surface. Generally, that prediction has turned out to be wrong. One of the real advances has been the use of relaxation and desensitization techniques to treat phobias. These work by getting the patient used to the phobia-creating stimuli while he or she is relaxed. *See* Flooding.

● Jo Melville, *Phobias* (1986); S. Rachman and R. J. Hodgson, *Obsessions and Compulsions* (1980).

Phonemes, the smallest units of sound that contribute to the meaning of a word. When we write, we put spaces between words. But when we speak, the words issue forth in a long babble of sound. The first task of the >hearing system is to break this down into manageable units. Phonemes are the first of these units.

Phrenology, the science of feeling the bumps on the head to determine character or personality. It was very influential in the early 19th century and helped stimulate interest in the anatomy of the >brain.

Physiological psychology. The branch of psychology which studies how the >brain, the >nervous system and the body affect behaviour. It has always attracted psychologists who are most interested in specific answers. Recent advances in biochemistry and genetics have made it a very promising area.

● Simon Green, *Physiological Psychology* (1987).

Piaget, Jean (1896–1980), Swiss psychologist whose theory of the intellectual development of children came to dominate psychology. Piaget first tested >IQ tests for >Binet's collaborator, Simon, and he learned to question children about why they got items right or wrong. He called this his 'clinical' method. By 1928, he postulated four stages of intellectual development: the >sensori-motor stage, the >pre-operational stage, >concrete operations and >formal operations. All children go through these stages, and as they do, they become more logical and can handle increasingly sophisticated modes of thought.

Piaget has been criticized for an over-emphasis on logic. He did ignore the emotional and social aspects of childhood, although he made some contributions to studies of moral development, >play and even >dreams. Piaget was always interested in philosophical questions and, because of this, his theories emphasized the intellect – for him, everything followed from that.

Piaget devised many ingenious experiments – for example, the one demonstrating >conservation – but they came under critical scrutiny when it became clear that he had underestimated what children could do. In addition, the design of some of his experiments was faulty: children were unable to grasp what they were being asked to do. When the experiments were recreated with better instructions, suddenly very young children could be unexpectedly logical. It's now clear, too, that children's minds develop through social and emotional >interaction – initially with their parents. It's strange that Piaget neglected this since his first subjects were his own children, whose behaviour he meticulously recorded. Like >Freud, he had inherited from the 19th century a belief in stages as powerful explanatory concepts.

Piaget spent much of his later career working on the problems of >perception, and in 1975, in one of the few high-level debates between theoreticians with fairly opposed views, he debated his ideas with >Noam Chomsky. *See* Child development.

- P. Bryant, *Perception and Understanding in Young Children* (1972); M. Donaldson, *Children's Minds* (1978); M. Piatelli Palmarini, *Language and Learning: The Debate between Jean Piaget and Noam Chomsky* (1980).

Pitch, perception of. This is complex, involving two different systems in the inner ear. High-frequency and medium-frequency sounds both make the basilar membrane vibrate, but they flex different parts of the membrane: high frequencies flex the front while medium frequencies flex the back. That signals pitch. Originally, it was thought that neurons (*see* Neuron) in the >hearing system signalled pitch by firing in synchrony with the vibrations of the basilar membrane. But axons, the long nerve fibres leading from the nerve cell body, can't fire fast enough for this to happen – a young ear can hear frequencies of more than 20,000 Hertz (cycles per second) but axons can't fire more than 1000 times per second. Frequencies lower than 200 Hertz make the tip of the basilar membrane vibrate in synchrony with the sound waves. The >brain counts these vibrations and thus detects low-frequency sounds.

Damage to specific regions of the basilar membrane can cause loss of the ability to hear specific frequencies.

Pituitary, the main gland of the endocrine system. It is connected to the >hypothalamus in the >brain and secretes hormones which are transmitted through the bloodstream.

Placebo effect. This has been known since the Middle Ages. Giving patients a totally neutral medicine – eg coloured water – often appears to help them. It's an example of the >mind triumphing over matter and of how we do our best to please doctors. Psychologists suggest that the placebo effect operates because of the attention that the doctor gives to the patient.

In methodological terms, it is an important factor that must be taken into consideration. Any new medicines have to be tested against a placebo to make sure that they do not work just because of the placebo effect. *See* Double blind.

Play, activities that are not 'for real'. Most behaviour has an obvious purpose. Play seems to be just for fun, but the concept is not as simple as that. Defining just what is and isn't play has plagued psychologists since 1900. There is some agreement that in both animals and humans, play has the following characteristics: it has no immediate obvious function; and it's usually (though not always) possible to tell that the players are playing because they emit special signals such as an exaggeratedly grinning face.

Observations suggest that one effect of play is to allow children to master both >cognitive and >social skills. Children first play at throwing rattles out of

P

their prams and then, after frequent repetition, learn a vitally necessary lesson about how objects fall if unsupported. >Freud argued that, in play, children can work out some of their emotional conflicts. Lowenthal seized on the sexual/obscene play of children during the >latency period to argue that, through such >jokes – especially jokes about bottoms – they deal with their sexual >anxiety.

Recently, developmental psychologists have charted out in detail the cognitive stages that affect the different ways young children play. Pretend play is especially important for this gives children the chance to test out both whether they can see events from a perspective other than their own and, according to some, other identities which may well be a way of helping them to discover the boundaries of their own selves. Given how theorists tend to play down infant capacities, it's interesting that all researchers agree that two- to three-year-old children know what it means to pretend to be, say, Batman – and that they are not Batman.

There are many different explanations for different kinds of play, but all current experts agree that we have been too ready to accept that playing stops at the end of childhood. Adults now don't play enough, yet playing with one's children is fun, rewarding and an integral part of helping the children grow up. *See* Child development; Piaget, Jean.

- David Cohen, *The Development of Play* (1993); J. Bruner, C. Garvey, *Play* (1977); J. Huizinga, *Homo Ludens* (1949); J. Moyles, *Just Playing* (1989); Jean Piaget, *Play, Dreams and Imitation in Childhood* (1952).

Play therapy, a form of >therapy in which children play with toys and dolls. The playing allows children a non-threatening way of representing fraught situations, and since it is relaxing, it opens the possibility of talking about deep problems. *See* Child abuse; Klein, Melanie.

- V. Axline, *Play Therapy* (1947).

Pleasure principle. According to >Freud, the >psyche is initially energized solely by the pleasure principle. This doesn't mean that we seek pleasure for its own sake but that we seek to avoid the lack of pleasure which is caused by growing tension, so we imagine ways of achieving the satisfaction of fulfilling our wishes. It's been suggested that the pleasure principle can be compared to the idea of >homoeostasis. Human beings cannot bear too much of a lack of balance. There are close links between this idea and that of drive reduction where the organism seeks to reduce excessive >drive by action – ie the hunger drive is satisfied by eating.

Pons, a large bundle of nerves in the brainstem which is critical for >sleep, wakefulness, movement and attention. *Pons* is Latin for 'bridge' and the structure was so named because large numbers of nerve fibres pass through it.

Population. Psychological research depends on studying particular >samples. A population is a group of people who are defined by certain characteristics. Medical students, housewives under 33, and old age pensioners are each distinct populations. It's important to distinguish those specific groups, *a population*, from *the population*, ie everyone in a country.

Position effect, how the position of a >stimulus affects its recall. For example, when a list is learned the fewest errors in recall occur for items at the beginning. The next most accurate recall is for items at the end of the list. The nature of the particular stimulus is largely irrelevant. The effect holds for poems, motor tasks (like typing), nonsense syllables. The only exception is if something is personally meaningful or for names which are recalled more evenly. The position effect also occurs whether subjects are asked to recall the list in the same order it was presented or to recall the items in any order. The effect is also known as the 'stimulus position effect' and is one of the best established facts in experimental psychology. *See* Ebbinghaus, Hermann.

Posthypnotic suggestibility. After >hypnosis, subjects may well carry out orders that they were given while they were in the trance state and which they have no recollection of at all. For example, someone may have been instructed by the hypnotist to say 'pink' whenever they saw him sitting down. Very often, it works.

● G. Pratt, D. Wood and B. Alman, *A Clinical Hypnosis Primer* (1985); D. Waxman, *Hypnosis* (1984).

Postnatal depression, also known as postpartum depression. In the 19th century, it was recognized that, after childbirth, women often became depressed. Research now suggests that this may well be due to a mixture of hormonal imbalances and the sheer exhaustion and change in lifestyle that having a small baby can bring about.

Post-traumatic stress. After the First World War, psychiatrists became aware that many soldiers had suffered >trauma in the trenches. This 'war neurosis' was initially seen as unique, a reaction to the horrors of the 'Great War'. It has become clear, however, that victims of other shocks often suffer from similar symptoms. The term 'post-traumatic >stress' has come to be applied, therefore, to the after-effects experienced by (among others) hostages, rape victims, dissidents kept in detention (eg in the USSR and South Africa) and road traffic accident victims.

Psychiatrists claim to have identified a consistent set of symptoms that most people will suffer from after such trauma, including >anxiety, sleeping problems, recurring nightmares, unwanted intrusion of images of their recent ordeal. Often, too, victims report that it is hard for them to become interested in anything. One of the best-documented incidents which led to post-traumatic stress was the accidental earthslip at a dam burst at Buffalo Creek in West Virginia in 1972. The survivors sued the mining company responsible, their lawyers claiming psychological damages. The Federal court insisted on a study of all the victims, and it was found that they suffered from >depression, loss of >libido, chronic anxiety and a general sense of hopelessness. They were awarded in all $9 million for psychological damages. While the condition has now been

P

widely accepted, it is not clear what can be done to treat it. Allowing the victims to talk about their experiences is clearly important – if they want to do so. There have been instances when, in their eagerness to provide help after a major disaster, the authorities have almost overwhelmed survivors with too much care. This happened in Holland after the 1975 train hijacking by the South Moluccans. The ex-hostages were furious because the authorities presumed that they had cracked under stress. *See* Loss; Rape trauma; Terrorism.

● Kai Erikson, *Everything Fell Apart* (1976).

Practice effects, the effect of practice on >learning. Studies show how well practised skills do survive long periods without being used.

Preconscious, an adjective referring to thoughts which are unconscious but not repressed. They can, therefore, become conscious fairly easily.

Prefrontal lobotomy. *See* Lobotomy.

Prejudice, an important topic in social psychology. Typically, the dominant group in any society will entertain many prejudices about those who are less well off and less educated. American society remains full of prejudices about blacks which surfaced in the >Jensen debate. Those in the lowest classes of any society also tend to have stereotypical beliefs and prejudices about those who are dominant. Idealistic social psychologists after World War II believed that if people knew more about different cultures prejudice would diminish. Information does help but it hasn't turned out to be wholly true that the more we know about different groups – especially >outgroups such as criminals or ethnic minorities – the less prejudice we feel. In an increasingly interdependent world, prejudices remain a serious problem in and between societies and the success of psychological techniques in combating it remains disappointing.

Premenstrual syndrome, feeling bloated, depressed and suffering mood swings before having a period. It is assumed that these symptoms are due to hormonal changes and it is now accepted that the behaviour of women can be affected severely by this. Premenstrual syndrome has recently been pleaded as a defence in court.

● Katherine Dalton, *The Menstrual Cycle* (1969).

Preoperational stage. The second of >Piaget's stages of intellectual development. It lasts roughly from when the child is two until he or she is seven years old. During this stage, the child is limited by its perceptions and remains deeply egocentric. In Piaget's view, children of this age cannot imagine the perspective of others. One of Piaget's most famous experiments showed that children would say there was more liquid in a tall glass than in a fat one when in fact they held the same amount. M. Donaldson and others argue this was the product of confusing instructions and that Piaget underestimated what children can do. Ingenious experiments have shown children can take the perspective of another person if given suitable help.

- M. Donaldson, *Children's Minds* (1978); J. H. Flavell, *The Developmental Psychology of Jean Piaget* (1962).

Presenile dementia, a form of >dementia which occurs before the onset of old age. *See* Alzheimer's disease.

Primacy effect, a concept that states that items which are presented first on a list tend to be recalled more easily. This doesn't just apply to learning nonsense syllables but to some aspects of person >perception. In 1980, Robert Zajonc identified a curious process known as 'hot cognitions', which basically suggests that our first impressions of people are, as Oscar Wilde observed, never wrong. This is mainly because what we are reacting to is emotional as well as cognitive.

Primary process, according to >Freud, the first kind of >thinking that the infant engages in. It shows condensation and >displacement. Condensation means that images become fused too easily so they can readily displace each other. It is governed by the >pleasure principle and ignores the restraints of time and space. Freud contrasted this with >secondary process in which logic and reason operate. It's interesting to compare Freud's stages with those of >Piaget: the latter's >sensori-motor stage has many of the same characteristics of primary process. Neither of the two great men acknowledged the fact, however, though many lesser folk have tried to achieve some integration of the two.

- P. Barros, 'Freud and Piaget Reconsidered' in *Psychology News*, 2, 5 (1989); Sigmund Freud, *An Outline of Psychoanalysis* (1940).

Primate studies, studies of great apes. *See* Ethology.

Proactive inhibition. When something new has been learned, it interferes with old >learning by inhibiting it.

Problem solving. Human beings are better at solving problems than all other animals. It has proved relatively easy to design elegant experimental problems that subjects can solve in the laboratory, although these suggest that humans are far from being totally logical. Psychologists have found that we are better at tackling certain kinds of problem. For example, if I have to seek examples that confirm a general rule, it is not hard for me to do so. Negative inferences are harder to deal with. In a study of scientific genius, Keith Simonton found that even great physicists like Einstein tended to avoid thinking of instances that might falsify their theories.

One factor which remains extremely interesting is the role of the >unconscious in creative problem solving. Some scientists such as the chemist F. A. Kekkule found that after a long period of >thinking about the problem of the chemistry of benzene rings of carbon atoms the answer appeared to him in a dream. He dreamt of rings. The great mathematician Henri Poincaré also dreamt the answer to a mathematical problem that he had worked on for years. Studies of more ordinary thinking don't dwell on this and, perhaps, miss

P

something as a result. No one understands how such solutions appear in >dreams but it is well documented that they do. *See also*; Cognitive styles: Convergent.

● K. Simonton, *Scientific Genius* (1989).

Projection, a term from >psychoanalysis. By projecting certain qualities, feelings or fears outside the self the on to other people, one achieves apparent safety. This is a form of 'casting out devils' form the self, often by the use of >denial. >Freud first mentioned the concept in 1911 in connection with delusions of persecution (*see* Paranoia). >Klein argued that this was a normal process of infant development, yet it can also be very counter-productive. Some commentators have suggested that fanatical movements like the Nazis, with their concept of racial purity, merely projected all their own inner evils on to the Jews. *See* Scapegoating.

● Wilhelm Reich, *The Mass Psychology of Fascism* (1970).

Projective techniques/tests, any >personality test where the subjects are asked to respond to ambiguous stimuli with the aim of having them project their own needs, feelings, attitudes, etc. The best known of these tests are the >Rorschach test and the >Thematic Apperception Test (TAT). Some projective tests are more focused than either of these, but all of them remain controversial. Considerable doubt as to the validity of these techniques exists because scorers often disagree on the interpretation of particular ink blots (Rorschach), stories (TAT) or other elements.

Psychiatry, the branch of medicine that deals with mental illnesses and which has attracted exceptional controversy over the last 20 years. (The Introduction provides an outline of some of the most recent controversies in psychiatry.) *See* Depression; Electro-convulsive therapy; Lobotomy; Mania; Schizophrenia.

● Books on the controversies include: A. Clare, *Psychiatry in Dissent* (1976); D. Healy, *The Suspended Revolution* (1990); D. Ingleby (ed), *Critical Psychiatry* (1981); R. D. Laing, *The Divided Self* (1960); M. Roth and J. Kroll, *The Reality of Mental Illness* (1986); T. Szasz, *Law, Liberty and Psychiatry* (1968); J. K. Wing, *Reasoning About Madness* (1977).

Psychoanalysis, the theory first developed by >Sigmund Freud.

Freud himself defined psychoanalysis as the procedure 'for the investigation of mental processes which are almost inaccessible in any other way'. He added that the name could also be used to describe a method of treatment for neurotic disorders and 'a collection of psychological information' which, in 1923 when he wrote this definition, was 'gradually being accumulated into a new scientific discipline'. Freud stated that the main aim of psychoanalysis was to make unconscious material conscious by patients using >free association and therapists providing interpretations for the patients' >dreams, their >resistances and their >transferences.

Ever since >Jung broke with Freud, there have been many schools of psychoanalysis, including Freudians, Jungians, Adlerians, Reichians, >neo-Freudians, Kleinians, the British school such as D. W. Winnicott and, more recently, the Lacan school. The works of the latter show at their most extreme the passions that analysis can arouse. Many see >Jacques Lacan as the greatest analyst since Freud; others snipe that it was never possible to understand what he was saying and that he wrote so obscurely because, in reality, he had nothing to say.

Psychoanalysis has been controversial from the outset. Freud saw himself very much as an empirical scientist, but more conventional scientists denounced psychoanalysis as both a secular religion and as nonsense. The main criticisms of psychoanalysis include the fact that it puts too much emphasis on sex; that psychoanalytic discoveries tend only to apply in the consulting room; that psychoanalysis is deterministic; that it is politically repressive; its often inter-minable length and, the greatest sin, that it isn't properly testable. >Eysenck carped in a memorable phrase that, in psychoanalysis, 'what is new isn't true and what is true isn't new'.

Many critics have honed in on the fact that psychoanalysis makes almost no truly testable predictions. For example, if a patient has been analysed as being unable to sustain a relationship with a woman because he has never resolved his >Oedipus complex, and then he goes on to make a decent marriage, this doesn't prove that the theory was wrong. Oh no – the wily patient is merely resisting the therapist! In other words, the theory provides a form of explanation for every conceivable objection and, as a result, it isn't really a scientific theory at all but more a theological system.

The vitriolic nature of the debates surrounding psychoanalysis has always been used by analysts to suggest that they have really hit on the truth – their insights are too uncomfortable. Weren't Galileo and >Darwin also persecuted? However, psychoanalysts after Freud have often behaved as zealots, which has not helped encourage proper, critical debate.

It was long considered impossible to record what went on in analytic sessions, and patients have often reported that they were made to feel guilty if they decided to drop out of analysis. A Sanskrit scholar turned analyst, Jeffrey Masson, has recently suggested that analytic cliques banish those who question the orthodoxy, a view that has been put forward, less contentiously, by others. But those who discount psychoanalysis often seem to revel in the act as if they are smacking down some pretentious upstart. Eysenck, for one, takes particular pleasure in deriding the theory, observing that Freud deserved the Goethe Prize, which he won in 1925, since it was a prize for fiction. However, increasingly, some philosophers of science such as B. A. Farrell, are arguing that psychoanal-ysis may not be testable but it does offer patients the chance of constructing a credible and organized story which explains how they have reached that par-ticular point in their lives.

Whatever the scientific validity of psychoanalysis, its social, medical and cultural impact has been profound. We live in a post-Freudian world: art, the cinema, our whole society has been altered by the success of analysis, and it has

P

provided a new >language for discussing the way we feel, think and are. It may, therefore, be that, while psychoanalysis wasn't true in the 1890s, it has become more true now, at least for certain small groups who analyse the way they act and react in Freudian terms.

Entry to the profession of psychoanalysis is now rigorously controlled in a way that Freud would have found surprising. Aspirants have to undergo training analysis, and many who are well qualified academically are rejected because they are not mature enough or 'well worked out' enough to qualify. In the United States, especially, psychoanalysis is an extremely lucrative profession.

- H. J. Eysenck, 'The effects of psychotherapy: an evaluation', in the *Journal of Consultative Psychology*, 16, 319–24 (1952) and *The Rise and Fall of the Freudian Empire* (1986); B. A. Farrell, *The Standing of Psychoanalysis* (1981); Sigmund Freud, *An Outline of Psychoanalysis* (1939); P. Kline, *Fact and Fantasy in Freudian Theory* (1972); J. Malcolm, *Psychoanalysis: the Impossible Profession* (1982) and *In the Freud Archives* (1984); S. Moscovici, *Social Influence and Social Change* (1976).

Psychodrama, a technique developed by >Jacob Moreno, who stated that it was a 'science which explores truth by dramatic methods'. In psychodrama, patients play the parts of various significant persons in their lives. Moreno argued that this would benefit them in two ways. First, they could discharge a considerable amount of psychic energy by playing these roles. Second, they could gain some insight into the feelings that their own behaviour aroused in other people. Despite its obvious appeal, psychodrama has always remained a rather peripheral technique in >psychotherapy. *See* Dramatherapy.

Psychodynamic theories, theories that locate the fundamental causes of human action in the social and emotional conditions in which children are raised. Psychodynamic theories play down the influence of heredity or of >organic disorders; they also discount the role of >learning. Most psychodynamic theories draw their inspiration from either >Freud or >Jung, but there has been a proliferation of such approaches which now include >Gestalt therapy, >transactional analysis, Kleinian therapy. Some of these are rigorous but many others are relics of faddish theories of >personal growth and psychobabble.

Psychokinesis, a term coined by the parapysochologist J.R. Rhine. Rhine argued that some of his subjects could affect the movement of objects by exercise of the will. *Psycho*, the mind, affects *kinesis*, movement. *See* Telekinesis.

Psycholinguistics, the application of linguistic theory to psychological problems. The study of >language has a long history in psychology, dating back to the behaviourist >J. B. Watson who tried to prove that >thought is actually silent language. However, both Watson and >B. F. Skinner spoke, deliberately, of 'language behaviour'.

The approach to the study of language changed radically when >Noam Chomsky showed how human beings are born with a 'language acquisition device'. Psycholinguistics has become an important area looking at how many variables affect the learning and use of language. A recent interest has been from feminists who argue that analysis of speech shows that women listen sensitively to men while the brutish blokes, on the other hand, never let women talk.

● Alan Garnham, *Psycholinguistics* (1985).

Psychological androgyny, the idea that every human being has a mix of typically male and typically female characteristics. Sandra Bem argued in the 1970s that the more psychologically androgynous a person was, the healthier and more successful they were. Bem found that women who could cope with car mechanics and men who could also change nappies were successful. The theory was very radically chic and heavily influenced by feminist aspirations. Good men would also turn out to be gentle, sensitive and able to discuss their emotions. A key point was that these men were not less masculine. They combined the perfect mix of male and female. Bem's ideas also owed something to >Jung's notions of >animus and >anima. Sadly, sophisticated analysis of Bem's results suggests that zeal got the better of evidence. Psychologically androgynous women were successful because they tended to score high on masculine traits and androgynous men were successful because they too scored high on masculine characteristics. In American society energy and determination are the usual requisites of success. Psychological androgyny remains an interesting concept but it needs critical application. *See* Behaviourism; Ethology; Psychoanalysis.

● S. Bem, *The Lenses of Gender* (1993).

Psychological tests, generally objective tests either of aptitude or >personality. Various techniques have been used to construct psychological tests, ranging from highly objective methods to fairly loose imaginative ones. Specific sorts of tests are examined in separate entries. *See* Idiographic; Intelligence testing; Jensen controversy; Objective psychological test; Personality tests; Q sort.

Psychologists, psychology of, a subject that is little studied but important since psychologists have to accept – at some level – that their ideas on how human beings function must also apply to themselves. Increasing attention is being given to this.

● David Cohen, *Psychologists on Psychology* (1977); T. Krawiec, *Psychologists* (1981).

Psychometric techniques, the mathematical and statistical tests which are used to determine either which >traits a person has or, more often, what illness they might be suffering from. Traditionally, psychometric methods are contrasted with clinical judgements. The main difference is that, in a clinical judgement, the expert uses expertise and the wisdom of experience to make

P

177

judgements while the psychometric test uses an additive model, totting up the number of symptoms and their severity, to identify the presence or absence of a particular trait or syndrome. In practice, many diagnosticians use a combination of both to determine just what is wrong with a person.

● P. E. Meehl, *Clinical versus Statistical Prediction* (1954); J. Rust and S. Golombok, *Modern Psychometrics* (1989).

Psychopathology, a term used when referring to the psychological and psychiatric problems of patients. It is employed loosely and often not just in respect of >psychopaths.

Psychopathology of Everyday Life, the title of a famous book by >Freud. He argued that nothing was accidental. The smallest slip of the tongue had a reason usually sexual or hostile. It was hidden from >consciousness and its real meaning or intent could only be divined by analysis. Freud asked, for example, why we forgot some names and suggested that unconscious associations might explain it. *See* Association theory.

Psychopathy, a form of behaviour disorder. The psychopath is meant to be evil incarnate, unable to distinguish right from wrong. There has been much debate on whether psychopaths are really mentally ill. The point is not just academic. Usually, it is only discovered that someone is a psychopath when they are found to have committed a major crime. The issue then is whether they are guilty or does their psychopathy mean that they have >diminished responsibility.

● W. H. Reid *et al*, *Unmasking the Psychopath* (1986).

Psychopharmacology, the study of drugs in relation to psychology and >psychiatry. This is an area that has reached increasing sophistication as drugs begin to be able to target more specific ills. *See* Antidepressants; Benzodiazepines; Chlorpromazine; Lithium; Monoamine oxidase inhibitors; Neurotransmitters; Psychotropic drugs.

Psychosexual stages, the stages employed by >Sigmund Freud to describe the emotional development of children, and first formally set out by >Anna Freud. They are: the >oral stage, the >anal stage, the >genital or phallic stage; the >Oedipal stage and >latency. At each stage, children are fascinated by, and derive most pleasure from, different organs. In the oral stage, the mouth is all; in the anal stage, excretion; in the genital stage, genitalia. For Freud, children have to move through one stage before they can tangle with the problems of the next, a general pattern that is the same as >Piaget's view of intellectual development.

The discovery of these stages changed our view of childhood, for before Freud it was assumed that children were not interested in sex until they reached puberty. Curiously, Freud arrived at his concept of these stages without observing any children. Many critics have mocked the theory, but there is actually a modest amount of evidence which suggests, at least, that at different phases of development children are more interested in different parts of their bodies.

Psychosis, a term that covers the most serious forms of mental illness, including >schizophrenia. Psychotic patients tend to have >hallucinations, and to lack >insight. It is harder for them to appear to function than neurotics, and doctors speak of 'psychotic episodes'. It was often charged that >Freud never dealt with a really disturbed psychotic patient as opposed to slightly self-obsessed neurotics. *See* Neurosis.

Psychosomatic disorders, from the Greek *psuko* ('mind') and *soma* ('body'). Somatic illnesses are diseases of the body. Psychosomatic illnesses are genuine physical illnesses which have, however, been caused by psychological conditions. *See* Life events; Stress.

P

Psychosurgery, surgical intervention on the >brain with the aim of removing the causes of psychiatric disturbance. The most common technique has been >lobotomy.

Psychotherapy, a global term covering a variety of approaches and treatments, most of which take a >psychodynamic approach. The idea is to get the clients to bring to the >therapy their problems, >fantasies, >dreams and wishes and to analyse them in partnership. Drugs play no part in pure psychotherapy.

>Behaviour therapy is not usually seen as psychotherapy; rather, it is psychologically based therapy. In addition, psychotherapy does not include >psychoanalysis but it does operate on similar principles. However, unlike analysis, psychotherapy does not depend on rigorous theory or a schedule of sessions five days a week, and relations between therapists and clients are not generally as formal. *See* Client-centred therapy; Gestalt therapy; Group therapy.

● Anthony Clare and Sally Thompson, *Let's Talk About Me* (1983).

Psychoticism, a somewhat vague term in >psychiatry and a precise one in terms of >Eysenck's >personality theory. In psychiatry, psychoticism is a form of serious mental illness. The psychotic is deluded, often paranoid, often – but not always – lacks >insight into his condition and can be dangerous. It is a sign of the confusion that surrounds the term that >schizophrenia is sometimes seen as a psychotic condition and sometimes not. In Eysenck's theory, psychoticism is a personality dimension. Like all personality dimensions, it is a continuum, running from those who score high on psychotic traits to those who score very low. There is no break point or set score beyond which a person is considered to be psychotic. Those who score high on psychoticism exhibit the worrying traits psychiatrists report.

Psychotropic drugs, initially used to refer to drugs such as mescalin and >LSD which would literally make the mind 'blow' – hence mind-blowing – because they created >hallucinations. Lately, the term has been used to refer to virtually any kind of tranquillizer or other mood-changing drug.

Punishment, an unpleasant event. It is important not to confuse this with >negative reinforcement which involves the withdrawal or avoidance of something which is aversive.

Pure word deafness, a form of >hearing disorder in which the person can hear sounds but cannot distinguish words.

P

Q

Q. In his *Project for a Scientific Psychology* >Freud used 'Q' ('quantity') to mark whatever denoted activity from rest.

Q sort, a psychological test that attempts to give some weighting to individual factors. The test involves getting subjects to sort out cards and blocks into groups and, then, it seeks to analyse the correlations between different categories the subject used. The technique is interesting because it offers both a degree of statistical precision and more room for individuality than most tests where results can be qualified precisely.

R

Race. *See* Intelligence testing; Jensen controversy; Prejudice.

Radical psychology, not so much a branch of psychology as a label given to certain kinds of work that have had frank political objectives, nearly always left-wing ones. Young psychologists in the 1970s became disillusioned. They knew Marx's famous maxim that philosophy seeks only to understand the world but the point is to change it. To this end, radical psychologists analysed how conventional science used its power to keep down workers, women and minority groups. There were studies of the way that 'the >language of discourse' justifies oppression. Undoubtedly, the most effective form of radical psychology was >feminist psychology. It showed how social attitudes, the unwillingness of men to give up power and women's own low expectations of what they could achieve all perpetuated a sexist status quo.

Analysis of the situation of workers and blacks tended to follow similar lines. Radical psychologists believed in listening to the 'disadvantaged' and consulting them. But increasingly radical psychologists saw that their work wouldn't lead to much change. They realized too that there was a paradox. They might be ideologically sound but they weren't powerless: they were professionals. A few bravely confronted the way they worked.

This confrontation has led in Britain to some interesting work especially in *The Politics of Mental Health*. In it a collective of Marxist and feminist psychologists saw that their own way of working depended on their using their power not against their clients but on their clients. Like radical social workers with whom they shared many characteristics, radical psychologists had long felt too guilty about the power they wielded to admit it. As a result, they were often extremely devious, manipulative and ineffective.

It's a sign of the change of ideological climate that we hear much less about radical psychology in the 1980s and much more about the ways in which psychologists can help businesses do well by producing everything from better >stress programmes for executives to education packs on creative >thinking.

• G. Banton *et al*, *The Politics of Mental Health* (1985); J. Henriques, V. Walkerine *et al*, *Changing the Subject* (1987).

Random sampling. This does not mean taking a >sample at random but constructing a >sample so that every member of a particular >population has an equally good chance of appearing in it. Theoretically, this is an excellent basis for a sample. In practice, however, it is extremely hard to achieve a proper random sample as biases of all kinds tend to creep into the choice of subjects. Good psychological research depends heavily on creating good samples.

Range, a crude measure of the variability of a group of scores, which is calculated by subtracting the smallest score from the largest score.

Rape trauma. Victims of rape suffer many immediate symptoms typical of >post-traumatic stress. These include shame, >anxiety, nightmares and the feeling, however, untrue, that they brought the rape on themselves. Society's treatment of rape victims often adds to the >stress; court proceedings in rape trials have been described as vicious. The defence often tries to prove that the victim 'asked' for it, that she had a bad reputation and/or that she 'provoked' the rapist. Groups for rape victims now exist to offer support and >counselling.

Some investigators have recently tried to claim that rapists often lack >social skills, that it is their inability to make 'normal' advances to women that drives them to rape. Some prisons now run skills groups for sex offenders in the hope that they will learn more appropriate ways of approaching women. Feminist organizations are understandably wary of such initiatives.

Rapid eye movement (REM) sleep. The French physiologist Michel Jouvet discovered that, in certain stages of >sleep, the eyes flutter rapidly under the eyelids – hence the name rapid eye movement (REM) sleep. This sleep stage usually starts about 80 minutes after the start of a period of sleep. Sleepers pass down through three different stages into deeper and deeper sleep, until finally the dominant pattern of brain waves is slow. Then, in a mechanism that is not yet understood, they spring into lighter sleep with REMs. The movement of the eyes suggests that the eyes were being used as in normal >vision, yet what were they seeing? It seemed plausible to suggest >dreams, and indeed, when subjects were awakened from REM sleep, they often reported being in the middle of dreams.

Some researchers tried to link the speed and direction of REMs with the content of the dreams that subjects had been woken out of. For example, if eye movements went from side to side, were people dreaming that they were watching a tennis match? However, it was never possible to match REMs precisely with dreams, and later work also found that people also dreamed during non-REM (*see* NREM sleep) sleep. REM sleep must perform some important activity: sleep-deprived humans fall almost immediately into long episodes of REM sleep, and Jouvet also showed that if animals are deprived of it they would eventually die. REM sleep is crucial but it's not clear what it's crucial for. Jouvet has suggested that it is an important element in integrating

R

>personality, although he has not been able to suggest how. An interview with M. Jouvet is in D. Cohen, *Psychologists on Psychology* (1977).

● *Ian Oswald*, Sleep (1980).

Rapport, literally a good relationship. Rapport makes it possible for one person to talk about sensitive issues with another. To possess it is an essential skill of the therapist.

Rating scales, used by psychologists for recording subjects' judgements, which may be about themselves, or other things, or other people. The common three formats reflect the three major subdivisions of >intelligence testing scales: numerical, spatial and verbal. A *numerical* rating scale uses numbers as ratings (ie from low to high). A *graphic*, or *spatial*, rating scale can have points along a line, just a line or just a space between two points representing the dimension being rated. A *descriptive graphic*, or *verbal*, scale uses verbal labels such as 'frequently' or 'not very often'.

There are problems with all three methods. The numerical scale may imply a >ratio scale to subjects where 2 is twice as much as 1, but experimenters want to make finer distinctions than this. The graphic scale is probably the least familiar to subjects and therefore runs the risk of bias, but responses to the unfamiliar format may be random. In addition, where graphic rating scales do not have equal intervals, but are made up of one continuous line or an unbroken space, results can be very difficult to score by hand. A descriptive graphic scale uses verbal labels for each point of the scale, but what do they mean? One pole may use any of the following: 'infrequently', 'rarely', 'seldom', 'not very often', 'now and again' – but each person may have a different idea of what each term means.

When >Alfred Kinsey was carrying out his massive survey on sexual behaviour, he wrote in a letter to a colleague:

> . . . We have had suggestions from a number of psychologists . . . that we should confine ourselves to a good, normal, middle-class group, such as college professors. In actuality, the histories [ie sexual histories] of this group represent one of the widest departures from anything that is typical of the mass of the population.

If psychologists who are not typical judge themselves to be typical, then their judgements using themselves as the baseline for what is frequent or infrequent will also not be typical.

Rational emotive therapy, a form of >therapy developed by Albert Ellis in the 1970s, which in many ways was the first form of >cognitive behaviour therapy.

Ellis argued that psychological problems stem from faulty cognitions (thoughts), and therapy should aim at changing people's beliefs. Ellis suggested that emotions flow from cognitions: a significant activating event (A) is followed by a highly charged emotional consequence (C), but A doesn't cause C; rather C is the result of the beliefs a person has, and >depression, >guilt or >anxiety can be abolished if the client changes these. The therapist, as a result, is very directive and confronts clients, insisting that they justify their behaviour, the aim being, says Ellis, to 'expose and annihilate nonsense'. In his battle against nonsense, Ellis compiled a list of 15 common irrational practices that we are all prone to. These range from the tendency to 'be overwhelmed by the great difficulty of changing, >thinking and acting' to 'overgeneralizing about events that have occurred in the past or may occur in the future'.

Follow-up research suggests that rational emotive therapy (RAT) can be good for those who profit from intellectual teaching and arguments – especially if they are very self-demanding. For others, it is less effective. It has been found useful in the treatment of >alcoholism but of little use in more 'emotive' disorders such as >agoraphobia or >schizophrenia. Some RAT techniques are employed by eclectic therapists who see them as useful aids rather than total insights.

R

- Albert Ellis, *Reason and Emotion in Psychotherapy* (1979).

Ratio scale, used by psychologists for recording subjects' judgements (*see* Rating scales). It is an interval scale that also has a true zero point, and measurements are directly proportional. For example, 8 metres is twice the length of 4 metres; 50 grams is half the weight of 100 grams.

Reaction times, how quickly a person reacts to a >stimulus. Usually, subjects are asked to press a buzzer as soon as they see or hear something that's been projected for them. Experiments involving reaction times carried out at the Leipzig laboratory between 1879 and 1890 were some of the earliest in psychology.

Experimenters have studied how making the stimulus more complicated, masking it or giving the subject difficult instructions affects the way they react. Obscene words, for example, are recognized more slowly (*see* Perceptual defence). Over the years, it has been established that a stimulus has to be visible for only a few milliseconds for a person to react to it, but much depends on how bright, or loud, the stimulus is, and, in vision, how far away it is. The thresholds at which the brain can work are very low. Work on reaction times can be used in unlikely places. The controversy as to whether the Canadian sprinter Ben Johnson anticipated the starting pistol in his 100m final with the American Carl Lewis at the World Championships in 1987 was eventually settled on the basis of reaction-time work: no one, said the researchers, can respond quicker to the gun than in 12 hundredths of a second, but Johnson did and was subsequently disqualified.

- R. Luce, *Reaction Times* (1987).

Reactive depression. *See* Depression.

Reality testing, the ability to tell the difference between, on the one hand, mental images and wish-fulfilments and, on the other, the truth of the external world. Classical >psychoanalysis argued that infants have no capacity for reality testing; for them, wishes and >fantasies are all. This is also true of people in the midst of psychotic episodes. The delicate process by which we acquire a sense of reality has never been convincingly explained by any theory. So far, rival descriptions are the best we have. >Adaptation to reality takes place; just how we don't begin to know.

Recall. *See* Memory.

Recency effect. A phenomenon of >learning. The item that was heard or learned most recently is easiest to remember.

Receptor, usually a sense receptor – a cell or specialized set of cells which picks up information either inside or outside the body. The free nerve endings on the skin which register to touch are receptors, as are the light-sensitive rod and cone cells on the >retina of the eye, which contains an estimated 130 million receptor cells. The receptors usually transform energy such as light into electrical impulses which are then sent into the >central nervous system.

Receptor site, part of the >neuron which is eased or made more 'receptive' by a >neurotransmitter.

Reductionism, the belief that the explanation for all behaviour can be reduced to physical and chemical causes. The origins of the idea can be traced to Rudolf Virchow, a 19th-century German biologist who believed that cellular anatomy held the ultimate clues to all psychological questions. There is some debate as to what the main version of reductionism was. Western psychologists argue that >behaviourism represented the climax of the approach. >Freud, however, certainly saw >psychoanalysis as a part of a reductionist science; his *Project For a Scientific Psychology*, written in 1895/6 but only published posthumously, explained all actions in terms of ENGRAMS or particles of energy.

In some senses, all schools of psychology have become reductionist. Few believe in the 'soul', or that there is any immaterial human substance though Sir John Eccles has disagreed. There are controversies, however, about how well we can ever understand how human biochemistry creates specific action. But many researchers increasingly doubt that simple scientific formulae can be used meaningfully in psychology. The attempt to make psychology fit the pattern of other sciences may be deeply flawed when its subject matter – human beings – makes it impossible so to do.

● J. Eccles and D. Robinson, *The Wonder of Being Human* (1985).

Redundancy, an information theory term for the extent to which a message doesn't convey new information. Languages are full of redundancy, which is why we can understand each other even if we communicate in rather noisy conditions. It has been claimed that the >brain is full of redundancy because, often, if there is damage to one part, patients can relearn their old skills in new ways. There is a connection here with >neural networks. *See* Language.

Redundancy at work, *See* Unemployment.

Reflex, automatic forms of behaviour that are not consciously controlled. If you put your hand near a fire, you will usually automatically withdraw it without >thinking. If you had to pause for thought, you would get burned. Reflexes are designed to protect. They operate quickly and rely largely on the more primitive parts of the >brain such as the >cerebellum. There are other reflexes that disappear as a person grows older. For example, if you touch a baby's cheek, it will turn its mouth towards the object, hoping that the touch will lead its mouth towards something (preferably a breast) to suck.

The fact that reflexes are so basic a part of our make-up has made them of interest to researchers, who see them as the building blocks of adult behaviour. The Soviet psychologist Bechterev and the early American behaviourists argued that complex human behaviour was the product of >conditioning chains of reflexes which turn into sequences of action. This view of the reflex seems, however, too generous. Many behaviours and actions are not related to reflexes at all. *See* Babinski reflex; Grasping reflex; Orienting reflex.

R

Regression, in general, a return to a more primitive form of psychological functioning. >Freud saw regression as a means of warding off >anxiety. In an emotional crisis, we regress – that is, behave less like adults and more like children, crying and becoming >egocentric. In psychoanalytic terms, we return to the libidinal pleasures that made us feel secure in infancy. There are situations in adult life when it is permissible to regress, but regression is usually a sign that the person is going through psychological trauma. It's a bad habit to get into, especially since some people are keen to reinforce it – to make others dependent.

Regression to the mean, in statistics, the tendency for the value of a variable, as predicted from a regression equation, to be closer to the mean than it should be. For example, in biology, while very tall and very short parents have children who take after them, regression to the mean determines that children are usually closer to the average than to their parents.

Reich, Wilhelm (1897–1957), psychoanalyst who was initially close to >Freud but then became too controversial for >psychoanalysis – especially in his evangelical views on sex. Reich set up the first sexual >counselling service in Europe in Berlin in the 1920s. He was at first an impressive thinker. He analysed better than anyone else the psychological distortions that lay underneath the growth of Nazism. He saw why the uniforms and the displays of brute power appealed to so many Germans. He devised the concept of 'character armour' which meant that people used certain personality traits to defend themselves against their wilder, more >id driven impulses.

He left Germany in the late 1930s, however, and became obsessed with the need for people to have orgasms. He argued that the essential problem all mankind faced was a lack of orgasms. Sex wasn't just good in itself but freed the person to be good. If the Nazis had had decent sex lives (impossible due to their character armour) they would never have been able to inflict such cruelties on others. Though one could trace a logic for such an argument in analytic theory, it was far too crude. Reich came to believe that sexual energy existed out there in the cosmos; it rained down on to the earth as showers of >orgone. Orgone was, in Reich's view, a real substance that was plentiful in the cosmos and encouraged sexuality. He imagined it as rays rather like X rays. The problem was how to get the orgone to the sexually deficient. In 1939, Reich moved to the USA where he claimed that the answer to the problem was to be found in orgone boxes. I have sat in an orgone box and was disappointed to say the least. It was an ordinary wooden box and, for me at least, did not produce throbs, thrills or even fantasies. Reich sold this exceptionally dubious device to credulous Americans. Few complained. He behaved oddly in other ways, claiming to have seen UFOs, and setting up a variety of experiments to try to control the weather. The authorities were suspicious and eventually the US Food and Drugs Administration prosecuted him. He tried to rally world science to his cause and to present himself as persecuted, but he had become bizarre and manipulative. From 1925 to 1940 he was certainly one of the most imaginative analysts. He died of a heart attack in prison.

- J. Croall, *Record of a Friendship*: *The Neill / Reich Letters* (1985); C. Rycroft, *Reich* (1980).

Reinforcement, a technical term for a reward which motivates either an animal or a human being. The term 'reinforcement' stems from the fact that a particular >stimulus – say, a pellet of food that is delivered when a rat has correctly pressed a lever – strengthens the likelihood of that behaviour being produced again.

The concept of reinforcement has been central to psychology since >John Watson's behaviourist manifesto of 1913. Psychologists have tried to discover the laws which govern how reinforcement affects behaviour, and they have had considerable success with animals. It's now clear that food, drink (eg sugar solutions), the chance to escape from a frightening environment and the chance to explore all reinforce behaviour. Much work has also gone into finding out how different schedules of reinforcement produce different patterns of response.

- *Fixed-interval schedule*: a schedule in which animals are reinforced at a fixed interval between presentations of a stimulus. So, for example, if the fixed interval is 40 seconds, it doesn't matter how many times a rat presses the lever, it will only get a reinforcing pellet of food after 40 seconds have passed. If a rat on such a schedule could read a clock, it would only press the lever every 40 seconds. If the experimenter sets a buzzer to go off as soon as the 40-second interval has passed, a rat soon learns to press the lever only after the buzzer has sounded. In real life, few rewards are based on fixed intervals, although some – such as our pattern of eating – loosely fit a fixed-interval schedule.

- *Fixed-ratio schedule*: instead of rewarding at a fixed interval of time, the reward is actually given, say, every third presentation. >B. F. Skinner argued that one of the best ways to train a rat to do a great deal of work for little reward is to start on a fixed-ratio schedule and then shift gradually to a variable ratio of reinforcement where the reward isn't so predictable.

● *Partial reinforcement*: a reinforcement schedule in which some, but not all, 'goal responses' are rewarded.

● *Variable-interval schedule*: the interval between deliveries of the reward varies. For instance, a VI.20 schedule would ensure that the animal got a reward *on average* every 20 seconds, but, during any given trial, this interval might be more (or less) than 20 seconds. In other words, the interval varies. This form of reinforcement has effects similar to partial reinforcement. It tends to produce a consistent rate of response which is hard to extinguish.

● *Variable-ratio schedule*: not every successful response is rewarded but only a certain number of them – hence the ratio. For example, in a 'VR 20' schedule, on average every 20th response would be reinforced. This produces a much quicker response rate than variable-interval schedules, suggesting clearly that animals become 'conscious' of the rate of reward in some way.

R

Initially, psychologists assumed that reinforcers were utterly obvious. In 1965, D. Premack suggested, however, that different animals have different preferences; psychologists can test for these and then use them to determine what will be the most effective reinforcer. Premack's principle draws attention to a paradox: what someone may think is reinforcing a particular desired behaviour may actually be having a very different effect. Take a mother who yells at her child to stop whining. The mother thinks that this is an aversive stimulus, assuming the infant doesn't want to be yelled at. But when she yells, she is paying much desired attention to the child, and so the whining is actually being reinforced and the mother's yelling is counterproductive.

With human beings, there are also subtle reinforcers that animal psychologists have ignored, such as >status, >self-actualization or even pride. A nice example occurs in T. S. Eliot's play *Murder in the Cathedral*, which tells the story of the murder and martyrdom of the 12th-century Archbishop of Canterbury, Thomas à Becket. In the play, he rebuffs three tempters. Then, he is surprised by a fourth. This tempter suggests that Becket is right to confront the king, Henry I, even if it means death – martyrdom is glorious. Becket should seek it; it would give him undying fame. Becket confesses himself tempted 'to do the right thing for the wrong reason'. Subtleties such as these which motivate many human actions aren't easily accommodated by reinforcement theories, which are accurate only about specific, obvious unselfconscious rewards such as food. But no understanding of 20th-century psychology is possible without a grasp of the varieties of reinforcement theory. *See* Behaviourism; Satiation; Secondary reinforcement; Vicarious reinforcement.

● W. F. Hill, *Theories of Learning* (1988); B. F. Skinner, *Beyond Freedom and*

Dignity (1972), *Science and Human Behaviour* (1953); S. Walker, *Behaviourism* (1984).

Reliability, a concept used in the testing of >psychological tests. A test is reliable if it gives the same result when the same >population is tested over time. The absence of variation makes it reliable. *See* Test-retest reliability.

Relaxation techniques. These are important in various forms of >behaviour therapy and in >meditation. They include making the client lie down, getting him or her to breath deeply and working on the patient muscle by muscle until he or she is relaxed. For very anxious patients, this procedure is in itself useful. Classically, the idea is to teach the patient to stay relaxed even when presented with noxious or frightening stimuli (*see* Stimulus).

Meditation involves some relaxation first though opinions vary on which is the most relaxed pose. Zen Buddhists favour the fairly controlled lotus position while therapists advocate lying down flat.

Religious behaviour. Psychologists have long been fascinated by religious behaviour. William James, for example, wrote lyrically of the force of religious experiences. James assumed that, although religious experiences were very various, they were real, and he would not have approved of the title of this entry for 'religious behaviour' implies that the experiences themselves aren't quite worth studying.

As psychology became more scientific, there was less sympathy for the truth of religious experiences. In his book *The Future of an Illusion*, >Freud suggested that human beings need to believe in God (or gods) to ward off the terrors of life in an uncertain world. We project the existence of deities 'up there' to help control life down here. Praying to rain gods, Jehovah and the woodland spirit of Pan are all efforts at reassurance. Freud claimed that the God of the Old and New Testament is a father figure in the sky. In a recently discovered manuscript, he said that it seemed likely that the early humans had invented gods not just because the natural environment was terrifying and uncontrollable but also to curb their own >guilt about desiring to murder their father. In *Totem and Taboo* (1913), Freud suggested that in early humans, the young male eager to mate killed his father and then, to ease his guilt, worshipped him in the form of a totem. It was not clear initially if Freud was thinking literally, drawing on the work of Victorian anthropologists, or symbolically. He may have partly misunderstood the anthropologists' ideas. But the thesis was crucial in suggesting to psychologists the unconscious origins of religion.

Such hostile attitudes towards religious belief meant that, from 1930 until the 1970s, there was little study of religious experience, although the British psychologist Michael Argyle published a monogram in 1952. In Britain, one of those who revived interest was the biologist Sir Alastair Hardy, who culled the newspapers through a cuttings service every ten years from 1925 on to see how religious attitudes had change. Hardy discerned a pattern. It wasn't one of growing scepticism. Rather, Hardy found that, at every decade, there were different concerns. In the mid 1970s, for example, he detected a new interest in faith. He did not distinguish this perhaps rigorously enough from flirtations with the occult which, especially in the USA, are very popular.

In the United States, it's estimated that over 60 per cent of the population have had mystical experiences. No existing psychological work can probe the truthfulness of religion, but Freud has turned out to be wrong – the illusion has prospered.

- Michael Argyle, *Religious Behaviour* (1952); Sigmund Freud, *The Future of an Illusion* (1932).

REM. *See* Rapid eye movement; Sleep.

Reminiscence therapy. *See* Ageing.

Repertory grid, developed and extensively described (in 1955) by George Kelly in the context of >personal construct theory. It consists of a grid, across the top of which the subject (S) fills in the names of a number of persons in his social environment. S is then asked successively to consider three of these people at a time and to decide in what way two are alike and different from the third. A series of 'constructs', or ways of perceiving others, is thus obtained. Each time S forms a construct, he places check markers in the grid under the names of the people or of roles such as 'teacher' perceived as similar in some way, and he enters the name of the construct (say kind/unkind) next to the grid. He is then asked to go back along the row and place check markers under the names of all those people who also come under that construct. For instance, asked to choose between himself, his mother and his father, S may decide that his mother and father are alike in being conventional whereas he is unconventional. If S's girlfriend, teacher and what S sees as a 'successful person' (another grid role) are also conventional, S will also check them off. This procedure yields a matrix of check patterns which represents how S perceives a group of persons. Kelly's theory argues that man is a scientist whose 'processes are psychologically channelized by the ways in which he anticipates events'.

In 1965, D. Bonarius reported research in which the >test-retest reliability of constructs thus obtained was high. However, as he pointed out, the technique may be used without total commitment to the theory. In the 1970s and 1980s, it became progressively more popular.

- F. Fransella and D. Bannister, *Inquiring Man* (1986); G. Kelly, *Personal Constructs* (1955).

Repetition compulsion, in psychoanalytic theory, an innate tendency to revert to earlier conditions. >Freud did not specifically refer to the behaviour of young children; rather, he conceived the concept out of the >dreams of his patients. Many obsessional patients suffered from the compulsion to repeat actions like hand-washing. Freud saw this as a neurotic defence. Yet, curiously, many observational studies of children's >play have found that they do frequently repeat patterns of play. Typically, a child will do so because play is a way of achieving mastery. You learn how to do something by 'playing it out'. The

R

parallel between obsessive adult repetition of actions and repetition in child's play is intriguing.

Repression, the process by which an unacceptable impulse is driven into the >unconscious. >Freud spoke of both primary and secondary repression. In primary repression, the initial idea doesn't even emerge fully before it is repressed; in secondary repression, manifestations of the impulse are kept unconscious. One key concept is 'the return of the repressed' in which ideas that have been driven underground keep breaking back into the conscious >mind.

Without repression, we could not adapt to the environment and the >ego could not develop because, then, we would be constantly indulging our instinctive >drives. Lust, violence and mayhem would leave no energy for the building of societies. In *Civilization and Its Discontents*, Freud argued that the achievements of civilization required repression, but human beings pay a price for this, for our lives often feel troubled and unfulfilled. Freud, nevertheless, clearly believed in the value of repression. Later theorists, such as Herbert Marcuse, argued that capitalism required >surplus repression to keep the workers sufficiently oppressed; in this way, they would not have the energy to demand a fair share of the spoils.

Although the concept of repression comes from psychoanalytic literature, it is accepted by psychologists of different schools. One reason is that there is considerable experimental evidence which suggests that often what we recall is not logical; and that we frequently forget things that we don't really want to remember. In his assessment of Freudian concepts, Paul Kline concluded that that of repression had been partially confirmed.

• Sigmund Freud, *Civilization and Its Discontents* (1930); Herbert Marcuse, *Eros and Civilization* (1958).

Resistance, opposition to treatment, either in >psychoanalysis or in other forms of >therapy. Critics of psychoanalysis are very wary of this concept because it can be used to justify anything. If a patient doesn't accept an interpretation offered by the analyst or if he fails to go into >transference, the analyst could say that resistance is at work, rather than accept any criticism of himself or psychoanalytic theory.

Response bias, a tendency of subjects to produce the response that is either socially desirable or that the experimenter wants. Hence, the responses are biased. *See* Experimenter effect.

Response set/style, like a >learning set, a fixed way of answering. In this case to a questionnaire or similar tests. There is no universal agreement whether there is a distinction between response set and response style, or if there is, how that difference should be defined.

Response style can be defined as the way in which something is written, said, shown or done, as distinguished from its substance – that is, a manner of responding that is not influenced by the content of the question (*see* Social desirability response set). For example, there is a tendency for some people to

R

answer questionnaires in a particular way and irrespective of the content. Extreme responders, no matter if it is a 5-point or an 11-point scale, will consistently endorse the extremes, while middle-of-the-roaders will endorse the mid-point at all times. Some psychologists use 4 point scales to stop subjects choosing the 'middle of the road'.

Retardation. *See* Mental handicap.

Reticular formation, also known as the reticular activating system; a collection of structures in the brainstem which function together to switch the brain 'off' and 'on'. The reticular formation includes the >pons and the medulla. It is crucially important in determining cycles of >sleep, wakefulness and attention.

Retina. The retina lines most of the inner surface of the eye. When light falls on the 130 million photoreceptors of the retina, impulses are transmitted to >neurons, the axons of which reach towards the optic disc at the back of the eye. All the axons leave the eye at the optic disc and join up to form the optic nerve which travels to the >brain. There are no photoreceptors in front of the optic disc, which is why that spot on the retina is blind – in fact, it is known as the 'blind spot'. Behind the photoreceptor cells, there are layers of bipolar cells and ganglion cells which can integrate the information from many photoreceptors.

The biochemistry by which light is changed into nerve impulses is clear. There are two kinds of photoreceptors in the human eye: *rods*, which are long and narrow and are sensitive to light and dark; and *cones*, which are shorter and bottle-shaped and are receptors for colour and sharp vision. When at rest, each photoreceptor is saturated with pigments. When light strikes a photopigment, the latter splits in two. The splitting causes a series of chemical changes that make the receptors transmit information to the bipolar cells. The 'used' photoreceptor which has been struck by light is said to be 'bleached'. The process of building up what we are conscious of seeing starts but doesn't end at the retina. For the rest of the story, *see* Vision.

Risky shift. Psychologists have been interested in the fact that a group will often take riskier decisions than an individual will. It is argued that when one person faces a risky decision, they feel wholly responsible for the outcome. That makes most, though not all, people conservative. In a group the responsibility is diffused so it's less weighty to take risks.

Ritual, literally, a formal pattern of behaviour for formal occasions. Psychoanalysts see ritual as an attempt to reduce >anxiety by setting up fixed patterns of behaviour that have the air (and almost the authority) of magical actions. Religious services can certainly be comforting; funerals can make it easier for the bereaved to cope (*see* Loss). Rituals can also be social or religious, and they often, but not always, carry a symbolic meaning. Some, such as the Jewish *Bar mitzvah* ceremony, mark a male's transition from boy to man. But there are also some anxiety-laden but still formal rituals such as introductions which carry no symbolic baggage or heavy meanings.

Contemporary authors on divorce take the view that one reason why divorce

R

is so painful is that, for most people in the secular West, there is no accompanying ritual. However, although there are in both Judaism and Islam divorce ceremonies laden with symbolism, there is little evidence that these make divorce an easier experience, especially for the 'weaker' partner. In general, rituals may be comforting not because they ward off anxiety but because they are learned set pieces of behaviour in which everybody plays their appointed >roles. In divorce rituals, this may not work because they occur so rarely in any individual's life that there's no way of learning the roles.

Roles and role therapy. The original idea for role therapy came from Shakespeare who noted that all the world's a stage and that, at different ages, we act out appropriate roles. In truth, however, role theory hasn't, despite the development of much jargon, advanced far beyond this initial >insight. We play social roles, and as we perform them, we take on some of their characteristics. For example, doctors generally act the part of the medical expert: they are, and feel themselves to be, knowledgeable, caring but a bit busy and, most important of all, powerful. Patients, on the other hand, are relatively weak, needy and dependent. These characteristic feelings are the product, not of basic >personality, but of the roles that are played out in a social transaction. Crossing role boundaries is difficult: when doctors become sick, they often make impossible patients because they are not used to that role.

Role theory has become very influential, but there are problems with it, especially in working out if there are real selves behind all these roles and, if not, why do we persist in feeling that there are. *See* Goffman, Erving.

- Erving Goffman, *The Presentation of Self in Everyday Life* (1956).

Rorschach test, a >projective test which makes use of inkblots. Subjects have to say what the inkblot looks like to them, the idea being that their answers will reveal what fundamentally motivates them. There are hefty manuals detailing how to score the Rorschach, but studies show that scorers, even though expert, tend to disagree on what a particular inkblot reveals. Many psychologists feel the test is misleading, and it could be taken as a 'blot' in the history of psychology.

- John E. Exner, *The Rorschach* (1986).

R

S

Sadism, a sexual perversion named after the Marquis de Sade (1740–1814), who spent 27 years in prison for sexual offences. The sadist enjoys inflicting >pain; cruelty is his delight. Sadism as a source of sexual pleasure was commented on by the Victorians and by Krafft-Ebbing.

It's not clear what turns a person into a sadist. >Freud argued that it is a manifestation of the earliest aggressive >instinct. However, he was slightly confused by sadism: at first, he thought it preceded masochism but then decided that, under the right provocation, the sadist could turn into a masochist; later, he changed his mind again and claimed that masochism was the first of these instincts because it was a manifestation of the >death instinct.

Surveys of sexual behaviour suggest that many people are masochists, but few are sadists (which must leave a lot of frustrated masochists around). Sadism need not be sexual; the 20th century has seen many instances of sadistic cruelty that have not been sexual. Perhaps because the subject makes us uncomfortable, we often make fun of it. *See* Masochism.

Salience, a term used in studies of visual >perception, denotes the quality surrounding an object or an event that makes it particularly likely to be noticed. Brightness and clarity are obvious instances.

Sample, the group upon which a psychological experiment is done. Great care needs to be taken with construction of a sample; it can be all too easily inappropriate. For example, far too many studies have used American undergraduates as subjects, and then assumed the results apply generally (*see* Kinsey reports). Experimenters also have to make sure that their samples aren't biased so as to make it more likely that meaningful results are produced. *See* Random sampling; Sampling error.

- S. Miller, *Experimental Design and Statistics* (1984).

Sampling error, literally, an error in sampling procedures. No matter how carefully any >sample is constructed, it will never be perfectly representative of a >population. Gross sampling errors will devalue the research done in an experiment.

Satiation, having no unmet needs for the moment, a rare state in life. Technically, in >learning theory, it refers to the state of an animal when food, drink or sexual contact no longer work as a reward. *See* Reinforcement.

Scapegoating, the process of blaming someone or some group for what has gone wrong. The concept, derived from anthropology, is used both in social psychology and in >psychiatry. According to one view of >family dynamics, families in difficulties often scapegoat one individual, and every problem then becomes the fault of that one deviant member. A similar process occurs in social psychology when one group, usually an >'outgroup', is blamed either for economic troubles or general decline. The Nazis scapegoated the Jews, for instance. *See* Prejudice; Projection.

S

Schedules of reinforcement. *See* Reinforcement.

Schema. In >Piaget's theory of intellectual development, a schema is a mental representation. Towards the end of the >sensori-motor period, at about 18 to 24 months, babies develop schemas of the world as they learn to coordinate their movements better. Piaget argued that they emerge as the child assimilates the flood of incoming perceptions and accommodates to them. The ability to form and recall schemas is a crucial stage in >learning to handle symbols. *See* Accommodation; Assimilation.

Schizophrenia, a serious form of mental illness which has been particularly controversial since the 1960s. Despite its popular image, schizophrenia has nothing to do with having a 'split personality' (*see* Multiple personality). Schizophrenia was originally described in the 1890s by Kraeplin and Bleuler, who held that it was basically an >organic disorder. The classic symptoms include >hallucinations, hearing voices and feeling controlled, often by 'aliens'. With these symptoms there is frequently a sense of withdrawal and lack of any emotional expression. This view was not challenged until the 1960s, when radical psychiatrists such as Thomas Szasz and >R. D. Laing pointed out that almost anything could be taken as a symptom of schizophrenia. This confusion, they argued, showed that schizophrenia was not an illness like measles or tuberculosis; rather, it was a way of labelling rebels, non-conformists and those who didn't meet the expectations either of society or of their families. In response to this theory, the World Health Organization set up an international pilot project, which found that, while most psychiatrists round the world agreed on what were the first-rank symptoms of schizophrenia – hallucinations and voices in the head – in two major countries, the US and the USSR, schizophrenia *was* diagnosed more widely. In the USSR, in particular, psychiatrists employed a diagnosis known as 'sluggish schizophrenia', in which the symptoms were so subtle that only a skilled psychiatrist could spot them – to the ordinary person, the so-called schizophrenic might look normal. This allowed abuse of patients to take place: mentally healthy individuals (often political dissidents) would be labelled schizophrenic despite appearances to the contrary.

The work of Laing and Szasz became popular outside the medical profession and did alter >therapy. Laing showed, in particular, how disturbed families might seize on one member as the 'sick one' (*see* Scapegoating) and give him or her contradictory messages. The contradictions would make that person behave very oddly, or 'drive them mad'.

However, in the 1980s, a reaction set in. E. Fuller Torrey, for example, has argued that schizophrenia is a >brain disease: there is evidence of brain abnormalities, especially in the ventricles which, in schizophrenics, are larger than normal. In 1988, Gurling and his colleagues claimed to have isolated a gene for schizophrenia. But even the 'organic lobby' accepts that environment may well also have some impact on the development of the illness. In families where there is a high degree of >expressed emotion – ie plenty of screaming, shouting and other emotional displays – schizophrenia is more likely to be triggered.

Such disputes have made the illness a political issue. Families of schizophrenics argue that the causes are biological and complain about the poor treatment that schizophrenics get in the community now that hospitals are closing down. Because schizophrenics evoke as much >fear as sympathy, politicians have tended to pay lip service to the need to fund care properly. Treatment is largely chemical, involving drugs such as >chlorpromazine, which suppress >dopamine transmission (*see also* Electro-convulsive therapy). Psychotherapy has been of little use in schizophrenia, although David Healy has recently argued that this reflects the timidity and lack of insight of many psychiatrists. Estimates of the number of schizophrenics world-wide suggests it is as high as 40 million.

- M. Boyle, *Schizophrenia* (1992); E. Fuller Torrey, *Surviving Schizophrenia* (1984); H. Gurling *et al*, 'A Gene for Schizophrenia', *Nature*, 164 ff (10 Nov. 1988); D. Healy, *The Suspended Revolution* (1990); R. D. Laing, *The Divided Self* (1965); T. Szasz, *The Manufacture of Madness* (1983).

Secondary process, the kind of mental functioning that is typical of the >conscious and >preconscious parts of the psyche. Secondary process accommodates to reality. It is reasonable and adaptive as opposed to the torrid chaos of >primary process.

Secondary reinforcement, a process by which a >stimulus which is associated with the original reward itself becomes reinforcing. So if doing well at exams allows you to get a job with high >status, you have the >primary reinforcement of a good job, plus the secondary reinforcement of the associated status.

Selective attention, a label that redefines the obvious. The >brain can't possibly notice all the perceptual stimuli (*see* Stimulus) with which its receptors are bombarded every second. It picks and chooses what seems important out of the 'flow'. This is usually not a conscious process.

The term 'selective attention' also has a second meaning: we accuse people

S

of having selective attention when they deliberately do not notice things that make them uncomfortable.

Self, the core of our identity. All the entries that follow which incorporate the prefix *self* throw some light on how psychology defines the self. There is a huge philosophical gulf between thinkers such as William James and Sartre who argue that our sense of self comes from within, from the stream of >consciousness burbling through our minds, and those such as >Skinner who see our sense of self as being derived from what others think of us. The first view suggests that, through our childhood and adolescence, we develop an internalized sense of our own identity; the reactions of other people are clearly important, but our sense of self is derived from internal reflection. The second view suggests that, fundamentally, a person doesn't have a sense of self. The >roles that you play and the reflections of your own self that you glean from other people make up your identity. You are not in the least in control. There's no way of proving empirically which version is true to date.

There are two particularly interesting strands to recent work on the self. First, ingenious thought experiments carried out by philosophers like Daniel Dennett, who are also interested in >artificial intelligence, keep on coming up against the fact that our idea of self requires a body. Philosophy often toys with the notion of disembodied selves; personalities floating about having metaphysical conversations with angels. But so much of what we take as crucial to our sense of self – our face, voice, ability to communicate – depends on the body. The self isn't really the soul revived in a non-materialistic form. The rootedness of the self in our bodies confirms how much our sense of personal identity starts from the physical.

Second, recent developmental work has examined when children develop the sense of self and recognize the most crucial of all human distinctions – that between Me and Not Me. It seems clear that this happens some time between the sixth and eighteenth month. By the age of three, intelligent children are perfectly well able to use the concept of self appropriately in conversation with adults. That is an enormous achievement and to date somewhat mysterious. Clearly, much of their sense of self comes from what adults reflect back at them. But the same is true of >language, as >Noam Chomsky has shown. Do we have an innate sense of self that is just confirmed or triggered by the way parents respond to us? The question is crucial and intriguing, and a convincing experimental way of testing it has yet to be devised.

- Daniel Dennett, *Brainstorms* (1985); Jonathan Glover, *Personal Identity* (1989); B. Lee, *Psychosocial Theories of the Self* (1979).

Self-actualization, fulfilling one's potential, which reflects the capacity of human beings to grow and become more emotionally and psychologically mature. K. Goldstein argued that it was only through battling with the environment that individuals reached maturity. >Maslow developed the idea, seeing self-actualization as the highest need in his >hierarchy of needs. Not many of us manage to become self-actualized; paying the gas bill and other everyday trivia usually get in the way. However, increasingly, people feel that they ought to grow, develop and make the best of their capabilities. The danger is that, as A. Symonds has suggested, these demands create new pressures. The culture that demands self-actualization causes >stress. Many psychotherapists claim that patients who experience >psychotherapy feel more self-actualized, but those who oppose the >psychodynamic view see 'self-actualization' as a fad of the 'me' generation – self-indulgent and rather neurotically demanding.

- Abraham Maslow, *The Psychology of Self-actualization* (1968); Carl Rogers, *On Becoming a Person* (1961); A. Symonds, 'The Stress of Self Actualization', *American Journal of Psychoanalysis*, 40, 293–300 (1980).

Self-concept, the idea that each of us has of ourselves. In >psychodynamic terms, to have a weak self-concept is to be vulnerable because you don't know who you are. >Sex differences are intriguing. Generally, men describe themselves in terms of their work, while women describe themselves in terms of their relationships – for instance, as 'mother' or 'wife'. This may be changing, however. In 1986, Susan Whitmore found that men highlighted their caring role in the family far more than before. It's not certain whether this change is real or an attempt to act in a way that is perceived as being socially correct. Men now know that they ought to have feelings and should not be obsessed with their jobs. At the same time, women now mention their professions more. *See* Psychological androgyny.

- Susan Whitmore, *The Me I Know* (1986).

Self-consciousness, literally, being conscious of one's >self. The term has two meanings: being aware of oneself and understanding what goes on in one's >mind; or being ill at ease with that self-knowledge. For example, we say someone is self-conscious if they are socially awkward and don't sparkle at parties. This second sense of self-consciousness is, however, derivative. The original sense refers to our relationship to our own mind, not a kind of shyness.

To be self-conscious is a mark of being human. The survival value of self-consciousness is unknown, yet it's one of those faculties that makes us different from other animals. H. Wellman has suggested that children as young as the age of three are self-conscious, and research is going on to examine how children begin to be so self-aware. William James claimed that the 'stream of consciousness' was the core of our identity. That 'stream' is really a constant self-conscious summary.

Once, the study of self-consciousness was banned from scientific psychology, but now the topic is very much on the psychological agenda again. In both >cognitive psychology and in >child development work, it is seen as an important area that psychology needs to encompass.

- J. O'Keefe, 'Is the Hippocampus the Way to Consciousness?' in D. Oakley (ed.), *Brain and Mind* (1985); H. Wellman, 'First Steps Towards Theorizing About

S

the Mind' in Janet Astington, P. Harris and D. Olson (eds), *Developing Theories of Mind* (1986).

Self-disclosure, a technical term describing the process of being self-revelatory. Studies of >love and attraction find that lovers self-disclose to one another a great deal at the start of a relationship.

Self-esteem, >thinking well of oneself or liking oneself. Psychologists have devised various tests to measure self-esteem. Low self-esteem is not good for anyone's psychological health. In a general way, it is assumed that good parents and a supporting environment give children a sense of self-esteem. Feminist psychologists such as Cline and Spender have argued that discrimination leads to lower self-esteem in girls, even though the family background may be conventionally stable. Plausible ideas but not easy to verify.

• S. Cline and D. Spender, *Reflecting Men* (1987).

S

Self-help groups, groups of people who all suffer from the same problem and believe that, by sharing experiences, they help each other. Those who have been helped are usually good leaders of such groups since they provide inspiration. Self-help groups have been one of the important developments of the 1970s and 1980s, although there is no theory that accounts either for their popularity or their relative success. *See* Group therapy.

Self-image, the image we have of ourselves. This is linked to our sense of >self-esteem and >self-consciousness. The self-image that you have depends initially on parenting, but in adult life, it is also affected by how people react to you. >Freud said that, secure in his mother's >love, he always felt like a 'conquistador'. That positive self-image gave him lifelong confidence. Negative self-images are damaging because they destroy one's confidence.

Self-monitoring. *See* Normal.

Self-report techniques. These are in effect a systematic form of >introspection. But where classical introspective techniques require the subject to report in detail on his sensations in a loose way, mixing narrative and reports of feelings, self report asks subjects to say (and often to quantify on a 5 point or 7 point scale) how they feel. For example, a test of >depression will list a series of symptoms and thoughts like: 'Do you wake early?' and 'Do you have suicidal thoughts?' The answers a person gives are generally assumed to be true and informative. Self-report techniques are now very prevalent in psychology but they do have risks associated with them. The most obvious is that people give the responses they think the experimenter wants and that are called 'socially desirable'. The self-reports risk being self-flattering; in general, however, psychologists believe them. *See* Experimenter effect; Idiographic; Social desirability set.

200

Semantics, in logic, philosophy and linguistics, the term 'semantic' refers to meaning. Early psychologists such as John B. Watson believed that human beings learned to recognize stimuli (*see* Stimulus) and >associations between stimuli. Children learn that a rose is a flower. But a rose can have different meanings. It can be a flower, a symbol of romance or a symbol of religious faith. You can't understand the particular meaning of the word 'rose' without understanding its context. It is one of the age-old puzzles of psychology that the >brain seems to code certain information not in terms of the actual stimuli it perceives but of the meaning that they have. >Chomsky argues, in fact, that the >deep structure of the >mind is essentially semantic not linguistic. We speak therefore of semantic >memory.

Semiotics, a branch of linguistics concerned with the study of the patterns and the manner of communication. It has become fashionable intellectually, and in psychology, its main impact has been on >psychoanalysis. >Jacques Lacan, the French analyst, was deeply influenced by it.

Senile dementia, mental confusion with growing age, nearly always due to >Alzheimer's disease. Surveys suggest that 20 per cent of those over 75 will suffer from it. The causes are similar to Alzheimer's disease and, indeed, the terms are often used interchangeably. A diet of white fish may help avoid it by stimulating production of the >neurotransmitter >acetylcholine. The increasing number of those over 75 and especially over 85 has focused attention on this condition.

Sensori-motor stage, the first stage in >Piaget's theory of intellectual development. Piaget charted how infants learn to coordinate their movements and to integrate sensory >perception and >motor skills – hence 'sensori-motor'. He claimed that babies are egocentric (*see* Egocentricity) and at the mercy of their constantly shifting perceptions. A key point in this stage is when the infant understands that, when objects disappear from view, they don't disappear for ever: a ball that has rolled behind a cushion hasn't dropped out of the universe; out of sight isn't either out of >mind or out of being. This tends to occur at the age of six months. The baby's task is not just to master grasping and moving but to begin to develop >schemas and symbolic representations. By the end of the period, the infant realizes that the world is 'stable' and that objects don't change randomly.

Unfortunately, Piaget's formulation ignores the role that people play in shaping babies' ideas. Almost all his descriptions centre on how babies handle things such as rattles. Much recent work stresses the role of social and emotional behaviour in creating an infant's sense of the world. Piaget bypassed all this. Nevertheless, the concept remains widely used and commented upon.

● M. Donaldson, *Children's Minds* (1978); J. H. Flavell, *The Developmental Psychology of Jean Piaget* (1962); Jean Piaget, *The Language and Thought of the Child* (1926).

Sensory deprivation, experiments in which subjects were deprived of light and sound. They found this very stressful and often began to hallucinate (*see* Hallucinations; Stress). This confirmed the notion that the >brain needs to

S

perceive to remain healthy. There were unethical reasons also for the experiments: the CIA hoped to understand through them how some American GIs had been brainwashed in Korea into accepting Communism.

- G. Thomas, *Journey into Madness* (1989).

Sensory neurons, >neurons which carry information from >receptors to the >central nervous system. They are designed to transmit information extremely quickly.

Separation anxiety, in >psychoanalysis, the term originally used to describe the >anxiety of a child who has had to leave his or her mother, who was held to be necessary for the child's survival. Films of children being taken to hospital graphically illustrated the distress they felt at 'losing' their mothers. When the mother didn't give the child a sense of living security, separation anxiety was worse. This lack could lead to adult neurotic separation anxiety, when some individuals feel they can't leave a lover. However, while this leaving may be sad, it shouldn't be ballooned into a psychological death.

>John Bowlby and D. W. Winnicott developed the concept of separation anxiety into that of >maternal deprivation. This states that if a child is away from his or her mother for a long period, this would cause long-term psychic damage. However, the statistical evidence for this is not clear cut.

- John Bowlby, *Attachment and Loss* (1972); D. W. Winnicott, 'Parental Deprivation and Mental Health', *The Lancet* (6 August 1966).

Serial processing, processing of one item of information at a time. Many models of cognitive functioning (>thinking) assume that the >brain works through serial processing but there is increasing evidence of >parallel processing.

Serotonin, a >neurotransmitter which is especially important in >sleep and mood. >LSD seems to be attracted to serotonin >receptor sites.

Set, a state of preparedness. A 'perceptual set' or a 'warning set' describes a state of readiness to receive certain kinds of stimuli or learning experiences.

Sex. *See* Sexual behaviour.

Sex differences. An enormous literature has tried to establish the psychological differences (if any) between males and females. There are three broad positions. First, sociobiologists (*see* Sociobiology) believe in profound biological differences: men were 'made' to hunt, women were 'made' to look after the babies, and this ancient 'truth' continues to affect behaviour deeply. Second, there is the feminist view which claims that men have exaggerated such differences for their own patriarchal advantage: the best way to keep women in their place is to persuade them that they are less able and less dynamic than men. Biological differences actually mean much less than has been believed; any woman can drive a tank or become prime minister like Mrs Thatcher. A third view argues that, although differences have been exaggerated, there is some biological validity to them.

One difficulty in assessing the literature is that female/male differences haven't been studied in any systematic way. In their massive tome, E. M. Maccoby and C. N. Jacklin analysed more than 10,000 studies of abilities ranging from mathematical skills to >motivation in sports. They concluded there were many unfounded beliefs about sex differences, including the notion that girls are more social than boys, that girls are more suggestible than boys, that girls have lower >self-esteem, that girls are better at rote learning while boys are better at higher-level cognitive learning. They also found that boys are not more analytic and that girls do not lack achievement motivation, but they did discover that boys tend to respond better to competitive environments. In other areas, the evidence was inconclusive. These included whether girls were more anxious, whether boys were more active and competitive and, interestingly, whether girls showed more maternal and nurturing behaviour than boys. Only four areas yielded clear-cut sex differences: girls do have greater verbal abilities than boys; and boys do have better visual spatial ability, are better at mathematics and are more aggressive. However, Maccoby and Jacklin's very careful tabulation shows how hard it is to generalize about sex differences. Morever, they themselves stated how well aware they were of how imperfect some of the evidence they collated is.

In the 15 years since their study, political pressure for women to have real equal opportunities has increased, yet many women say that it is still hard to succeed in a 'man's world'. They don't blame biology but social attitudes which are still prejudiced against women who seek to achieve. The problem has shifted from discovering what the sex differences are to finding out how to make it possible for people of both sexes to pursue the careers they want. Towards this end, some European countries have drastically improved child care facilities to help women, but female pilots and 'househusbands' still have problems and are often seen as eccentric.

- S. Golombok and R. Fivush, *Gender Development* (1994); J. Nicholson, *Men and Women* (1985).

Sex therapy, >therapy which aims to resolve the sexual difficulties of couples. There was no respectable sex therapy until >William Masters and Virginia Johnson's work in the 1960s. They set the rules for everything that followed. They insisted that all sex therapy had to be conjoint – ie treating a couple together. The couple as a whole needed treatment, not just the one person who allegedly wasn't good at making love, and it should be given by co-therapists, a man and a woman. Masters and Johnson didn't deny that sexual difficulties might be due to childhood experience, but they stressed that short-term remedial exercises could train individuals to be better lovers.

Sex therapy according to the initial Masters and Johnson formula involved patients booking into a hotel for a two-week stay. Couples would spend part of each day in discussion with their therapists and then be given 'homework' for their bedroom. The whole approach depended on freeing couples from 'performance >anxiety' by temporarily banning sexual intercourse. The hotel homework consisted of >learning to caress and stimulate each other in 'sensate focus' exercises, during which couples would focus on sensations in one part of the body. Over the 14 days, couples began on arms, backs and bellies and then graduated to focusing on their genitals, but intercourse remained taboo. This was a clever idea for it meant that couples were highly motivated and had nothing to be anxious about; they couldn't be afraid of >impotence or premature ejaculation. Masters and Johnson also developed new techniques for mapping what happened during sex, as well as curative tricks such as the 'squeeze technique' for premature ejaculation.

The success rate of their therapy was apparently phenomenal, and Masters and Johnson actually claimed a success rate with premature ejaculation of nearly 100 per cent. However, there were always critics – moral and scientific. Some simply wondered why people had to check into a hotel. Bernie Zilberfeld, in a paper wickedly called 'A case of premature congratulation', wondered if the results were really so good, while Thomas Szasz argued that sex therapy was morally dubious. It demanded people perform athletically in bed and often involved paid surrogates. Nevertheless, sex therapy is now well established, and all but a few therapists draw their basic inspiration from Masters and Johnson.

- W. H. Masters and V. Johnson, *Human Sexual Performance* (1970); T. Szasz, *Sex By Prescription* (1982); B. Zilberfeld, 'A case of premature congratulation: the inadequacy of Masters and Johnson', *Psychology Today*, 14–29 (1980).

Sexual behaviour. Psychologists have always been much more interested in abnormal sexual behaviour than in normal behaviour. Four main lines of inquiry in sexual studies have been pursued.

First, a number of physiological psychologists have tried to examine what attracts individuals to each other, and what happens when someone becomes sexually aroused. Physical signs include dilation of the pupils, faster breathing and, in some people, the face flushes. Many people recognize this state of arousal or excitement very well. Animal studies have suggested that in rats, at least, the areas of the >brain that control sexual arousal are in the >hypothalamus and in the >limbic system. In humans, however, the mixture of physiological and social cues is likely to make the story more complex.

Second, there have been many studies (the most notable of which are the >Kinsey reports) which have tried to plot actual behaviour. Essentially, over the last 50 years, people have become sexually active earlier and tend to be unfaithful to their partners more often. Today only 25 percent of men and 20 per cent of women are virgins when they marry – a marked decline from the virtues of pre-war America that Kinsey studied. Sexual surveys generally show that now there is more sexual experimentation, with people having more partners than before, although a recent American study suggests that more is said than done. Even in the US, with a high divorce rate, singles bars and a permissive ethic, the average male has only seven sexual partners in his lifetime, the average female, three. Nevertheless, sexual behaviour remains very individualistic; some people manage perfectly well without any 'outlets' as

Kinsey called them. Attitudes have changed enormously. As late as the 1950s, pre-marital sex was taboo, adultery a disgrace. Today, one marriage in three in the UK ends in divorce. Sex is no longer taboo; soft porn magazines are on sale in respectable shops; children receive sex education in most schools. What the early sexologists called perversions, such as >homosexuality, are now generally regarded as one form of sexual expression. The arrival of AIDS has produced something of a backlash to these more tolerant attitudes although this has been less than might have been expected.

The third approach is through social psychology, which has looked at the details of the social intercourse that precedes sexual intercourse. It is possible to plot the >eye contact of a couple as they start to fancy one another. Michael Argyle and his colleagues proved it is unwise to sit next to the person you desire since it cuts down eye contact, and eye contact is vital preamble to flesh contact. Psychologists have also mapped the areas of the body which people first touch and how sexual encounters usually proceed. Most people first touch 'safe' parts of the body such as hands and then move on to kiss and to the erogenous zones. The intricate ballet of look and touch has been mapped and psychologists are even able to show those who aren't skilled at it where they fall down. Classes for sex offenders have been introduced in some clinics to teach the requisite chatting-up skills. Fourth, psychologists have been interested in sexual preferences and in understanding why certain people don't conform to the heterosexual norm. There is considerable controversy as to whether homosexuality is a choice or determined by, for example, a slightly odd hormonal balance.

● Z. Luria, S. Friedman and M. D. Rose, *Human Sexuality* (1986).

Shaping, teaching a new form of behaviour by reinforcing responses which get closer and closer to the behaviour required. This form of >operant conditioning is central to >B. F. Skinner's thought, but for centuries, animal trainers had, of course, been 'shaping' animals without theorizing about it. Skinner found that he could get a pigeon to raise its head very high by, first, watching to see when it did raise its head and, then, rewarding it; he would then only reward the bird when it raised its head above a particular height. Skinner used this technique with exquisite patience and accuracy to train pigeons to play ping pong and even to develop the persistence to fly in missiles and, by appropriate pecking, to guide them, an area the military rejected as being impractical and cruel to birds!

Shaping has been used in some forms of >behaviour therapy, but its most useful applications have been in teaching mentally handicapped people to be more self-reliant. They can be taught to dress and feed themselves by breaking the behaviour required into smaller and smaller parts which they can master and then integrate into longer strings of behaviour.

Shyness. *See* Embarrassment.

Sibling rivalry. According to >psychoanalysis, siblings (ie brothers and sisters) are bound to compete for the >love and attention of their parents. Many observations confirm that the older child will hate the arrival of a new baby and

S

may even try to harm him or her, but it is only in some cases that this antagonism continues into later life. This concept has entered the popular imagination even though the evidence for it is rather flimsy.

Signal detection theory, a theory that explains how we detect weak signals through noise. It is suggested that we do so by cancelling out everything in the noise but the particular signal. *See* Hearing.

Significance level. *See* Null hypothesis; Significant difference.

Significant difference. Psychologists use tests to see whether a finding is statistically significant (*see* Statistical significance). When the >null hypothesis is not rejected, it is usually reported as having no significant difference. Usually a significant difference is reckoned to exist when there is a less than 1 chance in 20 that a particular correlation occurred 'by chance'. But it is important to separate the statistical and ordinary use of the word 'significant'. If, for example, a researcher tests the cognitive skills of a group of unemployed people and those in paid employment but finds no statistically significant difference, this does not mean that being unemployed/in paid employment or not having/having the opportunity to use cognitive skills in paid employment, is not significant to the individual. On a statistical level, the results may not 'reach' significance.

Skewness. A statistical distribution is 'skewed' if it is not symmetrical as it would be if it were the >normal distribution. In a positively skewed distribution, there are more low scores to the left, while a negatively skewed distribution has more high scores to the right.

Skill. Detailed studies have been made of how we acquire motor skills. Topics include vigilance, the ability to keep a pencil on a moving line and the effects of fatigue on performance. Essentially, we tend to learn skills in chunks. A skill is a smoothly joined series of sequences of action. Once learned, skills do not deteriorate easily. If you learned to type 15 years ago, you will re-learn the skill more quickly than a new typist. Skills such as driving are very complex. We can only use them because many aspects of them become automatic and we don't have to think about what we're doing in order to do it. They become part of what some authors call the brainstem >memory, that is, a pattern of actions that are so deeply embedded in the body's memory that they become automatic. *See* Learning.

Skinner, B(urrhus) F(redric) (1903–91), leading American behavioural psychologist. Wearing the mantle of >J. B. Watson, Skinner argues that >consciousness is an irrelevance and that the central role allotted to consciousness is baggage from the past. As an indication of his theories, he entitled one of the sections of his book *Science and Human Behavior* (1953) 'Man a Machine'. Skinner also dismisses all feelings, all motives, all intentions as, at best, byproducts. We attribute to the mysterious inner person the reasons for behaviour because we don't have a real scientific explanation for what we do. Skinner counters that the real cause of all behaviour is the past history of the organism, its actions, reactions and reinforcements: we are what we have done and what has been done to us. He elaborated these ideas into a view of behaviourist utopia in his book *Walden Two* where sensible > reinforcement led to an idealistic and cooperative society.

Skinner has been attacked for wanting a technocratic society much like that portrayed in Huxley's novel *Brave New World*, and the drift of psychology in the 1970s and 1980s, with its renewed emphasis on >consciousness, was in many ways against him. However, he remains one of the most challenging psychological thinkers of the mid-20th century. *See* Black box theories.

- B. F. Skinner, *Beyond Freedom and Dignity* (1972), *Particulars of My Life* (1976), *Walden Two* (1948).

Sleep. All animals need to sleep but it is not clear why. Different stages of sleep have been identified both in humans and other mammals. Initially, from wakefulness, which is characterized by alpha rhythm brain waves (8 to 12 cycles a second), a person dozes into Stage I sleep. In this, the electrical activity of the >brain is marked by slower cycles (3 to 7 cycles per second). Physiologically, the >reticular formation in the brainstem seems crucial in switching off wakefulness largely by a fall in the hormone >serotonin.

During the first 90 minutes of an average night's sleep, the sleeper progresses through different stages of sleep, each defined by a different pattern of brain waves. Stage II is marked by 'spindle' brain waves; stage III by mostly large and slow brain waves; and stage IV by only large, slow waves. The sleeper gradually drifts down into what seems to be deeper and deeper sleep. It's at the end of the first period of stage III sleep that the sleeping brain 'bounces' into 'paradoxical sleep', or >dreaming. It is now common to talk of different stages of sleep depending on whether there are, or are not, Rapid Eye Movements during them. In >REM sleep, people tend to dream or, at least, if woken up in a laboratory, to say they were just dreaming: in NREM, dreaming seems far less frequent.

Traditionally, sleep is considered the opposite of wakefulness, yet much filters through into the >mind during sleep. People seem to have some >memory of noises played to them during the night, and they will often wake to loud noises. Films of sleepers show that people shift endlessly while they sleep so our bodies are not inactive.

No one can really do without sleep, and the longest any person has gone without it is 14 days. After about 24 hours of sleep deprivation, people begin to do far less well on a variety of tasks. For another 24 hours or so, they can manage reasonably well if there is an emergency and they are highly motivated. After that, performance declines rapidly. If people go without sleep for a long time, at the first opportunity they immediately drop, not into deep sleep, but into paradoxical sleep in which they dream.

Radically different theories try to account for the need to sleep. It has been suggested that we require sleep so that the body and brain can repair themselves; that it allows our personality traits to consolidate; and that it is during sleep that our memories are firmed up. All other animals sleep, so, clearly, any theory needs to link human sleep with that of other animals. Ray Meddis has

S

sleep that our memories are firmed up. All other animals sleep, so, clearly, any theory needs to link human sleep with that of other animals. Ray Meddis has suggested that there is a sleep >instinct because, when asleep, animals are usually out of danger.

● J. Empson, *Sleep and Dreaming* (1989); J. Allan Hobson, *Sleep* (1989); R. Meddis, *The Sleep Instinct* (1985); Ian Oswald, *Sleep* (1980).

Slips, mainly Freudian. *See Psychopathology of Everyday Life.*

Smell, the least studied of the senses even though there is considerable evidence that smell is very important in sexual attraction. Some species secrete special kinds of sweat to announce that they are ready to have sex. The human sense of smell is much less well developed than our other senses. We smell far less competently than many animals. Even so, it is not that poor – for example, if you enter a room into which $\frac{1}{25,000,000,000}$ milligram of a chemical called mercaptan has been released, you will be able to smell it. Mercaptan is mixed with gas because it is so odorous.

The nose consists of two nostrils. Each nasal cavity is basically a tunnel which is lined with a mucus that is in perpetual slow motion. At the top of the nostrils, 100 million olfactory cells are packed into an area of about 2.5 million square centimetres which is shaped rather like a bulb of garlic. These cells project tiny hairs into the mucus, each hair being about $\frac{1}{100}$ the of the size of a hair on the head. Specific chemicals on these hairs react to smells in the air to create the sensation of smell. For human beings to become aware of a smell, what is to be smelled has to be volatile, or changeable. Only volatile substances release molecules into the atmosphere. Lead and glass, for example, don't smell because their molecules are immobilized, stuck within their substance. The molecules, then, have to be absorbed by the cells in the nose which means that they have to be mixed with water. The nose is full of water. Third, the molecules must register on the olfactory bulb as a change. No one has mapped all the smells we can smell. There appear to be seven basic scents – camphoraceous (like moth balls), musky, floral, pepperminty, ethereal-like, pungent and putrid. These seven make up our universe of smells. It is curious that psychologists have paid so little attention to smell given that our marketing-influenced culture is so conscious of smells. We are told that perfumes are sexy and some natural odours repulsive. The sense of smell is also crucial to our appreciation of >taste.

Social class, an important variable in much research and crucial for those psychologists who have been deeply influenced by Marxist ideas (*see* Marxist psychology). Class affects different aspects of life, from education, expectations from work and income to how one spends one's leisure time and how likely one is to develop illnesses as different as cancer and >schizophrenia. In Britain, the categories of social class that are almost universally employed are those of the Registrar General of the Office of Population and Census (A, B, C1, C2, D). These are based solely on occupation. Some controversy rages around these, especially as they lead to some paradoxes in how professions are rated. *See* Status.

most magnificent clothes on, he was in fact naked. The social construction of reality in that rather dotty court was that the Emperor wasn't naked. The social construction of reality is the claim that there is no absolute truth. Rather we accept as reality what the consensus claims it to be. The idea has been important in realms as different as physics and >psychiatry. Physicists still argue about the reality of sub-atomic particles or whether these aren't just a construction of physicists (that would make them a social construction too since physicists constitute a social group). In psychiatry, radicals like the late >R. D. Laing claimed that schizophrenics just refused to accept the social reality that 'normals' did. Hence they had to be labelled sick. An important critical concept.

Social desirability response set, the tendency for subjects to give replies, in questionnaire studies, which they judge to be socially appropriate. People try to present a good account of themselves. In analyzing results social psychologists have to be aware of the propensity subjects have 'to fake good'; to make their attitudes and behaviour fit what they imagine society expects.

Social identity. Usually a person is defined and defines himself/herself partly in terms of the group they feel they belong to. We are all born as members of a family. That family is the first group that provides our sense of social identity. As people grow up, they seek a more complex form of social identity. The school you go to, the job you have, the >social class you feel you belong to and your religious affiliations all make up your social identity. Often, individuals aspire to a higher social identity and attempt to move up the social scale to become part of a 'better' group.

Social interaction, literally, the action between (Latin *inter*) people. It's used to mean relating to other people.

Social skills, the skills needed to carry out effective >social interaction. In the 1960s, the concept was developed as it became clear that 'units' of social behaviour could be analysed much as units of >motor skills had been. In order to master the skill of playing the piano, for example, the pianist has to master a whole series of sub-skills from reading the notes to placing his or her fingers over the right keys. Social psychologists argued that any social interaction – from saying hello to a stranger to having an intimate meal in a restaurant – could be broken down in the same way, as a performance which required the participants to carry out sub-tasks using many sub-skills.

In order to have a conversation, for instance, you have to know when to talk, when to listen, what non-verbal cues (*see* Body language) to give and so on. If, while I'm trying to tell you how upset I am because my boss yelled at me, you turn your back and read the newspaper, our social interaction isn't likely to be very satisfying – for me at least. If you are doing this deliberately because you are angry with me, your callous display shows that you are a beast rather than deficient in social skills. But if you think that this is the right way to behave, then your social skills need attention.

Certain groups tend to be socially very unskilled, especially prisoners and psychiatric patients. Psychologists have used video techniques to analyse their

S

209

mistakes and structure groups to teach them how to interact better. In many hospitals and day centres, there are now social skills training groups which try to train subjects essentially to do better at life. Much work remains to be done on the way children pick up social skills, though it seems very likely that the quality of their early >mother/child interaction is an important determining factor. So far there have been no >longitudinal studies to examine this.

• Michael Argyle, *Bodily Communication* (1985); Peter Trower, Bridget Bryant *et al*, *Social Skills and Mental Health* (1978).

Sociobiology, a reductionist approach to the study of social behaviour which stresses the >innate. It suggests that there are specific genes that govern complex human activities such as aggressive behaviour. Politically, sociobiologists argue that the biological make-up of human beings determines much of our behaviour.

Sociometry, literally, the measurement of social factors. A technique devised by Jacob Moreno in which subjects reveal who their closest friends are by creating a graph of their relationships. The idea is to discover the links between members of groups and who is most strongly attached to whom.

Spearman's rank order correlation co-efficient, a measure of >correlation which can be applied to ordinal data and is used for small samples. Ordinal data is data expressed in rank order like positions in a class.

Species-specific behaviour, behaviour which is shown by all members of one species and by no member of another one. The most obvious example is >language in humans since even the most spoken-to chimp has been unable to learn to speak. Ethologists suggest that the elaborate courtship rituals of some species are species-specific, the aim being to avoid inappropriate mating between different species (*see* Ethology).

Speech acts, basically, actions to which a person is committed by what he or she says. The most frequently quoted speech act is promising. To say 'I promise' is just by itself an act. Nothing else is needed for the promise to be an act.

Speech therapy, >therapy which aims to remedy difficulties people have in speaking. The techniques used in speech therapy include much direct teaching by getting children to look at the way their mouth and tongue move while speaking. *See* Aphasia.

Split-brain studies, studies of what happened to patients after the severing of the >corpus callosum to relieve >opilepsy. The corpus callosum carries messages between the two hemispheres of the >brain. If it is cut, the two >cerebral hemispheres are largely independent. The early studies by Roger Sperry in the late 1960s showed that the 'right-half-of-the-brain person' and the 'left-half-of-the-brain person' often behaved very differently. Even odder, each part of the brain didn't necessarily know what the other part was doing. These findings were extremely exciting, and led to a revival of interest in >consciousness and >cognitive psychology. *See* Lateralization.

- R. W. Sperry, 'Brain Bisection Consciousness' in John Eccles (ed.) *The Brain and Conscious Experience* (1966).

Splitting, a psychoanalytic concept which describes the splitting of the >ego into two parts. One is usually the self which is seen as good. The other is the split-off part of the ego which is seen as bad. The person with the split ego is at the mercy of the interactions between these two halves of his or her self. They are often destructive. >R. D. Laing in *The Divided Self* used this concept to illustrate how many schizophrenics (*see* Schizophrenia) weren't mad but were trying to find a strategy for living in an intolerable situation. As a result, they created a self and a false self. The false, split self would, for example, often behave destructively and violently and appear to be 'mad'. It is a psychoanalytic (*see* Psychoanalysis) concept which has come to pervade psychological >language.

- R. D. Laing, *The Divided Self* (1960).

Spontaneous recovery, recovery without any treatment. It has two meanings. One is the strange process by which patients – and especially psychiatric patients – get better without receiving any treatment at all: time heals. This is an important methodological concept, for any test of how effective a new treatment is has to make sure that any benefits are due to it and not to the fact that some patients would improve anyway. In 1952, >Eysenck claimed that >psychoanalysis had no effect since many patients recovered spontaneously.

The second meaning is in >learning theory. If there is a sudden reappearance of a learned response after it was extinguished through lack of >reinforcement, this is said to be a spontaneous recovery.

S-R (stimulus-response) theories. These are theories which link the >stimulus to the response. They do not cover, and claim no interest in, what goes on physiologically within the organism. For example, if a pigeon learns to peck at a ping pong ball every 50th time it is fed, the theory notes that link but not how the >brain might achieve it. The best known example of S-R theories is probably >B. F. Skinner's >operant conditioning theory.

Stage theories, theories of development which assume that all children have to go through identical stages as they grow up. They are rather a carry-over from Victorian science where people 'progressed' to totally competent maturity. The most famous stage theories are those of >Freud and >Piaget. >Erik Erikson's eight stages of development – womb to tomb – have also been influential.

There are philosophical problems with stage theories. They tend to assume that the pattern in which these stages unfold is innate. The experiences that the child goes through are fixed, and there is a biological necessity to go from stage A to stage C via stage B. As a result, such theories play down the role of social learning. They also claim that all >normal children go through stages (and their associated substages) at roughly the same periods in their lives. There

S

would be something very bizarre about a child who was born with an >Oedipus complex as the complex emerges at around five years of age. Yet research into Piaget's theory, in particular, has shown a great deal of variability. Children master the skills that are typical of a particular stage of development at very different ages. The structure of each stage isn't very coherent. Both Freud and Piaget had to assume that all children 'graduate', that at a certain point, in a triumph of maturity, they reach the last stage and are truly grown up. However, much evidence on adult functioning shows that many individuals never reach either such intellectual or emotional maturity. This casts some doubt on the value of stage theories.

● M. Donaldson, *Children's Minds* (1978); K. Fischer, 'A Theory of Cognitive Development' in *Psychological Review* 67, 452–535 (1980).

Standard deviation, a measure of how much a set of scores deviates from the mean. >IQ scores, for example, scatter from 40 to 190. Simply knowing how widely apart the scores are doesn't mean much unless you know what the scatter of scores in a particular situation is. The standard deviation is calculated by taking the positive square root of the variance: $s = \sqrt{s^2}$.

Standard error. A group of subjects are sampled from a >population and measured on some >variable. This procedure is repeated several times, and the mean of each sample is calculated. The obtained distribution of those means is called the 'sampling distribution of means'. The >standard deviation of the sampling distribution is called the standard error of the means. The standard error of a mean tells us how large errors of estimation are in any particular sampling situation.

There are two major questions about the mean of a sample: one concerns >sampling error, due to not getting a representative sample, and the other is measurement error. Standard error of measurement is the standard deviation of an examinee's scores on a test administered to the individual several times. The larger the standard error of measurement, the larger is the uncertainty associated with an individual's score.

Stanford Binet test, the earliest >intelligence test developed in 1916 by Stanford University in California on the basis of >Alfred Binet's work. It gives just one score of IQ (*see* Intelligence quotient) as opposed to the >Wechsler test which breaks down IQ into various component parts.

Statistical significance. The significance of results is related to the extent to which an outcome is likely to be the product of pure chance. Such significance is usually expressed in terms of the relationship to 'p' – or probability. Traditionally, psychology has accepted that if 'p' is no more than 0.05 – ie if there is a likelihood of less than 1 in 20 that the results are the product of chance – the finding is significant and the >null hypothesis is rejected. In some areas, such as in testing for the effects of new drugs, far more stringent tests of significance are required. *See* Correlations in psychology; Significant difference.

Status, essentially a sociological concept. The status of any person is basically their rank in society. As societies have become less hierarchical, assessing status has become much tricker. Once, for example, a duke had the highest possible status within an aristocracy. Today, however, it is not at all clear that a duke has a higher status than, say, a famous television presenter. Status is linked to but not the same as >social class which is defined by traditional ranking of occupations. There, a vicar outdoes a television personality because a vicar is a professional.

Stereotyping, a process by which someone from a particular group is attributed supposed characteristics of that group, irrespective of what the individual is like. Stereotypes are generally nasty and reinforce prejudice. For example, Jews are rich and stingy; blacks are stupid. They can flatter too. Jews are clever; blacks sexual athletes. A determined policy to use the media to redress these images can work to some extent.

S

Stimulus, an entirely general term for anything to which an organism responds. A flash of light and an attractive person of the opposite sex can both be described as stimuli. Theorists speak of >S-R theories – a stimulus provoking a response.

Stimulus generalization, an identical response to a >stimulus which is not the same stimulus that first evoked the response.

Stimulus position effect. *See* Position effect.

Stimulus response learning, learning which associates a particular response to a particular >stimulus. *See* Conditioning; One-trial learning; Operant conditioning.

Stress, a curious concept developed by Hans Selye in 1956. Selye suggested that stress is the response of the body to any demands made upon it, and he found that there were three distinct phases in stress: alarm, resistance and exhaustion.

One difficulty with defining stress is that different individuals find different things stressful. I may enjoy examinations but hate skydiving. My friend, on the other hand, panics when he enters an examination hall but likes nothing better than to leap out of planes. Stress theorists suggest that stress is the result of an imbalance between capacity (ie a person's ability to handle a situation), demand and especially the individual's >perception of demand. The literature suggests that the members of some professions, such as pilots and doctors, are particularly vulnerable to stress. C. Cooper and M. Smith (1985) have also suggested that blue-collar jobs create stress, but of a different kind. Boredom, poor working conditions, lack of job satisfaction have consequences similar to being in a highly demanding situation. It's also claimed that there is a link between prolonged stress and >burnout.

Stress has had a bad press and we often assume that all stress is damaging. It is true that we feel 'under stress' when there are problems at home or at work, and that stress can result in physical ailments. People under stress are more likely to suffer colds and, of course, to drink and smoke too much: there is also much evidence which suggests that stress is involved in some major physical illnesses, especially cancer. However, Selye argued that stress is both good and bad. A certain degree of stress sharpens the mind (*see* Yerkes Dodson law).

Excessive stress can be damaging, especially if it continues for a long time. Work on learned >helplessness also suggests that, if there is nothing people can do to escape stressful situations, their health will suffer and they will become depressed. Recent studies of disaster victims show that many suffer the symptoms of prolonged stress (*see* Post-traumatic stress).

Techniques of stress >counselling have been developed. These rely largely on people (1) admitting they are under stress; (2) being given permission to talk about it freely; and (3) sometimes developing ways of relieving stress through relaxation exercises. Other techniques offer a way for people to learn to cope with and use their stress creatively. *See* Life events.

- C. Cooper and M. Smith, *Job Stress and Blue Collar Work* (1985); S. A. Fisher, *Stress and the Perception of Control* (1984); Hans Selye, *The Stress of Life* (1956).

Structuralism, an approach to psychology and also anthropology. The term may be used in different ways. Some claim that a theory is structuralist if it argues that the structure of the organism or of its surroundings affects the way it behaves. >Freud's theory of the organization of the mind into >ego, >id and >superego is thus a structural one. Others argue that what is important is that the relations between the elements of a system are seen as the crucial aspects of a theory.

Ferdinand de Saussure (1857–1913), a Swiss linguist, is generally accepted as the founder of structuralism. He made a basic distinction between the study of >language as *parole* or speech and its study as *langue* – the underlying system that makes up any language structure. The system is essential, he claimed, the *parole* contingent. >Noam Chomsky's notion of >deep structure owes something to this. One of the most influential extensions of these ideas was the work of the French anthropologist Claude Lévi-Strauss (b. 1908). He studied masks and the myths of South American tribes to see how these revealed the structures of their societies. He analysed 813 tribal myths and argued that they revealed a desire to deal with three main questions: why do humans prepare food and animals do not? why do humans take off clothes and barter them with foreign groups while animals do not? and how did this come about? These myths are an attempt to grapple with the issue of whether culture or nature determine how we behave. The essence of Lévi-Strauss's method is not to analyse each myth in isolation but to look at the relations between different symbols in the myths. Rather than examine what the lizard and the crocodile stand for in any particular myth, he focuses on the relation between the lizard as a land animal and the crocodile as a river beast in the myths. Lévi-Strauss argues that there is an unconscious structure to the human >mind. Psychologists have become interested in these ideas but don't easily grasp their implications.

- R. Jakobson and M. Halle, *The Fundamentals of Language* (1971); Edward

Leach, *Lévi-Strauss* (1970); C. Lévi-Strauss, *The Scope of Anthropology* (1967); D. Lodge, *Working with Structuralism* (1986).

Stuttering, a speech impediment concerning which many theories have been proposed. They range from a physiological flow to 'bad >learning'. Some evidence suggests that left-handed children who were made to write with their right hand developed stuttering. Often, the stutterer only speaks poorly under >stress. The condition can respond to treatment but not in every case.

Subconscious, that part of the mind which, in >Freudian theory, is not under conscious control or access. Psychoanalysts dislike the term which is popularly used as a synonym for the >unconscious, as they consider it vague.

Sublimation, popularly, to sublimate is to redirect sexual energy towards non-sexual ends. This is very close to the classical psychoanalytic view, which sees sublimation as a process whereby instinctual energies are shifted to non-instinctual subjects. For example, we speak of an artist whose libidinal energy is directed not towards sex but towards painting.

Subliminal perception, the >perception, without an individual knowing it, of stimuli (*see* Stimulus) whose appearance is too fast for conscious awareness. It has been shown that we react to and are influenced by subliminal perceptions. In most Western countries, so-called subliminal 'messages' – a few frames of film showing a particular product or a few words (eg 'You are thirsty') which are slotted into a perfectly innocuous film – are no longer allowed on television or in cinemas, precisely because of the powerful effect that they can have. *See* Threshold.

Suicide, killing oneself. The study of this phenomenon was crucial to the development of the social sciences. It was researched in detail by Emile Durkheim (1858–1917), one of the founders of modern sociology, in an attempt to prove that sociological laws could be applied to such a complex and individual event. Durkheim argued that people who committed suicide were less rooted than average in their society, tending not to have family ties or settled work. He called this lack of roots *anomie*. Durkheim also claimed that periods of economic change – slumps on the stock market or great rises – increased the number of suicides.

The statistics show that the majority of those who succeed at suicide are elderly – especially old men. Psychiatrists have been interested in how many suicides suffered from mental illness, and some studies have put that figure as high as 33 per cent. However, in 1985, in an analysis of the number of deaths from suicide in St Louis, Missouri, Eli Robbins found that far more than one third of suicides had actually tried to contact a doctor in the month before their deaths: they may not have been disturbed but they did perceive that they needed help.

Changes in technology have altered the methods used for committing suicide. Few shoot or hang themselves any more, and in most countries, gas has been rendered safe. Instead, sleeping pills and other drugs now offer a relatively

S

quick, clean and supposedly painless means. There are also fluctuations in the rate of suicide: it tends to fall in times of war and conflict – as it has done in Northern Ireland since 1970 – which suggests that Durkheim was right to claim that social cohesiveness reduced suicide rates. However, it is difficult to rely on international statistics; often coroners only give a verdict of suicide when they can't avoid it (ie when suicide notes exist). Two recent inconclusive debates have centred on whether the work of such organizations as the Samaritans actually does reduce suicide rates and whether unemployment increases them. There have been claims recently that a comparison of European statistics in the 1970s and early 80s definitely shows that high unemployment pushes suicide rates up.

Psychiatrists differentiate suicide from a >'cry for help' – ie attempted suicide – which is committed by members of different groups (usually young girls) for different motives.

- Emile Durkheim, *Suicide* (1897); Sally O'Brien, *The Negative Scream* (1985); Eli Robbins, *The Final Months* (1985); Erwin Stengel, *Suicide and Attempted Suicide* (1961).

Superego, one part of the trilogy of the unconscious mind in >Freud's theory, the other parts being the >ego and the >id. Popularly, we take the superego to mean the conscience, but in classical >psychoanalysis it plays a slightly different role. According to this, it is that part of the ego which employs self-observation to effect self-criticism, and it arises from a child's tendency to internalize his parents – and the rules they live by. Initially, Freud claimed that the superego is the voice of the father forbidding many instinctual pleasures, but later analysts have suggested that it is formed earlier. It isn't, Freud stressed, an ethical idea but a psychological one. The superego includes unconscious elements such as >fear of one's parent. The values of the superego may well include prohibitions which are at odds with the conscious values that a child who has grown into an adult now holds. The energy of the superego comes from the id. *See* Unconscious.

- Sigmund Freud, *The Ego and the Id* (1923).

Surface structure, a term used by the linguist >Noam Chomsky to refer to the grammar and sentences of an existing >language. He distinguishes it from >deep structure, which is grounded in meaning.

Surplus repression, a concept developed by Herbert Marcuse, who argued that capitalist society needed to prevent workers using up their instinctual energies by imposing more repression than was necessary.

- Herbert Marcuse, *Eros and Civilization* (1964).

Survival value, a concept from evolutionary theory. The survival value of a phenomenon is the way it helps us survive. The survival value of many human behaviours is not well understood.

Symbolic representation, the ability to create and understand >symbols.

Symbols, something that stands for something else. A letter is a symbol. So is the statue of a god when the statue is taken to represent that god. Human beings are the only species to understand symbolic behaviour but understanding what symbols mean is a complex process that takes much learning. In >Jean Piaget's theory, the child's ability to understand symbolic behaviour comes as it internalizes a number of schemas (*see* Schema). The ability to master the use of symbols – the earliest being in >language, where certain sounds stand for certain objects or persons – is crucial to becoming fully developed as a human being.

• Jean Piaget, *The Child's Conception of the World* (1929).

Synapse, the junction (or space) between two neurons. For an impulse to fire from one >neuron to the next, it has to pass across the synapse. When it does so, it produces the connection between neurons. The >brain's functioning depends crucially on the proper functioning of the synapses so that impulses travel to and from their correct destinations and do so quickly. *See* Neurotransmitter.

S

T

T-group, a form of >encounter group which is unstructured (ie there is no clear group leader or fixed agenda of what can, and can't, be addressed) and free floating. The idea is to promote communication between members and, through the honesty of that communication, to help resolve problems. They are thus rather similar to many encounter groups.

T-test, a statistical technique in which the scores obtained in raw data are compared. The two means of two samples of data are compared to see whether the differences between them are statistically significant. If the means of two sets of data (say the >IQ scores of people who have been to college and the IQ scores of people who left school at 15) are very different, the T-test will provide a measure of how much more they differ than one would expect by mere chance. *See* Statistical significance.

Tachistoscope, a machine which presents visual stimuli (*see* Stimulus) at different speeds. It was much used by early psychologists to flash dots, lines and letters at subjects to test how fast they could react to them. The tachistoscope, although very simple, was one of those marvels of Victorian engineering without which psychology would never have developed. *See* Reaction times.

Tardive dyskinesia, a disorder caused by taking various forms of >neuroleptic drugs for too long. The patient's face becomes disfigured; tics develop; and the tongue flops around, out of control. In 1981, the American Psychiatric Association published an exhaustive report which argued that tardive dyskinesia was a considerable risk and that psychiatrists should be very careful about the overprescribing of drugs. Once the symptoms are established, they tend to remain even if the drugs that caused them are withdrawn.

Taste, one of the five senses. The stimuli (*see* Stimulus) that create taste are the substances that touch the surface of the tongue. Yet, the sensations of taste that these produce are profoundly influenced by >smell, texture, temperature, even colour. That's why, in many countries in the West, fruits are dyed – the colours of the natural fruits aren't luscious enough to taste good. The >receptor cells for taste are in the taste buds, of which there are about 9000 on the human tongue. Each bud comprises a dozen individual receptor cells bunched together. The cells are constantly dying and being replaced so that, over seven days, a whole set of taste cells is renewed. There is some evidence to suggest that, as we grow older, a permanent change occurs in our sense of taste. Different parts of the tongue are more sensitive to different kinds of taste: sweet things are 'tasted' on the tip of the tongue, and the buds specializing in salty, sour and bitter tastes are located progressively further back. Of all the senses, taste has been of least interest to psychologists. This is perhaps curious, given the extent to which hunger and thirst have been basic in developing theories of >reinforcement.

TAT. *See* Thematic Apperception Test.

Telekinesis, the ability to shift objects at a distance. In one famous case, the Israeli Uri Geller bent spoons by rubbing them lightly and, even more bizarre, stopped watches in houses all over the UK during a television appearance. Intense interest in >paranormal phenomena has meant that, for the past 100 years, anyone who seems to have such a talent tends to become something of a music-hall turn.

Sceptics such as the magician James Randi allege that it's done by legerdemain, mirrors or fraud. Yet strict scientific investigations, such as one conducted by the Department of Physics at London University, suggest that a few individuals may affect objects without touching them. If telekinesis does exist, it would mean that >mind can affect matter, a concept that would require a profound paradigm shift in how we understand science. Not surprisingly that is resisted.

● Brian Inglis, *The Paranormal* (1984).

Telepathy, the ability to know what someone else is >thinking through some form of mental communication. Believers in such parapsychic powers claim that telepathy often happens at emotionally charged moments – you know when someone you care for is in danger or happy even though you are not with them – but such dramatic incidents can't be tested scientifically. Sceptics have long argued that since positive evidence of telepathy would render many of our scientific ideas obsolete, proof of it has to be far more rigorous: the more improbable the theory, the tougher the criteria.

The best psychological evidence comes from the work of J. B. Rhine in the United States. Rhine gave subjects cards with simple shapes on them, and asked them to transmit these patterns to other people. Those on the receiving end of these telepathic messages had to visualize the shapes – a square, a circle or wavy line. If they simply relied on guesswork (ie chance), they had a probability of 1 in 4 of getting it right on each presentation. Some subjects, however, performed spectacularly well, a number managing to beat chance resoundingly. In some cases, the probability that they could have scored as highly as they did in a series of trials was less than one in 500. Rhine found that the skill seemed to fade with time and that some subjects became very resentful at being made to flaunt their skill time and again. Rhine eventually founded the Institute for the Study of the Paranormal at Duke University. His last years were marred by a scandal in which one of his associates was discovered to have altered results to favour telepathy. As the history of parapsychic claims has been riddled with imposters, this badly affected Rhine's standing within the scientific community. Nonetheless, work on telepathy continues, and it has been given a boost with the founding of the Koestler Chair at Edinburgh University. Certainly, psychology can't ignore the possibility of such psychic skills. Also important is the fact that people tend to believe in them and appear to want to. Fascination with the paranormal is common and, given the West's generally sceptical culture, perhaps slightly surprising. *See* Paranormal phenomena.

Temporal lobe, the lobe of the >brain that lies underneath the parietal lobe and in front of the occipital lobe. Its main sensory function was once seen as >hearing, but it has also been found to be involved in >vision, >memory, >personality and social behaviour. Brain physiology no longer sees the function of lobes in such gross terms and tries, increasingly, to be more specific. It acknowledges complex networking between different parts of the brain.

The primary auditory >cortex is located in a fold (gyrus) of the lobe. The auditory association area is on the sides at the back, near the occipital lobe. Damage to the left area (known as Broca's area) reduces the ability to understand speech and decode speech sounds (*see* Aphasia). But often their talk becomes laden with jargon. Those with damage to the right temporal lobe often become compulsive talkers, suggesting a loosening of controls. The neuropsychologist L. Mishkin has conducted a series of experiments in which he found that damage to the area of the lobe near the lower edge of the cortex led to visual difficulties. In particular, monkeys could no longer discriminate certain features of objects, even of familiar monkey faces. As with other sections of the brain, studies tend to ignore the links of the temporal lobe to other lobes, and to regard it in perhaps excessive isolation.

Tender v tough minded, two opposing concepts that describe >personality types and attitudes. William James first suggested the distinction, which was later elaborated by >Eysenck. Tender-minded persons tend to be gentle, soft and idealistic. Tough-minded people are brisk, hard and pragmatic.

James didn't see the distinction as illuminating political attitudes but recently this has been done: tender-minded types are 'wets', 'lefty liberals' who love to be kind to prisoners, immigrants and those on Social Security. Touch-minded individuals, on the other hand, are usually right wing and have no sympathy for the deserving or undeserving poor ('Social Security scroungers'); all poor people, criminals and outcasts are *ipso facto* undeserving. To the tough minded, if they pulled their socks up and didn't winge, they'd make good, make money and not make demands. It's an interesting example of how a concept which has lain dormant in the literature of psychology for a long time is suddenly taken up when it fits current political ideologies. Tests for 'tough v tender' also suggest a link with >locus of control, with the tough favouring inner and the tender outer locus of control.

Territoriality, a concept taken from studies of animal behaviour (*see* Ethology). Animals will defend their territory, that part of ground or nest that they identify as their own. They will be aggressive on it even against larger, more dangerous beasts. At the edge of their territory, when they are about to enter another animal's space, their attitude changes. >Aggression turns to hesitation, attack to flight. The concept is now used to account for some forms of human behaviour, especially the fact that people feel attached to their homes and become fraught when they have to move away.

Terrorism. The effect of being kidnapped or held hostage by terrorists is a classic cause of >post-traumatic >stress. Some countries where there is a greater likelihood of terrorist incidents have developed good psychiatric services for coping with their aftermath. In Israel, it has been realized that it is important for communities to maintain regular links with emergency services, even when there is no crisis, for crisis services to work well. Otherwise, when help is offered after a terrorist attack, residents of the town or kibbutz may feel intruded upon. That was very much the feeling in north Holland during the Moluccan sieges in the 1970s and in the small British market town of Hungerford after a crazed gunman slaughtered a large number of residents.

The personal motives of terrorists have been studied, but no very definite conclusions have been drawn.

Testing, politics of. *See* Jensen controversy.

Testing psychology. *See* Personality tests; Psychological tests.

Test/retest reliability. A >psychological test is of little use if, at different sittings, the same subjects produce widely differing results for no good reason. Validation of tests should, therefore, include giving the same test at different intervals. Test/retest reliability is usually expressed numerically. So if 20 out of 100 answers differ on the retest, the test/retest reliability will be expressed as 0.80. >Intelligence and >extroversion tests tend to have a reasonable test/retest reliability of about 0.80, while others are less consistent. However, even IQ test results change more than one might expect in some experiments, such as M. F. Petty's and L. J. Field's four year study of children. It is an invaluable concept in assessing the usefulness of a test.

• P. Kline, *Handbook of Psychological Testing* (1993).

Thalamus, a part of the forebrain right at the top, near the >cortex. About 10 per cent of the nuclei in the thalamus are very specific, and damage to them leads to specific deficits – auditory or visual. The remaining 90 per cent of the cells are non-specific and are probably involved in associative thinking. In general, the thalamus appears to act as a reception area to the cortex for fibres from the eyes, ears, skin and some motor areas. The thalamus then transmits the impulses from these fibres on to the cerebral cortex.

Norman Cook has argued that the upper brainstem 'is involved in as yet poorly understood mechanisms of arousal, attention and association'. The thalamus's function of relaying information is important but only part of the story.

● Norman Cook, *The Brain Code* (1986).

Thematic Apperception Test (TAT). In this subjects are asked to write or tell a story based on a given set of pictures. The test assumes that the form of the story will reveal underlying motivations – especially >achievement motivation or >nACH. For example, if the picture shows a boy playing a trumpet, a story that says that he is practising to get into a jazz band would score high on achievement motivation. However, a story that says that he enjoys making a noise to frighten the neighbours would score low, as it would suggest a rather less ambitious >personality.

TAT has been used to measure the need for achievement both in individuals, contemporary societies and cultures in the past. David McClelland has argued that the scores of particular individuals on the TAT were consistent; otherwise it wouldn't be so useful. Nevertheless, later research has suggested that the test scores are not consistent, and as a result the test ought to have lost much credibility. However, it still continues to be widely used. *See* Projective techniques/tests; Rorschach test.

● David McClelland, *Human Motivation* (1988).

Therapy, a term now used loosely to cover a whole galaxy of psychological interventions, ranging from formal, five-times-a-week >psychoanalysis to much less formal arrangements. An 'A to Z' of the different therapies available would run from Adlerian analysis to Zen >psychotherapy. There are entries covering many therapies throughout this book.

● Anthony Clare and Sally Thompson, *Let's Talk About Me* (1983).

Thinking. The ability to reason and think abstractly is, Aristotle suggested, the capacity that sets humans apart from brutish beasts. In most other areas, when psychology began to emerge as a scientific discipline in its own right, it had little to build on, but not so with thinking.

Thinkers had studied their own thinking from Descartes on. Philosophers of the Scottish Enlightenment such as Hume and Hartley had discovered the laws of association (*see* Association therapy) which show how thoughts follow on from one to another. Such a body of knowledge made psychologists confident – perhaps overconfident – that research into thinking would advance quickly. The first main technique used was >introspection, which was meant to reveal the 'atoms' of thinking. However, the failure of the work of the introspectionists and the rise of >behaviourism meant that, from 1920 to 1950, relatively little work was done on thinking, although >Piaget studied >child development very much through the thinking of the young.

Eventually, however, it became clear that psychology couldn't really avoid this subject. Initially, studies of thinking concentrated on >problem solving, and

T

clever experimental designs teased out how subjects solved problems. Thus, using a design based on card games, Goodnow, Bruner and Austin found that subjects were better at making confirming instances than at framing questions that would really test the truth of a theory. For example, if I want to test the proposition that 'oranges have to be grown in California', it doesn't matter how many positive instances I turn up, the proposition won't be proved. A million Californian oranges will make the theory more plausible but not conclusive. To make it conclusive, I have to scour all the countries of the earth seeking a negative instance – ie an orange not grown in California but in Paris or the Antarctic. It is said to be hard to prove negatives but scientific progress depends on this. It was only when chemists proved that the ether didn't exist that chemistry managed to make important progress. In the Bruner, Goodnow and Austin card study, they saw that subjects had more problems with disproving theories. They found it easy to confirm that all hearts were red but harder to disprove by, for example, trying to find a black heart.

However, there were clear limitations to this very artificial 'card game' technique, and since 1975, >cognitive psychologists have focused on other aspects of thinking, ranging from logical puzzles to how we think about real-life situations. P. Wason found that we are not very good at manipulating negative inferences, which rather invalidates Piaget's claim that all teenagers attain >formal operations. On the other hand, there have also been studies of the different kinds of intelligence that people apply to different kinds of problems.

There are some elementary facts that are in great need of discovery. For example, in an ordinary day, how much of our time do we spend thinking and of what? In 1982, E. J. Dearnley monitored himself and found that he spent less than 2 per cent of his time in any form of analytical thought. As he was not just an academic but an academic who was motivated enough to study himself, it might be his results would have come as a shock to Aristotle! In a 1984 study of what people spent their time thinking about, Mihail Czinentmihalyi also found that human beings spend far more time thinking about what to eat, who they will meet, when they are going to do their laundry than about Socrates and syllogisms or anything remotely abstract.

To make matters even more complex, recent work on >consciousness suggests that we should regard ourselves not as having one >brain but an interrelated series of brains that sometimes compete, sometimes complement. Do these various brains think different thoughts at different times? There is some understanding of how we solve problems and what kinds of logical mistakes are easy to make, but this is far from providing a global theory of thinking. The linguist >Noam Chomsky has suggested pessimistically that the human >mind may not be able to understand how the human mind works – 'thinking about thinking' is an activity doomed to disappointment. For Chomsky, that doesn't mean that the subject should not be pursued but just that the solutions we can achieve may be far more partial than we would like.

Interestingly, the rise of cognitive psychology has answered some questions about thinking and opened up new questions. It has certainly put thinking back on the agenda of psychology. Current studies can be divided into a number of areas: problem-solving; creative thinking; what computers can tell us about the way we think; brain studies; improving our thinking.

● D. Dennett, *Consciousness Explained* (1993); K. J. Gilhooly, *Thinking* (1982); R. Sternberg and R. Wagner (eds), *Practical Intelligence* (1986).

Thorndike, E. (1874–1949), leading American psychologist now remembered for his law of >effect. His work helped pave the way for >behaviourism. His two main books – *Animal Learning* (1911) and *Educational Psychology* (1903) – were landmarks in their time.

Thought disorder, a term often used to describe the mental processes of >schizophrenics. Much evidence suggests that not only do they have >hallucinations but they do not make inferences in the >normal way. For the schizophrenic, cause and effect are not linked in a normal way because they attribute causes to impossible entities. Aliens tell them to breathe; the TV set flashes messages in the middle of golf competitions just meant for them. Their thoughts are scrambled. >R. D. Laing suggested one could find meaning in these confusions but he was rare in that generosity.

Threshold, the lowest amount of a >stimulus that will evoke a response. It's important in the study of all forms of >perception. It has been shown that we remain aware of something even if a stimulus is presented 'below the threshold' (*see* Subliminal perception).

Time and motion studies, a technique developed by Charles Taylor in 1903 in which he analysed the movements of workers in factories with the aim of improving efficiency. Managements welcomed this extension of >industrial psychology (and, indeed, these studies contributed to its rise), but workers often found that these studies and Taylor's recommendations dehumanized them. Taylor paid virtually no attention to the psychological needs of workers; concepts such as >job satisfaction were of no interest to him.

Token economy, a programme based on >B. F. Skinner's ideas of >reinforcement. In a token economy, inmates of prisons and other institutions are rewarded for acting responsibly and cooperatively. For example, if they keep their rooms clean and contribute to group discussions, they will receive certain privileges, graded from, say, one extra hour of television a night to a home visit. The term 'token economy' stems from the fact that items of good behaviour earn 'tokens' which can be exchanged for the rewards. There have been some successes with token economy in tightly organized programmes, but these tend not to last. The training doesn't transfer well to real life.

● B. F. Skinner, *Walden Two* (1948).

Topdown theories, those which work from the top downwards. An example would be a theory explaining the way an organization works by studying the style of its leaders.

Touch. Of all the senses, touch is the most enigmatic. Our whole body is wired to feel and respond to touch. It is the one sense that transcends that old bugbear of the human condition – isolation. Touch provides the sense of intimacy so that we feel we aren't alone. Babies need to be touched – and so do adults usually. The study of touch tends to be pursued by three sorts of psychologists: neuropsychologists who try to map the ways in which >pain is registered by the >brain; social psychologists interested in non-verbal communication (*see* Body language); therapists who see touch as healing and claim that, in a repressive society, it's the one sense that is taboo. For example, in the 1960s, Herbert Marcuse argued that capitalism requires >surplus repression to control workers and, therefore, discouraged touching.

The whole surface of the human body is covered by >sensory neurons that convey information to the >brain. Some have become specialized so that they are sensitive to particular stimuli (*see* Stimulus). The most common type of nerve fibre is the free nerve ending which looks rather like the root of a plant. These are found on the palms of hands, and also surround the hair follicles in hairy skin, firing if the hairs are bent. The Pacinian corpuscles are the largest of these nerve endings; they are thought to be sensitive to vibration and continuous pressure.

Sensory psychologists define touch as the sensation of very light contact and differentiate between it and pressure, which is more intense. Different areas of the body are differently sensitive. The lips and the fingertips are the most sensitive and command, together with the sexual organs, the most processing space in the >cortex of the brain. There is a famous cartoon of the human body which has been drawn in proportion to the amount of processing space used by each part; the resulting creature has a large head, immense lips, big genital organs and huge hands, but spindly limbs and trunk. Traditionally, sensitivity to touch is measured by a curious technique using a pair of dividers. How far apart the legs of the dividers have to be before the subject says that he or she feels two separate legs indicates how sensitive that part of the body is.

Psychologists have been dissatisfied with the traditional notion of the five senses. They have argued that we should see touch as just one of the 'somato senses', others of which are the ability to respond to pressure, temperature and pain. The neurophysiology of touch is relatively well understood, but psychologists are much less sure about how human beings learn to use it and to understand what it means.

Tourette's syndrome. *See* Giles de la Tourette's syndrome.

Training. Psychologists have become much more involved in training as it has become clear that interviews and >psychometric tests don't predict too well who will do a job best. The increasing pace of technological change has also made companies see that they need to 'refresh' their work force from time to time. Good training schemes in whatever the field have similar principles – build on what there is, offer clear information, instil confidence. It's important to break down the skills that have to be learned into manageable chunks and to provide feedback. Students need to know what they have done well and what they have

T

done badly. All aspects of industry – from the Post Office to high tech industries – are now involved in training. The area has become something of a boom for psychology.

● J. Hartley and A. Branthwaite, *The Applied Psychologist* (1989).

Trait theory, a theory of >personality which argues that personality can be measured in traits such as >extraversion/introversion. Originally developed by R. B. Cattell, it was embellished by >Eysenck.

Tranquillizers, drugs used especially in agitated patients. The best-known tranquillizer is valium, one of the >benzodiazepines. The prescribing of valium in the 1970s and 80s was often indiscriminate as GPs tended to give it to patients who were anxious and/or depressed for perfectly valid reasons: their lives had reached crisis point, and drugs could not resolve anything. Two special problems occurred – addiction to valium, and the use of valium to attempt >suicide. Prolonged campaigning by pressure groups like MIND and in the media has alerted doctors to the dangers of over-prescribing but the problem has not been eradicated. Some valium addicts have set up self-help groups to help them withdraw. A few with multi-drug experience say that getting off tranquillizers is more difficult than withdrawing from heroin. In some crises, tranquillizers can nevertheless be useful in conjunction with other treatments.

Transactional analysis, a form of >therapy developed by Eric Berne. Berne argued that social life is a kind of exchange of transactions. Berne argued that the >ego used set games and scripts as a defence against reality. He popularized this by focusing on the actual *transactions* or social exchanges in which we take part. We play different parts with each other – as adults, as child and parent and so on – not usually knowingly. Often we form relationships that are problematic, because, for example, my child may want to pick a partner who is rather dominant. This can lead to conflict as my personality isn't wholly 'child' and my 'adult' may battle with the dominant partner. Berne hoped that transactional analysis by its very clarity would quickly engage patients. They would not be put off by the mystifications of >psychoanalysis. But these virtues have also led to some oversimplifications – mainly that people *are* one of these three basic types all the time.

● E. Berne, *Games People Play* (1968).

Transcendental meditation. *See* Meditation.

Transference. When someone is in >psychoanalysis or >psychotherapy, they usually become very emotionally attached to their analyst or therapist. The first time this occurred was when Josef Breuer, >Freud's partner, became terrified when one of his patients, Anna O, had a phantom pregnancy and accused him of being the 'father'. Breuer fled respectable Vienna. Freud slowly uncovered the principles of psychoanalysis as a consequence of asking patients to re-think and re-live early memories (*see* Memory) and, by doing so, evoked in them the kind of >love that parents and, later, lovers would evoke. Freud insisted that, although transference might appear to be risky to the analyst, it was a vital part of the therapeutic process. Only by working through the transference could the person be healed. The therapist is also at risk through >counter-transference.

Transfer of training. This occurs when learning to do one task makes it easier to learn a second one. This is a feature of ordinary >learning. Psychologists have tried to find formulae which will maximize such transfers. There have occasionally been results which suggest that injecting brain material from one animal to another produces such transfers.

Transformational grammar, a linguistic concept developed by >Noam Chomsky. Chomsky argues that the >brain codes sentences basically in terms of meaning, not of grammar. In order to create speech, that meaning has to be transformed into an utterance, and transformational grammar specifies the rules by which this transformation occurs. *See* Deep structure; Psycholinguistics; Surface structure.

- Noam Chomsky, *Syntactic Structures* (1957); J. Lyons, *Chomsky* (1975).

Transitional object, a term first used by D. W. Winnicott to refer to a baby's first possession and the way in which he or she uses it to move from a subjective (and false) feeling of total omnipotence to a reality-based relationship with the outside world. This transitional object is both 'me' and 'not me'; it acts as a defence against >fear of annihilation, of ceasing to exist. Winnicott argued that this function made the object especially important for the infant at bedtime. Common transitional objects are blankets which babies cling to for dear life.

- D. W. Winnicott, *The Child, the Family, and Home* (1974), *Home is Where We Start From* (1986).

Trauma, either a physical or a psychological injury. The term covers anything from being brain damaged to being the victim of rape (*see* Rape trauma) or being in an earthquake. Psychiatrists have become increasingly aware of the impact of >post-traumatic >stress.

Trial-and-error learning, a form of >learning first described by >Thorndike in his work on cats (*see* Effect, Law of). The cats learned how to undo the catch of a cage by trial and error. But once they had learned it, their strategy changed completely and they quickly honed in on the right answer.

Turing, Alan (1912–1954), a mathematician who developed two key psychological concepts. The first was the Turing Machine. This is not really a machine but a design for a machine. Its theory was crucial in the development of >artificial intelligence, and was proposed by Alan Turing in 1937. He suggested that the machine could be imagined as an infinitely long string of squares on which there may be numbers, or squares may be blank. The machine can read one square at a time and can move back and forwards over the squares. It can also erase what is on any of the squares. He showed that such a simple machine could

T

specify the steps needed to resolve any problem which could be resolved by specific rules or procedures. The actual material that such a real machine might be constructed of was irrelevant. In 1950, Turing elaborated these ideas in his Imitation Game. This has three players – a man, a woman and an interrogator. The interrogator has to find out which player is male and which female, relying just on questions that tease out their mental attributes. Next a machine is substituted for one of the two being questioned. The machine communicates with a teletype. In some skills people would do badly – say in arithmetic. But Turing suggested that the test offered the best format for distinguishing between men and machines. To date, no computer would pass it. Turing was a central figure in showing how the study of computers would matter to psychology, and how the study of psychology would matter to computers or, at least, to computer scientists.

- A. Garnham, *Artificial Intelligence* (1986); Ian McEwan, *The Imitation Game* (1983) (a play based on Turing's life); S. Turing, *Alan M. Turing – a Life* (1959).

Twin studies. Two sorts of research designs are included in twin studies. First, there are those that look at both biologically identical (monozygotic) twins and fraternal (dizygotic) twins. If two identical twins show the same pattern of behaviour or level of skill and two fraternal twins don't show that, the result suggests that the particular behaviour or skill is inherited genetically. Second, twin studies are carried out on identical twins who have been reared apart in different households. If these twins show similar capacities or personalities, this strengthens the case for heredity determining those particular things. However, detailed research has shown that often twins are reared either by relatives or by people with very similar characteristics, so the data obtained are hard to interpret. Moreover, this is an area in which some data used have turned out to be fraudulent – especially in the studies of heredity and intelligence carried out by Sir Cyril Burt. *See* Genetic factors.

- L. Hearnshaw, *Cyril Burt* (1980).

Two-tailed hypothesis, a hypothesis which predicts that there will be a change of behaviour at both ends of the >normal distribution. A good example is that both extreme left-wingers and extreme right-wingers in politics will be more authoritarian. *See* One- and two-tailed significance tests.

U

Unconditional positive regard. In >client-centred >therapy, this is the attitude that the therapist is supposed to have towards the client. Carl Rogers argued that the therapist must be warm, empathetic and give the client total attention and caring. It has been found that the degree of *empathy* a therapist 'exudes' correlates highly with the outcome of the therapy – more empathy, more cure! It may well be that one reason for the success of client-centred therapy is the emphasis that it places on such empathy.

Unconditioned stimulus, a raw >stimulus that human beings or animals respond to – such as food. In experiments in classical >conditioning and >operant conditioning, psychologists usually try to associate a different stimulus with it (eg >Pavlov's bell) so as to evoke a learned response.

Unconscious, that part of the >mind which is not conscious. This is a key topic in the psychoanalytic literature. >Freud argued that the mind is driven by unconscious energies, some of which, those wild longings of the >id, become unconscious from birth. Other parts of the unconscious are the product of >repression and censorship. Much of the >superego – that patient presence that forbids instinctual pleasures and disciplines the mind – is unconscious too.

The task of analysis, said Freud, is to make the unconscious conscious. He believed that the analysis of >dreams offered a key into these hidden processes, and he called dream interpretation 'the royal road to the unconscious'. >Jung posited a less biological unconscious (*see* Collective unconscious). Even experimentalists agree that unconscious processes exist but differ on their meaning.

● Sigmund Freud, *The Interpretation of Dreams* (1905).

Unemployment. Psychologists didn't really concern themselves with unemployment until the 1970s when it became a major problem in the Western world. Then they discovered that, as far back as 1931, there had been studies of its consequences in the Austrian town of Marienthal, where it was found that men who were unemployed became depressed, resented the loss of their >status as breadwinner, lost their >libido and, in general, felt life was no longer worth living. In the 1970s, despite the development of the welfare state, very similar consequences were found and, as a result, this research has had some impact on social planning.

Recent work has made some novel discoveries. It is now known that unemployment tends to run in families: often, when a man loses his job, his wife (if she is employed) also gives up her work – almost as a way of ensuring that she does not exceed his status. There is some evidence that children of unemployed parents are more likely to be unemployed. It has also been found that long-term unemployment is very damaging to mental health.

The physical impact of unemployment is considerable. One study shows visits to GPs up 60 per cent, a 70 per cent increase in episodes of illness and a 200 per cent increase in visits to hospital outpatients. Nevertheless, attempts to prove a correlation between unemployment and >suicide have never quite managed to make the connection stick. *See* Stress.

- M. Jahoda, *Employment and Unemployment* (1981); R. Smith, *Unemployment and Health* (1987); P. Warr, *The Psychology of Work* (1979).

Universals. In psychology, the question is whether there are some aspects of human nature in behaviour which can be found in every culture and are thus universal. The answer is *yes*. All human beings have some form of capacity for >language, for example. However, culture is so various that the only universals in psychology are very general.

V

Validity, a technical term used in the assessment of tests. The validity of a measure defines the extent to which it quantifies what it is claiming to measure. There are essentially four main kinds of validity:

- *Construct validity*: It's important to be sure that a test isn't just statistically valid but that it also reflects real life. Construct validity is assessed by seeing whether the scores on a given test are linked with behavioural differences which a theory assumes are associated with a particular trait. For example, one would expect extraverts as defined on the Eysenck Personality Inventory (*see* Eysenck) to be more likely to go to parties than introverts.

- *Concurrent validity*: a measure of whether two tests correlate properly. One would expect, for example, a test of how good someone's vocabulary is to be concurrently valid with a test of the ability to write good English. If not, there is something badly wrong.

- *Face validity*: a test has to appear on the surface to deal with the subject under discussion. For example, a >personality test would have no face validity at all if all its questions were mathematical. Although it may be hard to see how writing stories about pictures connects with problems of >motivation, judging the face validity of a test isn't a statistical procedure but a matter of common sense.

- *Predictive validity*: a measure of how well the results on a test predict performance in a real task or job. To measure it, one has to compare later success in the real task with previous test results.

There is no accepted way of combining the measures of all these validities to arrive at a figure that fixes the overall validity of a test. As a result, arguments about the validity of particular tests are often ambiguous. Tests are faulted on both the grounds of statistics and common sense, and on what is perhaps best described as a form of textural criticism: Item A, for example, may prove to be 'asking for' different responses to those the testers imagine.

Valium. *See* Benzodiazepines.

Variable, what is tested and manipulated in an experiment. A good example is if group A is tested on how well they hear a message through a noisy channel, while group B only gets the chance to hear this same message after taking two tranquillizers. The administration of the tranquillizers is the variable.

Variable-interval schedule. *See* Reinforcement.

Variable-ratio schedule. *See* Reinforcement.

Variance, a measure of the scatter of test scores. It is obtained by subtracting each score from the mean of the >sample, squaring these differences and averaging them. One benefit of this procedure is that scores which differ only a little from the mean don't count for much, while those that are distant from the mean contribute a great deal.

Ventricles, cavities of the >brain underneath the >cortex which, in >schizophrenics, are enlarged.

Verbal behaviour. *See* Language.

Verbal IQ. *See* Wechsler scale.

Vicarious reinforcement. Social learning theory argues that >reinforcement occurs when someone watches a model being either rewarded or punished. For example, I see another person being kissed or beaten on screen. This is an important element in the study of the effects of pornography on television, especially as it has been argued that watching violence is reinforcing and may lead to a viewer committing acts of violence.

Victims. *See* Post-traumatic stress; Rape victims.

Vision, the sense that is probably better understood than most. The eyes contain the only part of the >brain – the nerve fibres from the >retina to the optic nerve – actually to interface with the outside world. Light falling on the retinas is converted into our experience of our one image of the world.

As adults, most of us can see amazingly well, yet we are born half blind. The eyes, closed at birth, open soon afterwards, but most babies spend much of their first week of life asleep, in part so that their eyes can get used to the light. Babies obviously can't be *taught* how to see, but they have to *learn* how to do it. By the age of four weeks, most babies can focus; by six weeks, they can distinguish patterns; by ten weeks, they can usually follow a moving object.

Experiments with cats have shown the damage that can be done to the visual system of kittens brought up in special containers made up of either only straight lines or only curves. Kittens reared in the square world cannot see curves; those reared among curves cannot see straight lines. Not only is general seeing required but also specific experiences of particular stimuli (*see* Stimulus).

For example, in children with a 'squint' (ie one eye looking in a different direction from the other) the less centred eye tends not to focus and the brain learns not to respond to it. The eye is healthy but the brain does not note its information. Wearing an eye patch over the good eye 'retrains' the lazy eye. If one eye is kept shut from birth, the >neurons that would relay that eye's 'messages' into the brain don't develop properly.

Our eyes are essential for survival. We can respond very quickly to visual stimuli, even those seen with our peripheral vision. We can see things at a distance and judge how far they are. The brain computes the angle at which each retina is turned towards the object in view; it knows the distance between the two eyes and so can calculate distances. With one eye, it's much harder to do that.

Our visual system is remarkable. Its key anatomical components are the retinas, the optic nerves, the optic chiasm (where the two optic nerves meet in the brain), the lateral geniculate nuclei, the superior colliculus and the primary visual >cortex. The eye has often been compared to a camera. The cornea, a thin transparent membrane covering the outer eye, starts focusing, which is completed by the lens as it becomes thicker or fatter depending on what it is focusing on. The iris, a circular muscle, controls how much light enters the eye; it can open wide or shut much like the aperture of a camera. These adjustments are called *accommodation*.

The light falls on the retina at the back of the eye. The retina is a highly structured organ which converts light into electro-chemical messages that convey information about what is seen. The retina contains five different sets of neurons, including the primary sensory >receptors – the rods and cones. These connect with bipolar neurons which, in turn, connect with ganglion cells, the axons of which travel from the back of the retina into the optic nerve and up into the brain proper.

Pinpointing just what has been seen where is crucial for the visual system. Each ganglion cell responds to light in a defined receptive field on the retina – some when light is in the centre of that field, others when the light is off-centre. Additional cells, called horizontal cells, restrict the spread of information so that the ganglion knows exactly where the light it is reacting to is coming from. Cones, which are important in colour vision, contain pigment. Each cone is specialized and reacts only to one colour or wavelength of light depending on which of three visual pigments (red, blue or green) the cone contains. A cone responds only to light of the colour that its specific pigment is able to absorb. The cone's pigment is bleached out when it is 'hit' by blue light and the bleaching out triggers responses further up the visual system.

The output cells of the retina tell a slightly different story when it comes to colour vision. They respond to red, blue, green and yellow light. Yet there are no cones which are specifically sensitive to yellow. Investigations, including asking people the colours they could see under different conditions, suggested that contrast was important in colour vision and led eventually to the >opponent process theory.

Understanding the ways in which information is processed after it leaves the retina and travels into the brain is more complex. Experiments have shown that there are cells in the visual cortex which respond to individual features of a stimulus. David Hubel and T. Wiesel found that particular cells respond to very specific stimuli such as movement left, or movement at an angle of 40 but not 60 degrees, and to particular shapes, for example corners. Researchers were surprised that there should be individual cells for such precise specific features. These results suggest that a mosaic of cells fires to tell the person what they see.

Recently, more detailed neurological studies have suggested that the visual system requires parallel processing. What an object is, its features, and where it is located may be processed at the same time in different places of the cortex in parallel. No one is sure yet how the visual system reintegrates the information that has been broken down from the retina onwards. Research shows that people tend to see what they expect to see, so that there must be room for information from the retina to be either 'misread' or incorrectly matched with memories (*see* Memory).

Increasingly, as people live to a greater age, there is more interest in the deficiencies of the visual system. Research on patients who have glaucoma (which destroys peripheral vision) proves the extent to which head movements can compensate for retinal failure. Often people do not realize that their peripheral vision has deteriorated so badly that they can only see out of the centre of their eye. Vision is also affected by >stress and >emotion so that people do report sometimes blurred vision when they feel overloaded. This complex mix shows that understanding the anatomy, physiology and neuropsychology of vision is not enough to understand how it works. Like all our senses, vision is affected by what we feel and what we expect.

- Richard Gregory, *Eye and Brain* (1980); D. Rose and V. G. Dobson (eds), *Models of the Visual Cortex* (1985).

Visual cliff, a device invented by the perceptual psychologist James Gibson with the aim of testing whether animals and babies have an innate >perception of depth. The visual cliff is a glass plate which is placed over a drop in floor level. If an animal has a sense of depth, it will not venture on to the glass. The cliff is designed so that it looks terrifying but is quite safe.

Experiments with human babies showed that they became rather alarmed by the visual cliff, but since babies can't move as soon as they are born, the meaning of this result is ambiguous. Gibson tested infants aged four months, by which time they would have had plenty of opportunity to learn some depth perception.

Voice recognition systems, computers that can recognize the sounds of words. It's an important area in the development of >artificial intelligence.

Volley principle. In >hearing and in other sensory systems, the intensity of a >stimulus is signalled by the rate at which the electrical impulses are fired to the >brain. Neurons can fire very quickly, but they have certain limits because of their refractory periods – that is, how long it takes them to recover after firing. If presented with very intense stimuli, neurons fire in relays or sets – like a volley of guns. The brain therefore receives the impulses at a rate which wouldn't be possible if the neurons were firing in the normal way. *See* Neuron.

Warning set. *See* Set.

Watson, J(ohn) B(roadus) (1878–1956), American psychologist who was the founder of >behaviourism.

Watson came from South Carolina, studied under the philosopher John Dewey and became professor of psychology at Johns Hopkins University in Baltimore, Maryland, at the age of 30. He was known as an 'animal man' for his studies on how rats and monkeys learn. Inspired by the ideas of >Pavlov on >conditioning, he became convinced that human behaviour should be studied as objectively as animal behaviour (*see* Ethology). It took great courage to argue this since it equated humans with animals at a time when religious conservatives were still vigorously (and often successfully) fighting against any attempts to have >Darwin's theories of evolution taken seriously in schools and elsewhere. Despite being advised to keep these views to himself, Watson declared them in a series of lectures in New York, which remain the credo of behaviourism.

Watson wanted psychology to be a science but a practical one; he wanted it to study what we did in the office and in the bedroom. To this end, he initiated studies on >child development (before >Piaget), on how we think and on how alcohol affects behaviour. During the First World War, he conducted a massive study on sex education for the US government which aimed to teach GIs to resist the siren attractions of European prostitutes. Watson also has a claim to be the founder of >behaviour therapy: his work on a child known as 'Little Albert' showed that it was possible to instil, and cure, acute fears by conditioning, though recently some historians have questioned Watson's role in this work.

In 1920, Watson's world crashed when he was found to be having an affair with a student, Rosalie Rayner (whom he later married). He was forced to resign from Johns Hopkins, and no other academic institution would touch him. At the age of 42, Watson, possibly the greatest scientific psychologist of his generation, had to become a rubber boot salesman. Eventually, the advertising agency J. Walter Thompson hired him as an account executive and, using his vast knowledge of psychology, Watson transformed advertising. He hit upon the idea of creating an image for products, arguing that what sold products was not their intrinsic merits but emotional responses to them. He devised images for many products, including those of Johnson & Johnson – good mothers have clean babies whose bottoms are powdered three times a day (despite the fact that, as far as babies' health was concerned, this was totally unnecessary). By 1928, he was the guru of Madison Avenue.

Watson did try half-heartedly to get back into academic psychology, but he found that there was much prejudice against his own image as an 'immoral' man. On the outside, he grew richer but sadder. His wife Rosalie died when she was just 36, and he increasingly took to the bottle. In fact, it was something of a surprise to psychologists when, in the mid-1950s, it was discovered that Watson was still alive. Following this discovery, the American Psychological Association decided to award Watson its Gold Medal in 1956 but, bitter at the way his colleagues had previously rejected him, he refused to go to the presentation. He died that same year.

Watson did more than any other psychologist to create a climate in which psychology aimed to be scientific. Yet he wasn't narrow and would have been surprised by how behaviourism came to be trapped in the laboratory.

● D. Cohen, *John B. Watson* (1979).

Wechsler scale, with the >Stanford Binet test, one of the great >IQ scales. It offers the chance to break >intelligence down into its constituent parts. The Wechsler includes scales for verbal IQ, mathematical IQ, performance IQ and even musical IQ. *See* Intelligence testing.

Wernicke's aphasia, damage to the area of the temporal lobe which is particularly involved in the decoding and understanding of >language. *See* Aphasia.

White noise, sound containing many frequencies with about equal energies. It is used in experiments into >hearing to mask signals.

Wilcoxon test, a non-parametric test which is used instead of the >T-test for correlated samples when the assumptions underlying the T-test are not met. It is especially useful when there are two observations or scores which can be compared, rather than making comparisons between different groups of subjects.

Will, an important attribute in the philosophy of mind, which implies a conscious decision to achieve something. In modern psychology, will and intention have tended to be studied only obliquely as parts of >motivation.

Culturally, will has been important. The Victorians, for example, believed in willpower, ie that anything could be achieved through effort of the will. Psychology, however, has helped to relegate the will by suggesting that we are victims of our upbringing: it would seem unfair to expect motivation in a child from an underprivileged background. This theory is brilliantly lampooned in the song 'Officer Krupsky' from *West Side Story*.

Withdrawal symptoms. When addicts try to get off drugs or alcohol, they can experience a variety of unpleasant symptoms including vomiting, diarrhoea, tremor, and a great deal of >anxiety. The mystique of >addiction holds that the experience of withdrawal is agonizing. 'Drying-out' clinics, drug rehabilitation centres and other facilities where addicts can go 'cold turkey' exist, but there are increasingly fewer of these. In fact, there is a growing body of evidence that suggests that the horrors of withdrawal, and particularly from heroin, have been exaggerated. Strange collusions may be at work: addicts want to portray withdrawal as the hardest thing on earth in order to justify not trying or failing to stay 'clean'; this also reinforces society's view that heroin is diabolical. However, many argue that withdrawal from tranquillizers such as Valium is physically far worse.

- Tam Stewart, *The Heroin Users* (1987).

Work, *See* Ergonomics; Industrial psychology; Time and motion study; Unemployment.

Wundt, Wilhelm (1832–1920). He is regarded by many as the father of experimental psychology because he set up the first experimental psychology laboratory in Leipzig in 1879. Wundt attracted many students to his laboratory, especially Americans, who returned home and started similar labs in the United States.

Wundt also wrote the enormously influential *Grudzuge die Physiologischen Psychologie* (*Principles of Physiological Psychology*, 1874) and set up the first psychology journal, which was called ironically *Philosophische Studien* (*Studies in Philosophy*). Wundt saw his experimental work as only a small part of psychology and was eager for it to remain close to philosophy. By the time of his death, he was very disheartened by the progress of the discipline that he had helped found.

- R. W. Reiber (ed.), *Wundt and the Making of Scientific Psychology* (1980).

X chromosome, a distinctive chromosome which contains information crucial for sexual development. In women, the X chromosome is paired with another X. In men it's paired with a smaller chromosome called the Y chromosome. There are some men who have an XXY chromosomal make-up, a condition known as Klinefelter's syndrome which occurs in about 1 in 700 live male births. They are usually considered male but show some secondary female characteristics.

Y

Yerkes Dodson law, a psychological law which states that the level of performance of a person depends on his or her state of physiological arousal. Too little arousal means that people aren't motivated enough to try hard, while too much makes them over-anxious and equally likely to spoil their performance. *See* Stress.

Yoked control, an experimental technique in which everything that happens to a subject in the experimental group also happens to the subject in the >control group. They are said to be 'yoked' together in everything apart from the one independent variable which applies to one and not to the other.

Yoga, a form of Eastern >meditation. There are many different schools of yoga but most seem to aid relaxation and, in certain circumstances, and only with those who are masters, to allow the performance of remarkable – and well-documented – feats.

Young Helmholtz theory, a theory of colour >vision developed by 19th-century physiologists, Thomas Young and H. Helmholtz. It attributes colour vision to three >receptor systems based on blue, red and green. The colour we see is the result of the summation of the saturation in these receptors. It differed from the >opponent processing theory.

● R. Gregory, *Eye and Brain* (1980).

Z

Zero sum game, a concept in game theory. In a zero sum game, if one person is to do better then someone else must do worse. Social psychologists have made the dispiriting finding that, even when people aren't in a zero sum situation, they act as if they were. In other words, they will behave in such a way that the other side suffers even when that doesn't help them. A blow against idealism.

Zipf's law, a law which states that the longer words are, the less likely they are to occur in a >language. Thus it may be fitting that the last word in a dictionary of psychology should be a familiar one that is quite frequent – the end.